B-29
COMBAT MISSIONS

B-29

COMBAT MISSIONS

FIRST-HAND ACCOUNTS OF SUPERFORTRESS OPERATIONS OVER THE PACIFIC AND KOREA

DONALD NIJBOER • STEVE PACE
FOREWORD BY WALTER J. BOYNE

METRO BOOKS
NEW YORK

This 2011 edition published by Metro Books by arrangement
with Elephant Book Company Limited, 35 Fournier Street,
London E1 6QE, United Kingdom.

Editorial Director: **Will Steeds**
Project Editor: **Kevin Wiltshire**
Designer: **Philip Clucas** MCSD
Photographer: **Dan Patterson**
Production: **Robert Paulley**
Color reproduction: **Modern Age Repro House Ltd**, Hong Kong

Jacket and front cover illustration: *Spearhead to Victory* by Roy Grinnell.

Metro Books
122 Fifth Avenue
New York, NY 10011

ISBN: 978-1-4351-2542-1

Printed and bound in China

10 9 8 7 6 5 4 3 2 1

Roy Grinnell, Official Artist of the American Fighter Aces Association and the American
Combat Airman Hall of Fame (Commemorative Air Force), was an honors graduate of the
Art Center School in Los Angeles. He has received many honors and awards, including the
R.G. Smith Award for Excellence in Naval Aviation Art, becoming an Honorary Ace of the
AFAA and, most recently, the opening of the Roy Grinnell Gallery in the American Airpower
Heritage Museum (CAF) in Midland, TX. He is also well known for his Western and Native
American art. Grinnell's oil paintings have been displayed in museums and private collections
throughout the world. His work also features on the covers of *B-24 Combat Missions* and
Spitfire: Life of the Legend (website: www.roygrinnell.com).

Elephant Book Company and the editor particularly wish to thank Dana Bell for his help
in preparing this book. Dana is a full-time researcher and author who, in addition to his
interest in the growth of US military aviation, has specialized in aircraft technical
development, military aviation organizations, aircraft colors and markings, and the
history of aircraft designations and names.

Contents

Foreword

Airpower was undoubtably a mighty force in the European theater of conflict during World War II, but it did not quite reach the peak it had appeared to promise early in the war in Europe. It did so in Japan, thanks in no small part to the American people, who as well as sending warriors into combat in their name, also placed them in the high ranks of political office—in the Congress and in the Presidency. The great instrument of airpower reaching its peak in the Far East was the Boeing B-29 and the aerial firepower it could deliver in 1945.

In this unique book, Steve Pace and Donald Nijboer have captured the times, the people, the planes, and the great adventure that saw airpower meted out in ways that Douhet, Trenchard, and Mitchell had never dared to dream of—with a force, a mass, a velocity, and a result that compelled the relatively small military cabal ruling Japan eventually to release the Japanese nation from their control, and to seek peace.

The demands of writing a book such as this one far exceed the more prosaic ones of time and experience. Most crucial is a love of the subject, followed by a knowledge of where, and how, to research to find the facts that really count, rather than just the facts that have made the headlines. No one is more capable in this respect than the authors of this book, and the results are apparent in these pages.

As you, the reader, enjoy this book, it is as well to place some things in context. Consider the short time span between the first flight of the B-29 and the first combat. Wonder at the myriad engineering problems that had to be solved by invention first, then integrated into the final aircraft and its ultimate weapons' system, the atomic bomb. Think not only about the devastating air raids, under the finest aerial commander in history, Curtis E. LeMay, but also of the training and effort required to plan new factories, new tools, educate new work forces, establish new logistic concepts, new reporting concepts, and most important, new bombing strategies. Think, too, about a nation that was willing to fight, and that did not know the meaning of what have since become cliched phrases—terms such as "political correctness," "winning the hearts and minds of our enemies," and "minimizing collateral damage." Think of a nation that was threatened, saw the threat, geared up and defeated the threat decisively, and then went back and succored the very nations it had defeated. Consider all of this, and you will see that "Superfortress" and "America" have a deeper relationship than you might imagine.

Walter J. Boyne
Author/Historian, National Aviation Hall of Fame Enshrinee, Class of 2007

Introduction

Beautiful; streamlined; awe-inspiring: the B-29 was an aircraft of purposeful design and gleaming inspiration. With a wingspan of 141ft (43m) and length of 90ft (27.5m), it dwarfed both the B-17 and B-24; its gross weight of nearly 70 tons was double that of the B-17 Flying Fort. The B-29 Superfortress was the most expensive weapons' system in America's wartime arsenal, costing over $3 billion to develop and manufacture. Remarkably, it cost about $1 billion more than the atomic bomb project with which it will forever be associated. And the B-29 was an aircraft of firsts: it was the world's first pressurized bomber; and it employed the largest piston engines, the most sophisticated radar, and the most advanced fire control system in existence. Shaped from 27,000lb (12,247kg) of sheet aluminum, it also comprised 1,000lb (454kg) of copper, 9.5 miles (15.3km) of wiring, 2 miles (3.2km) of tubing—and 600,000 rivets, just to hold it all together.

But, despite the innovation and technical prowess, when the B-29 first took to the air in September 1942, it was far from combat ready. Those who flew the aircraft experienced the consequences of its rushed development first hand; consequences that included explosive decompressions at altitude and inexplicable engine fires. But the most formidable problem encountered by B-29 air and ground crews was the notorious and ongoing unreliability of the Wright Cyclone Duplex R-3350 engine. But even with these inherent faults, the B-29 became a success story beyond the wildest dreams of its innovators.

From their bases in India, China, and the Pacific, B-29 crews flew the longest bombing missions of the war, with unenvisioned success. B-29 combat operations began on June 5, 1944 and would end on August 15, 1945 (B-29s would see action again during the Korean War, from 1950 to 1953). In 14 months of combat, B-29s dropped 170,000 tons of bombs and 12,000 aerial mines. The cost was heavy, though: 414 aircraft were lost, 147 of which were actual combat losses. Sadly, more B-29s were lost to mechanical failure, operational malfunction, and causes unknown, than were shot down in combat. But compared with the 4,600 B-17s lost in Europe between 1942 and 1945, B-29 crews could perhaps be considered fortunate.

For the crews, life on a B-29 base was far from ideal. Compared with their brothers in the 8th and 15th Air Forces, their creature comforts were primitive. From the heat and monsoons of India and China to the blazing sun in the Pacific, B-29 crews were forced to live under canvas for long periods of time. Missions were long and distractions and luxuries between missions were few. On some of the recently captured island bases, Japanese soldiers were still active, requiring each person to carry a side arm when venturing to the latrine at night.

The B-29 was never a perfect aircraft, but it was capable enough to burn almost every major Japanese city to the ground and to bring the war to an end with two devastating atomic bombs. The men who flew B-29s were fiercely loyal to their aircraft, and also knew the odds and their chances of survival. But they were steadfast in their belief that what they were doing was—however appalling—the quickest and most effective way to end a barbaric war. This is the extraordinary story of the remarkable B-29 Superfortress, and the courageous young men who flew her.

Donald Nijboer

Part 1
History & Development

Preparing for a Mission

History and Development

"The B-29, along with the two atomic bombs, ended World War II months, and maybe years, sooner than would have been the case without the B-29."

—Robert M. "Bob" Robbins, Boeing XB-29 project test pilot (October 21,1943 to August 15, 1945)

The B-29 will be remembered as the bomber that helped bring World War II to a conclusion earlier than predicted. For, on August 6 and 9, 1945, two B-29s—*Enola Gay* and *Bockscar*—brought devastation to the Japanese homeland cities of Nagasaki and Hiroshima. Those controversial actions prompted Japan finally to surrender, saving the lives of countless people who would have perished in Operation Downfall, the planned invasion of Japan's home islands, due to begin in October 1945. Yet there is far more both to this story and to the history of the B-29, which had to fight another war before it could retire.

In the late 1930s, the chief of the US Army Air Corps (USAAC), then major general Henry H. "Hap" Arnold—the beloved "Father of US Airpower"—believed that the defense of the United States of America required a fleet of very-long-range (VLR), heavy-payload, high-flying bombardment aircraft. He envisioned a bomber that could reach far out from American shores and was capable of carrying heavy loads of bombs; a "super bomber" equipped with modern devices and highly trained men who would direct those bombs to the annihilation of any threatening force. Thus, in late 1939, General Arnold passed his plan along to the USAAC Air Materiel [sic] Command (AMC), and specifications were drawn.

The USAAC AMC issued additional requirements on January 29, 1940 (Request for Data R-40B) for what had become known as the VLR "super bomber" type—a bomber with a top speed of 400mph (644km/h), a maximum range of 5,333 miles (8,583km), and the capacity to deliver

Left: *J. Howard Miller's poster for the Westinghouse War Production Coordinating Committee became a defining image of women workers in World War II, collectively known as "Rosie the Riveter."*

a 2,000lb (907kg) bomb load at the halfway point. On April 8 of that year, the USAAC AMC increased its demands with Type Specification X-218-A, which called for a much higher bomb load of 15,000 to 20,000lb (6,810 to 9,080kg), fully pressurized crew accommodations, and a service ceiling of 30,000 to 40,000ft (9,144 to 12,192m). (The USAAC became the US Army Air Forces (USAAF) on June 20, 1941, and US Air Force (USAF) on September 18, 1947.)

As a result, four airframe contractors—Boeing, Lockheed, Douglas, and Consolidated Vultee—were awarded design and engineering contracts for their respective proposals: the XB-29, XB-30, XB-31, and XB-32. The entries from Douglas and Lockheed were soon eliminated from the competition, and Boeing and Consolidated Vultee were awarded production contracts to build two experimental prototypes each, a number that was later increased to three.

To get the most available horsepower at altitudes that would exceed 30,000ft (9,144m), both airframe contractors selected four supercharged 2,200hp Wright R-3350 Cyclone 18-cylinder, twin-row, radial piston engines to propel their aircraft. Yet the R-3350 was an unproven power plant and, as such, risky business; nevertheless, its development and production proceeded for these two aircraft. In September 1942, the first of three Boeing XB-29 aircraft was ready for flight-test evaluations. And on September 21, with famed engineering test pilot Edmund T. "Eddie" Allen at the controls, the Premier Superfortress, as it would be called, made a successful first flight. (The Consolidated Vultee XB-32 had made its first flight two weeks earlier, on September 7.) Allen also piloted the second XB-29 on its first flight, but on February 18, 1943, tragedy struck the program when his aircraft crashed to destruction, killing ten crewmembers, including Eddie. His last words were, "Have fire equipment ready. Am coming in with a wing on fire."

The crash of XB-29 number two meant that flight-testing operations were put on hold for quite some time. Nevertheless, due to pressing wartime priorities, B-29 manufacturing processes continued, and flight testing finally resumed in the summer of 1943 as faith in the program burgeoned once more.

The B-29—the Boeing Model 345—was engineered, designed, developed, and produced as a large piston-powered and propeller-driven four-engine heavy bombardment airplane for the US Army Air Corps. It was unofficially called "Super Bomber," "Very-Long-Range Bomber" (or VLR bomber), "A-bomber," and "Superfort," but its official name was "Superfortress." Its many names aside, the aircraft was indubitably the world's first dedicated heavy-class bombardment airplane—fully missionized and optimized for the primary duty of strategic bombardment.

Boeing initiated all-out production of its B-29 in 1943 at its Wichita facility in Kansas. In addition, and due to strong wartime demand, the Bell Aircraft Corporation and Glenn L. Martin Aircraft Company

Above: *Bob Robbins replaced Eddie Allen as chief B-29 test pilot for Boeing after the latter's tragic death. Robbins is seen here following another test flight, this time of* The Flying Guinea Pig, *XB-29 number one.*

produced numerous other B-29s, in Atlanta, Georgia, and Omaha, Nebraska, respectively. Subsequently, Boeing produced more B-29s at its Renton, Washington, plant.

For the most part, B-29s were produced in round-the-clock, ten-hour shifts, six days a week. Boeing went on to build 2,766 B-29s; Bell produced an additional 668; and Martin manufactured another 536, to give a grand total of 3,970 aircraft, consisting of XB-29, YB-29, B-29, B-29A, and B-29B. The last Superfortress built, a B-29A, rolled off the Boeing-Renton Plant 3 production line on May 28, 1946. The USAAF had originally ordered 9,052 B-29s prior to VJ Day (Victory over Japan Day). After VJ Day, orders for 5,082 B-29s were canceled.

As an aside, the Consolidated Vultee B-32 Dominator went into production as a backup to the B-29; this was in case the latter failed to deliver, which it did not. Thus, the 118 B-32s that had been built were removed from service and scrapped shortly after World War II.

Above: *The B-29's Wright R-3350 Duplex-Cyclone was one of the most powerful piston engines produced in the US during World War II. It produced some 2,200hp in its full military power setting; thus, each B-29 could flaunt up to 8,800hp.*

The process of building the thousands of B-29s required by the USAAF was fraught with difficulty. In early 1943, in order to meet General Arnold's demand for at least 175 combat-ready B-29s by the spring of 1944, the Boeing-Wichita factory in Kansas started producing components, and then a run of 14 YB-29s in early 1943, before starting on building production aircraft by the autumn. Soon after the fatal crash of the second XB-29 that killed Eddie Allen, USAAF Colonel Leonard Harmon came up with a plan to coordinate the process of working the "bugs" out of the new B-29 aircraft, most notably the engines. The objective was to take control of the entire program of production, aircraft modification, flight tests, and training. Approval for the "B-29 Special Project" came directly from President Roosevelt, who had been advised

Above: *Several thousand B-29s were produced to help defeat Japan in World War II. Shown here are but a few of them coming down the Martin-Omaha assembly line in mid-1944. Boeing, Bell, and Martin joined forces to build 3,970 Superfortresses.*

by General Arnold. Notwithstanding this directive, the B-29 program was about to run into trouble.

By mid-January 1944, 97 B-29s had been built at Wichita; unfortunately, only 16 of these airplanes were airworthy, with most of them grounded at "Modification Centers" or on the huge parking/delivery apron at the Wichita plant, pending urgent modification. The basic design of the B-29 was sound, but significant shortcuts had been taken in the race to get it into service, causing numerous defects and

quality problems. The Boeing-run organization that should have been getting the B-29s ready for battle collapsed under the strain.

The biggest headaches were caused by the new R-3350 engines, which were constantly overheating. Other problems arose with defective pressure seals around the cockpit windows and sighting blisters, which required precise fitting to prevent leakage. The sighting systems (four analog computers) for the remote-controlled defensive armament also caused problems, as well as the turrets themselves. Then came electrical failures caused by faulty Cannon plugs, which supplied connections throughout the ten miles (16km) of wiring. Substandard glass in the cockpit transparencies meant the pilots had trouble seeing through them clearly, and a minor "beef-up" was found to be needed on the wing structures.

When General Arnold visited the Wichita plant on January 11, 1944, he was expecting 175 combat-ready B-29s for the XX Bomber Command. As he was shown around the assembly lines, he picked out the 175th fuselage section and signed it, commenting, "This is the plane I want. I want it before the first of March." When he discovered two months later that no B-29s were actually combat-ready, and, worse still, that some had been sitting waiting for parts for two months or more, Arnold was livid. In March 1944, General Bennett Meyers was given full authority to act under Arnold's name to get the B-29s modified and combat-ready. Specialist USAAF ground crew and technicians were called in from all over the country, and 600 workers were pulled from the Wichita assembly lines. Subcontractors were told to stop all work on non-B-29 components until they had fulfilled their commitments.

The 1,200 technicians who had gathered at the Wichita factory and the Modification Centers were asked to update each bomber inside and out. First, the wings needed to have some of the plating removed, the required "beef-ups" were added, and then each piece of skin was riveted back in place. At the same time, the cowl flaps, which controlled airflow through and around the troublesome engines, were being modified. Each piece of glass installed in the nose had to be pulled out and replaced with new distortion-free panes. After that, the pressurization had to be rechecked: 75 B-29s in total needed new glass. Internally, every electrical plug had to be removed, disassembled, and resoldered—a total of 586,000 connections in completed aircraft, plus those on the assembly lines and in wiring bundles ready for installation. Making things even more challenging were the frigid temperatures and frequent snowstorms: with the thermometer often reading below zero, it was so cold that crews could only work for 20 minutes at a time, since most of the jobs required delicate handling.

One particularly challenging project was pulling all R-3350-23 engines out of already completed B-29s and modifying them to R-3350-23A "war engine" standard. This entailed disassembling and rebuilding them with additional baffles to accelerate the airflow over the cylinders, new exhaust

ranging from the release of small incendiary bombs to high-yield atomic bombs. In the Korean War, instead of carrying nuclear weapons, B-29s dropped conventional high-explosive bombs, including the very large radio-controlled Razon and Tarzon bombs, primarily for the destruction of bridges. During its tenure, the Superfortress served with the USAAC, USAAF, the USAAF Air Rescue Service (ARS), the US Air Force (USAF), the USAF Air Resupply and Communications Service (ARCS), the USAF Air Weather Service (AWS), the USAF Tactical Air Command (TAC), the USAF Air Training Command (ATC), and the Strategic Air Command (SAC).

The first B-29 strikes to be flown against Japan in World War II were flown from four forward air bases: Kwanghan, Kuinglai, Hsinching, and Pengshan,

Left: Thumper of the 497th Bomb Group, 870th Bomb Squadron, was one of the more famous stars of the Superfortress brood. Here she is being shown to Boeing employees upon her return home in October 1945.

Below: This B-29 was the 1,000th one built; it was manufactured by Boeing at its Wichita, Kansas, facility.

valves with improved metallurgy, new rocker arms (drilled with small holes, to allow better oil flow), and modified nose casings and engine sumps, again to improve oil flow. Given the subzero temperatures, the work was arduous, especially when it required struggling with stiff and brittle fuel and oil lines and hard-to-reach clamps, bolts, and screws.

Other necessary modifications included replacing the rudders with strengthened units, replacing all main landing gear tires, and reinforcing the main gear leg structures. The B-29 AN/APQ-13 radar sets had to be fitted, too. Finally, long-range fuel tanks were installed in the bomb bays. After about five weeks of exhausting work, the first combat-ready B-29s started taking off on the first leg of the long journey to their bases in the CBI (China, Burma, India theater of operations); General Arnold had won the "Battle of Kansas" and was finally getting his 175 combat-ready Superfortresses.

The Boeing B-29 Superfortress featured a number of innovations that had never before been applied to heavy bombardment-type aircraft. These included dual (in tandem) bomb bays, pressurized and heated crewmember stations, tricycle landing gear, a computerized remote-controlled machine-gun armament system, and two computerized radar-directed bombardment systems: the AN/APQ-13, and AN/APQ-7 Eagle.

The B-29 was vigorously used in combat, serving in both World War II and the Korean War. It performed a variety of bombardment duties,

all seated around Chengtu in the southern central part of China. Combat-ready Superfortresses began to arrive in India in March 1944, and by mid-June they were ready to strike. However, these forward bases in China did not have adequate supplies of the fuel, spare parts, and weapons needed for the B-29s. Such critical materials therefore had to be transported from the permanent bases in India to the staging bases in China by flying over the so-called "Hump"—the eastern end of the Himalayan Mountains (see pages 34 to 35). Furthermore, many of the materials required were transported over the Hump by the India-based B-29s themselves. The first combat-ready B-29s to operate in the CBI theater of operations belonged to the 58th Bomb Wing (Very Heavy) of

Right: *Cartoons are meant to be humorous. However, in this particular illustration from the gunners' manual, the truth is clear, too: "B29ers" loved their Superforts.*

Below: *Little Organ Annie was a B-29-55-BW (42-24893) of the 794th Bomb Squadron, 668th Bomb Group; she is seen here in all her glory while en route to West Field on Tinian in the early spring of 1945.*

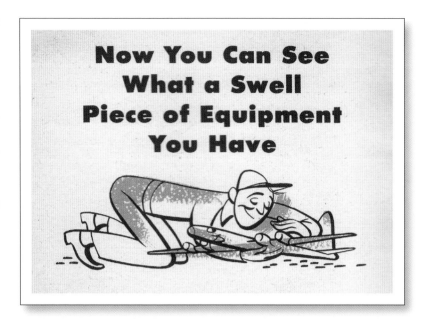

XX Bomber Command, 20th Air Force, made up of four bomb groups with four bomb squadrons each.

While waiting for basing closer to Japan, these 16 bomb squadrons continued to fly over the Hump and strike against Japan. Since these bombardment missions were flown over vast distances comprising well-defended Japanese-held territories, the losses of B-29s and their crews flying out of the CBI were enormous.

The first combat mission flown against the Japanese mainland by B-29s operating out of Chengtu, China, on June 15, 1944, had as its target the Imperial Iron and Steel Works at Yawata. This was only 20 months and 25 days after the first flight of the premier XB-29; this remarkable time period from "first flight to first fight" set a record that has never been broken. The bombardment missions from China lasted until the spring of 1945, when all of the B-29s based in India could finally be transferred to the island bases of Guam, Saipan, and Tinian in the Western Pacific. Other

B-29 attacks flown from China upon Japanese-held territories included raids on Burma, the Dutch East Indies, Manchuria, occupied China, and the empire of Malaya. Many other missions were flown over Japan by photographic reconnaissance F-13s. (It is interesting to note that CBI-based XX Bomber Command flew more photographic reconnaissance missions with its F-13s than it flew actual B-29 bombing sorties.)

In the meantime, US Navy and US Marine Corps personnel were battling hard, with significant loss of life, to take the Mariana islands of Guam, Saipan, and Tinian, as well as Iwo Jima and Okinawa, in order to get B-29s as close as possible to Japan. This was accomplished, and XXI Bomber Command, 20th Air Force, fielded four bomb wings: the 73rd and 313th on Saipan and Tinian respectively, and the 314th and 315th on Guam. A fifth B-29 bomb wing—the 316th of the Eighth Air Force—began to base its four squadrons on Okinawa just as VJ Day loomed. The 313th Bomb Wing (VH) at North Field on Tinian received a fifth bomb group in the spring of 1945—the 509th Composite Group (CG), with its single highly classified 393rd Bomb Squadron. Iwo Jima was primarily an escort fighter base occupied by P-51 Mustangs, but it was used time and time again by B-29s for emergency landings, refueling, and repairs.

It was this last bomb group/squadron that was assigned the fleet of 23 "Silverplate" B-29s produced by Martin in Omaha, Nebraska; 15 of them were used in combat. Silverplate was the code name for what was called Secret Project MX-469 by the USAAF AMC. These specially built B-29s, stripped of their upper and lower gun turrets, and with modified bomb bays, were the first atomic bombers in the world. Among the 15 Silverplate B-29s used by the 509th CG were two Martin-built B-29s named *Enola Gay* (B-29-45-MO, 44-86292) and *Bockscar* (B-29-35-MO, 44-27297, sometimes seen as *Bock's Car*). It was these two atomic bombers that laid waste to Nagasaki and Hiroshima on August 6 and 9, 1945, respectively. The other Silverplate bombers were primarily used for the bombardment of Japanese cities with the specially developed five ton "Pumpkin bombs." These bombs were very large ellipsoidal, high-explosive, conventional orange-colored bombs, similar in shape to the "Fat Man" atomic bomb dropped by *Enola Gay*; the "Little Boy" atomic bomb was dropped by *Bockscar*. (Including the prototype, a Boeing-Wichita-built B-29-5-BW, 65 Silverplate bombers were eventually delivered to the 509th CG, 393rd BS. Of these, 57 were built by Martin and eight were built by Boeing. They were based at Roswell, New Mexico, after World War II.)

B-29s were also converted for other purposes. During World War II, 15 B-29s and one B-29A were converted to serve as air-sea rescue aircraft for downed crews (see page 88); these were designated SB-29 and called "super-dumbo." They carried A-3 Edo lifeboats, and when crews were forced to ditch their B-29s at sea, the SB-29s dropped their lifeboats for the rescue of the crash survivors.

After World War II, up until the Korean War, numerous Superfortresses were converted to serve in many capacities other than strategic bombardment. Primarily, these were KB-29s used to refuel aircraft in

Left: *The War Department produced numerous official war films to instruct the troops at home and abroad. This one, primarily shown to up-and-coming B-29 crewmen, introduced them to "their" B-29.*

flight, RB-29s used for the gathering of electronic signals intelligence (ELINT) and photographic reconnaissance, TB-29s for combat crew training and pilot training and transition, and the WB-29 for weather observation.

During the Korean War, the USAF initially fielded five bomb groups equipped with B-29s. These groups included the 19th Bomb Group (BG) (Medium)—Kadena Air Base, Okinawa; 22nd BG (M)—Kadena Air Base, Okinawa; 92nd BG (M)—Yokota, Japan; and 307th BG (M)—Kadena Air Base, Okinawa. Respectively, these groups had three bombardment squadrons, except for the fifth group, the 98th, which had four. A separate squadron—the 91st Strategic Reconnaissance Squadron (Very Long Range) of the USAF Strategic Air Command—also operated from Kadena Air Base during the Korean War. (The 92nd BG (M) and its three bomb squadrons returned to the US in the fall of 1950 to convert to the B-36, which left four bomb groups to do battle in the Korean War.)

The Superfortress also served with the Royal Air Force (RAF) Bomber Command of Great Britain as the Boeing Washington B1. The RAF borrowed 88 B-29s, mostly Renton-built B-29As. These aircraft were primarily based at RAF Coningsby, Lincoln, RAF Marham, King's Lynn, and RAF Watton in Norfolk, beginning in the early 1950s. They were also based on the islands of Cyprus (RAF Akrotiri) and Malta. A few B-29s remained in the UK for use by 192 Squadron for ELINT operations until 1958.

While the USAF waited for its first jet-powered strategic bombers, and as B-29 development progressed, there were numerous improvements made to the Superfortresses' basic airframe. These ultimately led to the proposed B-29D model, later redesignated B-50A and unofficially dubbed "Superfortress II."

In the final analysis, the B-29 proved to be a remarkable war fighter, and the thousands of men who manned their Superfortresses grew to love them. But getting ready to do combat in such a revolutionary and unproven aircraft was a major undertaking for both ground and aircrews.

Preparing for a Mission

"At these meetings crewmen were always tense, for the information given out in this hour would tell everyone about the mission—whether it would be a milk run or pure hell, a piece of cake or a shard of hot steel."

—Kevin Herbert, tail gunner

The Japanese knew the B-29 was coming; their experience with the rugged and hard-to-shoot-down Boeing B-17 had given them a bitter taste of what was to come, and American intentions to mount a strategic bombing campaign against the Japanese home islands was no secret. The combined bombing campaign against Germany by both the USAAF and RAF Bomber Command was a clear indication of not only what the Allies were capable of, but also, and more importantly, what they were prepared to do to win the war.

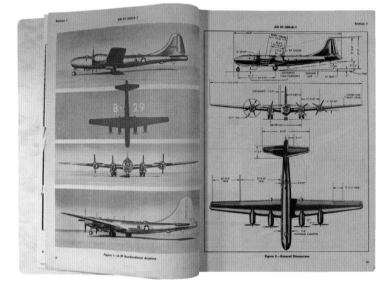

Left: The B-29 was big on every scale. It was the largest, most advanced US bomber built during World War II; it was also the most expensive.

subject to shortages and crippling delays. In many respects, the training time available for B-29 crews was incredibly limited. Crews were often allowed only a few flights before flying out to the Marianas. Captain Davis Bunn of the 505th Bomb Group remembers: "We were living in the barracks waiting for a '29 to be assigned to us and as soon as it

Reacting quickly to information of the B-29 prototype, the Japanese expanded their intelligence-gathering capabilities. And what concerned them most was the new bomber's range. They had already managed to identify some of the Superfortress's design features: a mid-wing, four-engine aircraft with a total weight of about 40 tons. Bomb load was estimated at 9,900lbs (4,500kg) with four to six 20mm cannons for defense. Remarkably, the Japanese concluded that the new bomber would be pressurized, have an operational ceiling of 32,000ft (9,754m) and top speed of 372mph (600km/h)—all very accurate. Even armed with this information, the Japanese did remarkably little in the way of preparing their cities for the coming assault. And what they didn't know was how massive the B-29 production and training program really was.

However, like the production of the B-29 itself, which was fraught with myriad technical problems, the training program for its crews was also

was we didn't get any flying practice, except for one flight to get off the ground and land and then they gave it to us and told us to fly to Tinian."

The B-29 was an extremely advanced aircraft that had demanded a new approach to training. The first crews were originally drawn from those who had operational experience and those with previous four-engine time; other pilots were plucked from among the instructors in multi-engine flight school. But a shortage of aircraft meant that early crew training was done in B-17s and B-24s.

The crew compliment of the B-29 was standardized early and consisted of 11 men: aircraft commander, pilot, bombardier, navigator, flight engineer, radio operator, radar operator, central fire control gunner, left and right gunners, and tail gunner. And the training was centered on the crew concept—crews would train together as a team, to be changed only in the event of wounding or death.

B-29 operations emphasized high-altitude, long-range navigation and the use of radar for both navigating and bombing, and these three requirements demanded a much closer integration of the crew and were unique to the Superfortress. Ivan Potts—a pilot with the 40th Bomb Group—remembers seeing one for the first time: "The first time I saw a B-29 up close I couldn't believe something that big could actually get off the ground and fly. Structurally they were very strong. No US Army Air Force plane made was more challenging or exciting to fly. We hated it on occasion but loved it most of the time."

The shortages of B-29s for training, and the accelerated need for combat crews in the Pacific, created a training regime that was efficient in numbers, but lacked the quality required for such a sophisticated aircraft. (The USAAF recorded 52,651 training accidents resulting in 14,903 deaths in World War II.) And when the B-29 first entered combat, it was still a very immature weapons system; however, the pressures and momentum of war called for its urgent use. As a consequence, shortcuts had to be taken, and crew training suffered the most. It was a situation that did not ease until the very last months of the war.

Above: *The Aircraft Commander was responsible for ensuring his crew was ready for combat.*

Left: *The crew button with a photo is from Castle Air Force Base, California. The other badge was used to gain access to the flight line (where the aircraft are parked).*

Kevin Sherbet, a tail gunner with the 873rd Bomb Squadron, observed the results of the inadequate training firsthand: "One yahoo [in this context this means 'idiot'] brought in a gleaming new B-29 from Wichita, but forgot to check the landing gear was fully down and locked. Needless to say, the plane was somewhat used when the gear collapsed and it finally skidded to a halt at the end of the runway."

When the 58th Bomb Wing (the first B-29 Wing in the Army Air Force) was established in Kansas during the summer of 1943 it was short of just about everything, including B-29s; as a result, some squadrons trained on Martin B-26 Marauders and B-17s. Combat-experienced pilots were also in short supply, but, ready or not, the 58th began leaving Kansas in late March 1944, destination Calcutta, 11,500 miles (18,507km) away. It was

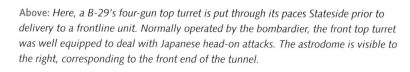

Above: *Here, a B-29's four-gun top turret is put through its paces Stateside prior to delivery to a frontline unit. Normally operated by the bombardier, the front top turret was well equipped to deal with Japanese head-on attacks. The astrodome is visible to the right, corresponding to the front end of the tunnel.*

an inspiring journey; young aviators, some barely out of their teens, were spanning oceans and continents in the world's most advanced aircraft. From the central United States, 150 B-29s headed east to Newfoundland, Canada, then 2,800 miles (4,506km) over the Atlantic to Morocco, across North Africa to Cairo in Egypt, then to Karachi, and finally to Calcutta in India. Considering that fewer than half the aircrews had completed the training syllabus, it's amazing that only five B-29s were lost en route. From here and bases in China, the 58th would launch the first strategic bombing raids against the Japanese mainland.

Even though B-29 crews had been trained to be a unit, they did not always remain that way. Occasionally crews were split up as soon as they arrived on Guam, Tinian, or Saipan (the Mariana Islands, western Pacific); it was simply military logic—crews that had suffered combat deaths or wounded individuals required replacements. And for newly arrived crews expecting to stay together, it was known for them to have their shiny new B-29 taken away and the crew to be separated.

Crews arriving in the theater were often shocked by the hostile environment in which they now had to live; after facing a cold and windy Kansas winter, the 58th Bomb Wing now faced the sweltering heat and humidity of the Asian subcontinent. On Guam, Tinian, and Saipan, which were within 15 degrees of the equator, the temperature varied only between 70 to 85°F (21 to 29°C) year-round, and it would rain every day. Early accommodation consisted of tents—the lucky ones had wood floors. As more men and supplies poured in, the tents were replaced by Quonset huts (semicircular, corrugated steel prefabricated buildings), and more permanent structures were established. William H. Carter, a CFC gunner with the 60th Bomb Group, remembers the scene:

"For the first couple of days on Guam, we were required to live in a 12-man squad tent until our Quonset huts were built, and then we were separated from our officers. These Quonset huts provided living quarters for three crews of enlisted men. We had showers, which had huge tanks of water and high walls to provide privacy. We waited until the afternoon after the sun had warmed the water to take our showers. In our squadron we had black air personnel who drove trucks to take us to and from the hard stands. A hard stand is a circular concrete area where the planes were parked. Many of these men also worked on the runways changing them from coral runways with landing mats to concrete runways. During that era we were segregated by race, and the black men had their own living quarters."

There was nothing routine when it came to flying combat missions; while the preparation may have become a well-established ritual, the actual missions were not. Before a mission was planned, aircraft

Far left and above: *The gold leaf insignia signified the rank of major, one rank above captain; crews are briefed on their target, its geography, and likely opposition.*

availability was the first consideration—if it was a major strike, the maximum effort was required, and that meant every combat-ready aircraft was assigned to the mission. In this situation, crew selection was automatic; the crew and alternate crew were allocated to an aircraft. Because B-29 bases in the Pacific were so huge, the best and most efficient way to inform crews assigned to a mission was through the public address system.

A typical B-29 briefing and mission was a 24-hour affair; each day, aircrews would rise, eat, and confront the pre-mission jitters that never seemed to go away. If it was a daylight strike, they would have a few hours to kill before the briefing; some would make their way to their aircraft and begin the process of preflight prep: fuel, bombs, and ammunition would be loaded, engines checked, and radio, radar and navigational equipment tested and made ready. William H. Carter of the

60th Bomb Group describes the type of ammunition he loaded and in what order:

"Our ammunition consisted of five different types of ammunition. We had tracers, armor-piercing, incendiary, which produces a very hot fire when it explodes, and the regular lead bullet. Each gunner made his own decision as to his choice of bullets. Most of us belted the five types of ammunition in that order. In other words, each fifth round would be tracer, armor-piercing, et cetera, and each gunner loaded his own ammunition. There were two large canisters in the tail section of the plane into which I replaced my belted ammunition. I, therefore, had close to about 1,000 rounds of ammunition."

At around 16:00 hours the briefing would begin—all briefings took place in the group's headquarters (HQ) Quonset hut, which was just big enough to hold the bomb group's three squadrons. It was typically a crowded affair and, as the crews filled the hut, the body heat rising from the closely packed men would add yet another level of discomfort to the stifling conditions. In front, an elevated stage and podium would stand empty waiting for the Group Commander and Briefing Officer to arrive.

As the men settled in, the nervous jokes and chatter would join the chorus of shuffling feet and squeaking benches. The briefing officer would enter and make his way to the stage; the men turned their attention forward. A large map behind the podium showed the course to and from the target, and the vital details would follow: bombing altitude, enemy defenses in the form of flak batteries and fighters, radio frequencies, and navigation points. The men would take notes quietly.

If it was to be a day mission, other vital factors would be discussed: on a large blackboard behind the briefing officer would be the all-important order of battle; here in great detail each squadron was designated as first, second, or third into the attack. Each crew had its position designated by its number and the commanding officer's name. Other vital information would be opposite each squadron listing: time of the flight, engine start-up, time to taxi into line, and, most important, time for takeoff. Flying to Japan required a trip of 1,500 miles (2,414km) one way. In order to avoid the strain of formation flying all the way to the target, the B-29s would fly individually to a designated rendezvous

point off the enemy coast. These small volcanic islands with names such as Sofu Gan, Aoga Shima, and Hachijojima (the Izu Islands, south and east of Japan) would serve as a rallying point for the groups of B-29s. Here, the aircraft would circle and gather into their designated squadrons and set the order of battle before heading to the target.

Above: When fully loaded, the B-29 could carry 5,470 gallons of fuel (around 300 automobile tanks).

Right: Flying suit, type K-1, standardized in 1944. This one was used by Kenneth W. Schmidt, a tail gunner/bombardier on B-29 and A-26 aircraft.

scheduled for the mission. At the same time, fuelers would start filling the wing tanks with high-octane aviation fuel (6,803 US gallons, or 25,752 liters) and other ordnance men would collect the .50-caliber ammunition and deliver it to the aircraft.

Bomb loading crews would start the heavy work of moving incendiary and high-explosive ordnance from the remote bomb dumps to each aircraft; the vehicles most commonly used were Dodge trucks fitted with a special hoist mounted over the rear axle. Prior to the bombs arriving, an armorer in each bomber ground crew would start the "putt-putt" (auxiliary power unit, or APU), a two-stroke gasoline-engine generator, to boost the aircraft's electrical supply.

Release mechanisms for the bomb racks would be tested to ensure that they were functioning properly prior to loading and, once the bombs were in place, the nose and tail fuses would be screwed in and secured with a pin and wire to prevent the arming vane from spinning and arming the bomb; these pins and wires would be removed just before the target was reached. Bomb loading was a dangerous and arduous task—in the confined space of the bomb bay it was easy to sustain an injury. And, if a mission was "scrubbed," all the bombs would have to be removed and returned to the bomb dump.

Before each mission, all aircraft would undertake a preflight check. This vital task was performed by the crew chief and his assistant. Their first job was to "pull through the props." Each prop had to be pulled through (rotated) in order to remove any fuel that had accumulated in the cylinders from the last mission. With the assistant crew chief standing ready with fire extinguisher in hand, all four engines would be started and put through their paces. Oil pressure, turbo-supercharger, and magneto performance would be checked. Propeller feathering (optional rotation of each blade to reduce drag in case of engine failure) would also be tested along with all electrical and hydraulic functions. With all lights in the green, the engines would be shut down to wait for the arrival of the crew.

As the meeting continued, other briefers would take the stage and describe the weather, target specifics, air-sea rescue services, and alternate fields. (Weather prediction in the Pacific was a rather sketchy affair at best; the weather services did the best they could, but for Jim O'Keefe, navigator with the 40th Bomb Group, it was always a mystery: "I never understood how, with so many ships and planes in the area, we never got better forecasts.") And then the briefing would be over. As the men filed out they would break into smaller groups and head for specialist briefings: navigators over here, radar operators there, bombardiers in that building, and gunners to their aircraft.

If this were a night mission the briefing would have followed a different schedule. It would have been a morning briefing with takeoff usually set between 18:00 and 19:00 hours and arrival over the target between 01:00 and 02:00 hours next morning.

While aircrew were being briefed, ordnance would be given the bomb load specs and the list of aircraft

While the flight testing was going on, aircrews would have time to eat. Depending on the target and what they had been told about their

Right: Lt. Col. Elmer E. Elmer, mascot of B-29 Deacon's Distress *was a familiar sight at mission briefings and flew on all missions; he wears a dog tag, with his name (the "E" stands for Elmer) and his blood type is C, for cotton—information from* Boeing Plane Talk, *March 16, 1945.*

mission, some crewmen could fill their plates with abandon, while others would pick at their food, their appetites suddenly AWOL (sandwiches and fruit juice were usually picked up and put aboard each plane). For a daylight mission, takeoff time was usually scheduled for 02:00 to 03:00 hours. This meant that arrival over the target would be around 09:00 hours, giving sufficient daylight for the long trip home. After the dinner meal, some men would try to sleep; others would catch a ride to the hardstand and simply wait.

Getting to an aircraft required a motor vehicle since the distances on a B-29 base were measured in miles. Men would jump aboard whatever transport was available—usually a GMC 2.5-ton truck or weapons carrier. And with thousands of vehicles in motion, traffic jams were not uncommon. Once at their destination the crews would unload their gear, and the pilot and flight engineer would start their walk-around inspection. While the pilot checked the control surfaces and other aspects of the airframe, the engineer would climb on to the wings and check each fuel tank was full and that caps and access covers were secured.

But before a B-29 was turned over to the pilot, he would have to sign form 1A; this indicated the current engineering status of the aircraft, and was used by the crew chief to record servicing and repair work. Then, before the rest of the crew boarded the aircraft, the "personal equipment check" had to be carried out. Each crewmember had to make sure he was properly equipped for the mission: fitted oxygen mask, sustenance vest, Colt .45 semi-automatic side arm with shoulder holster and birdshot ammo, parachute and one-man raft attached, Mae West life preserver, flak jacket, helmet, throat mike, headset, flashlight, and E/E (escape and evasion kit). With all gear checked, the aircraft commander inspected the crew one more time. Once aboard, each member settled into his station to begin the preflight checks.

And then it would be time—"start engines." Clouds of blue smoke signaled good health as 72 pistons began to fire. As power surged through the aircraft a tension would fill the cramped spaces—each man, alone in his thoughts, readying himself for the mission. Before them lay hours of tedious routine and the uncertainty of what lay ahead. Would a flak shell reach its mark? Would a Japanese fighter, bent on suicidal glory, make it past the guns? And would their courage hold? As one B-29 pilot recalled, amid the chaos of battle he swore, "'If I ever get out of this one I'm through flying'—and at the moment I really meant it." Many crews probably felt this way at one time or another, but now they had one more mission to fly, one more to survive, and one more that would bring them a little closer to home.

Above: An ordnance technician making sure that each and every one of the 500lb (227kg) bombs are properly attached to their shackles prior to the mission. The cylindrical object above his head is the communication tunnel that connected the forward and rear crew areas.

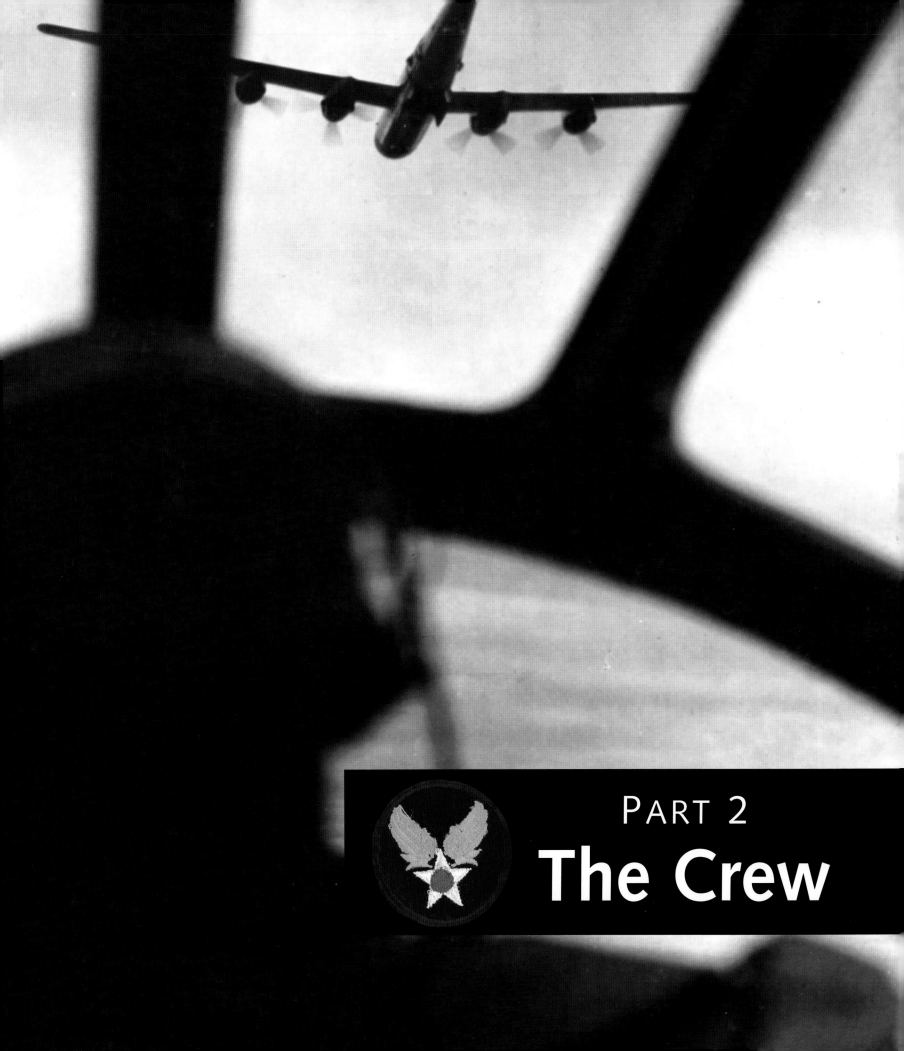

PART 2
The Crew

The Aircraft Commander and Copilot

"You would have to coax an overloaded airplane off the ground while sweating out an engine failure, fire or explosion . . . then endure the stress of a seven- or eight-hour flight to the target . . . then you had to fight the Jap . . . maybe he would get you—or hurt you or damage you enough so that it would be difficult for you to get home—or maybe you couldn't get home . . . and your friends died . . . welcome to war."

—1/Lt. Gordon Bennett "Ben" Robertson Jr., 314BW (VH), 29BG (VH), 43BS (VH)
North Field, Guam (A/C of B-29 *Grand Slam*)

The B-29 aircraft commander (A/C) was the pilot, in charge of the airplane and its crew, but the copilot was fully capable of taking over operations of the airplane if the aircraft commander fell ill or worse. This held true during all Superfortress operations in World War II and the Korean War, and all postwar operations. In fact, some of the more experienced and capable B-29 copilots served as aircraft commanders as well, and all aircraft commanders and copilots were officers.

Initially, the B-29 crewmen had to fly 25 combat missions to qualify for going home; this number was soon upped to 30 and finally 35. In World War II specifically, all B-29 bombardment missions against Japan were flown from China and the Western Pacific islands of Guam, Saipan, and Tinian. In the Korean War, B-29s bombed North Korean targets from Yokota Air Base and Kadena Air Base—both of which are located on the Western Pacific island of Okinawa, Japan.

A B-29 combat mission could be extremely long in duration, anything from 13 to 16 hours. And that did not

Left: The instrument panels on the flight deck of the B-29 were relatively sparse; certainly, they are pared down when compared with the more modern strategic bombers of today.

take into account the pre- and post-flight times for the pilots and other crewmembers, of around four hours: two hours pre-flight, two post-flight. All in all, each combat mission could eat up some 17 to 20 hours of the crewmen's lives.

Once the aircraft reached its initial point (IP)—the beginning of the bomb run—the aircraft commander let the bombardier take control. In action, then, the bombardier literally "flew" the airplane until all the bombs were released. If it was nighttime or cloudy, the radar operator fed targeting information to the bombardier, who in turn adjusted his Norden bomb sight to correlate with the radar fix. So, while the radar operator and the bombardier worked in unison on a bomb run, the aircraft commander and copilot were hands-off.

World War II B-29 pilot 1/Lieutenant Henry F. "Ford" Tolbert of the 482nd BS (VH), 505th BG (VH), 313th BW (VH) on Tinian—22 combat missions—relates how the B-29 compared to the B-17 in flight: "I only flew the B-17 in training at Hobbs Army Air Field, New Mexico, so I have no idea how the loaded B-17 flew, but in the training planes I found the B-17 handled easier [was more responsive] than the B-29s I trained in at Pyote

Army Air Field, Texas, in level flight, and it was much easier to maneuver. Yet the B-29 was much easier and smoother to fly in rough weather. And once you determined where the 'step' [the attitude of the plane to get the best speed/fuel efficiency possible] was on the B-29, it was a pleasure to fly. I'd set up the '29 on the 'step' slightly nose down and keep watch that it did not 'fall' off the step, and about seven hours later you were home if nothing bent or broke."

The B-29's flight controls were conventional and the forces necessary to move them were light, even at high flying speeds—a fact surprising to most pilots the first time they flew one. The elevators were similar to those on the B-17; the ailerons, although considerably larger than those on the B-17, were rigged so that they could easily be moved 18 degrees up or down. The rudder gave maximum possible control yet

could be moved easily without the use of power boosts, and the wing flaps and tricycle landing gear were lowered and raised by reversible electric motors. The Fowler-type flaps, which provided lift and drag, traveled on track and roller mechanisms in such a manner that they projected beyond the trailing edge of the wing when they were extended; and under normal operation the landing gear could be lowered in just 40 seconds.

Prior to landing, the pilots performed 14 checks, which included crew notification, reeling in the trailing antenna, turning off the autopilot, stowing the gun turrets, starting the "putt-putt" (a gasoline auxiliary power unit (APU) situated in the tail, which supplied power during taxiing, taking off, and landing until engine number three was started), lowering the landing gear and checking that the down and locked indicator lights were on. These checks also included the reduction of propeller speed to 2,400rpm, and seeing that the flight engineer's checklist was complete.

After landing and taxiing to the assigned hardstand, the aircraft commander and copilot checked off their final 13 duties, which culminated in a final crew inspection. This last crew inspection was to verify that they, too, had completed their respective checklists and that they were of sound mind and body.

Little Brown Book

B-29 crewmen, especially the aircraft commander and copilot, carried a little brown book entitled *Flight and Operational Manual*, upon which they heavily depended. Featured within its pages were invaluable facts and figures related to combat operations, including detailed descriptions of the enemy aircraft they would encounter (see below). It also explained many of the Superfort's systems critical for successful operations throughout the combat missions.

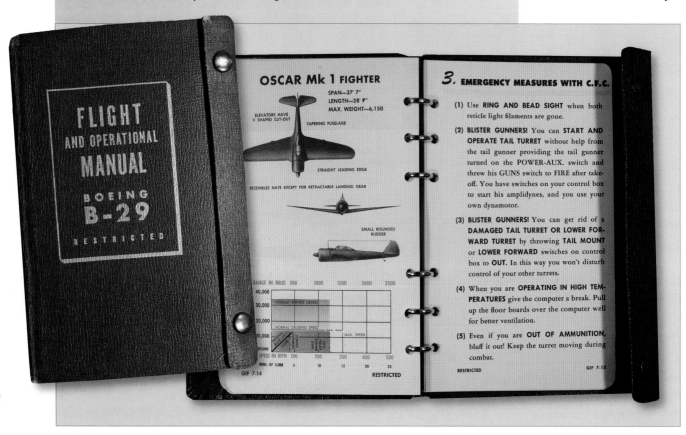

Page right, clockwise from top left: *This boss, found in the control column center of all B-29s, served to remind the aircraft commander of his most critical priorities; the aircraft commander's instrument panel was no more cluttered than our road vehicles of today; a view to the illuminated inside of a B-29's flight deck, which housed the all-important pilots and bombardier; the B-29 airspeed indicator pegged at 400mph (643km/h)—but, for the most part, speeds in excess of 310mph (498km/h) were frowned upon.*

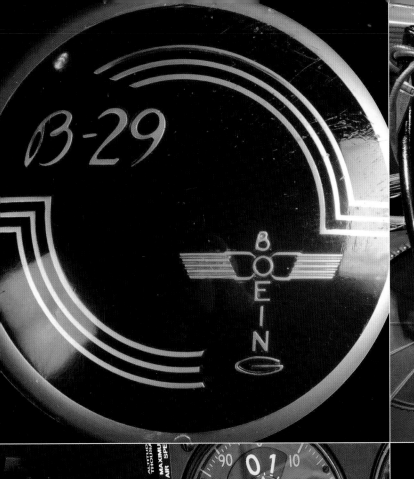

220 M.P.H. MAX. AIRSPEED FLAPS 2° - 20° DOWN
130 M.P.H. MAX. AIRSPEED FLAPS 20° - 45° DOWN

345 MPH MAX. AIR SPEED ABOVE 105,000 LBS

THE BOEING B-29A
Superfortress

Anything can happen

Lieutenant Colonel James R. "Jim" Farrell was A/C of *Frisco Nannie* of the 500th Bomb Group, 882nd Bomb Squadron, stationed at Isley Field on the island of Saipan. Nursing a damaged bomber home required a great deal of skill and determination; forced to break off a "windmilling propeller," Farrell found out just how skilled a pilot he was:

"On one occasion during a high-altitude mission over Nagoya we were hit by over a dozen fighter attacks which knocked out our number three engine. The 'feathering motor' [each of the blades can be twisted by a motor to reduce the drag of an inoperative unit] was destroyed in the process, making it impossible to feather the propeller.

"After making it safely back to the coast of Japan there was no way that we could possibly make it back to Saipan with a 'windmilling propeller'; in this situation the propeller creates a great deal of drag. Faced with the inevitability of ditching at sea I decided to try to shake the propeller loose by aggravating the situation. By this time we were probably down to around 29 to 28,000ft [8,839 to 8,534m].

"I put the bird into a fairly steep 60- to 65-degree dive angle (a little past the 305mph [491km/h] red line), and when the propeller shaft turned molten red from over-speeding I leveled off and gave the control yoke a sharp jolt. This caused the propeller to fly off like a rocket. It went straight ahead for about 3 miles [5km] or so before it finally stopped and hung there like a picture hanging on a wall. Believe me, seeing a giant hunk of metal over 16ft [4.9m] in diameter hanging motionless (other than it spinning) at more than 25,000ft [7,620m] in the air was an almost hypnotizing sight to behold.

"Then just as we came abreast of it (maybe 200 yards [183m] off to the left of us), it suddenly arched right across the top of our fuselage, missing us by no more than 20ft [6m]. It was like it was 'coming home to roost,' right back to the spot on our number three engine. With just three engines we diverted to Iwo Jima and landed safely."

Air Commander Nolan Strange was one of very few pilots who served in both the European and the Pacific theaters of war. After flying 27 missions in B-17s with the Eighth Air Force he returned to the United States in late 1944 and learned to fly one of the specialized versions of the Superfortress: the B-29B F-13. Photo reconnaissance was a vital cog in the Allied war machine; targets had to be found and bomb damage assessed:

"I was in the 91st Reconnaissance Squadron; we flew out of Guam, the Northwest Field. We were flying the B-29B F-13 model, which was the long-range photo reconnaissance version. It didn't have any turrets, except for the tail gunner, no blisters on the side, but it did have an astrodome on the top for the navigator. In the bomb bay we carried six cameras: three K-17Bs, two K-22s, and one K-18. It knocked down the weight pretty good and I think we weighed in at 110,000lbs [55 tons]. All of the cameras were operated by the photo-navigator; his position was up where the bombardier usually worked. Of course we didn't carry any bombs and that made us a lot lighter than the bomber boys—they called us 'hot rods.' A normal fully loaded B-29 would take almost the entire runway for takeoff—8,500ft [2,592m], but because we were much lighter it took us only 7,000ft [2,134m]; we flew a little bit faster and a little higher.

"We flew a number of different missions: photo-reconnaissance, weather recon, and fighter escort. We would take pictures before a strike, after, and sometimes during.

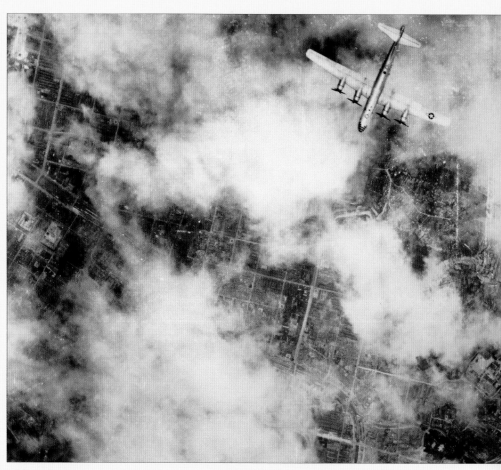

Below: A B-29 encounters overcast skies over the target. Pacific currents and frigid winter winds from the Asian continent conspired to produce almost perennial cloud over Japan. Bombing through Cloud (BTO) using radar became standard procedure.

Above left: *The propeller feathering buttons were located just to the right, and within easy reach, of the A/C.*

Right (inset) and above right: *The B-29 altimeter; each prop had to be "pulled through" so that there were no liquid locks in the lower engine cylinder.*

"On the fighter escort missions, we acted as a navigation ship—we'd shepherd up to 50 P-51s at a time. We'd take them to a specific point off the coast of Japan and off they'd go. On their return they'd look for our big red tail and form up on us— that was the name of our plane—*The Red Ass.*"

Friendly-fire incidents during World War II were sadly a common occurrence: ground troops suffered the most from stray artillery shells and fighter-bomber attacks by their own aircraft, and thousands were killed in this manner. Allied aircraft were not immune, either. On December 20, 1944, copilot John Elliott and his crew received instructions to transfer a B-29 from Hsinching, China, to Chakulia, in India; that night over Burma they were shot down by a British Beaufighter in the dark:

"That evening we took off for Chakulia. At the time the sky was overcast, and because of the earlier Japanese raids there was a radio blackout; we couldn't receive any weather broadcasts. We were given meteorological data prior to takeoff but we couldn't confirm it due to the overcast. Our flight plan was to take us south to Ipin and then southwest to the Assam Valley, which we would follow to Calcutta. We were not carrying any bombs and our guns were not loaded—we didn't believe we were in any danger. It was all very relaxing, and we were equipped with IFF (Identification Friend or Foe— a device [that], when activated by friendly radar, would transmit the right identification codes). It was operating properly and was set on the designated code channel for that day.

"The first indication that anything was wrong was the rat-tat-tat of bullets hitting the plane. I looked out the right side of cockpit and saw our number three engine on fire. Bob (the A/C) told me to feather and activate the fire extinguishers, but heavy flames continued to trail; we were in danger of blowing up. Bob gave the order to bail out and rang the alarm bell— I lowered the landing gear so the crew in the forward compartment could go out through the nose wheel well.

"I'm not certain, but I believe Chuck Biehle was the first one out. I followed, and when I hit the airstream feet first I began to tumble head over heels. I pulled the ripcord, and after my 'chute opened I stopped tumbling.

"I looked down and saw that I was over the large estuary of the Ganges River, about a half mile in width. It was very difficult to judge distance in the light of the moon, which was about 30 degrees above the western horizon. Coming down from 10,000ft [3,048m], I drifted over Sandwip Island. When I landed, I sort of slid down the side of a springy tree which slowed my speed but it was a little jarring. Since I was not certain of our location, I rolled up in my parachute and spent the night where I was. After daylight the next day, some local people gathered around, and they escorted me to the headquarters. Some of the other crewmembers were there, and that's when I learned a message had been sent to Chakulia informing authorities of our location. An OA-10 (Air Force PBY) was sent to pick us up."

The heat is on

Aircraft Commander Ernest Pickett was one of the first B-29 pilots to be shot down and made a POW. Having endured torture, starvation, and being sentenced to death, Ernest found that his unmarked POW camp was in the path of a B-29 incendiary raid; his graphic account tells us what it was like to be on the receiving end of a B-29 IA (incendiary attack; most bombing missions to Japan were IA raids):

"Shortly after midnight on the morning of March 10, 1945, we awoke to the sound of air raid sirens and the drone of heavy aircraft overhead. The noise, even in the barracks, was deafening. The boom of antiaircraft fire,

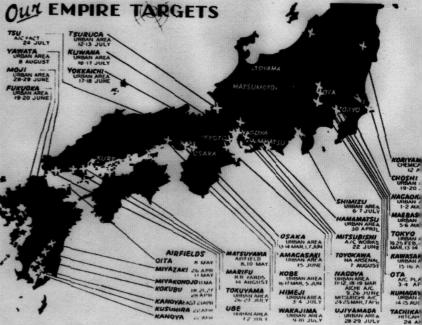

Above: *This target map, created after the war, shows the principal Japanese cities that were attacked using incendiary bombs, with the percentage of each city destroyed.*

Left: *An IA mission in progress—a view of the war from the bomb bay. 100lb (45kg) M-47 incendiary bombs rain down on the docks of Kobe, June 5, 1945.*

the explosion of bombs, and the sound of pandemonium in the streets all added to the roar. Within five minutes the room was lit up from the outside as if it was midday. It was an incendiary raid! The city was on fire.

"Guards, manic and frightened, ran into the barracks, ordering us outside. Their hate for us boiled in their eyes, but they couldn't kill us. They needed us to fight the fire.

"We could see them bombing to the north of us. Instead of flying in formation, the B-29s made individual bomb runs. Each bomb fell as a huge ball of fire dropping from the belly of the plane. It sparkled like an enormous inverted Christmas tree. The fire was an inferno; the heat was incredible—almost too hot to breathe. Smoke and cinders blew in swirls around us, creating a wind of its own. The raid probably lasted a couple of hours. Between the bombs, the fire and the guards, it had seemed as if there was no way to survive. My fear had been overwhelming; and then it was over. We were dismissed to the barracks where we sank to our mats, exhausted, and slept.

"Here and there, the carcass of a horse rested in the streets, roasted. We had one meal of horsemeat—it was the only meat I ever ate in Japan."

Above: *Goin' Jessie was named by pilot Capt. John D. Fleming. She completed 51 successive missions without an abort, and dropped more than 330 tons of bombs.*

Charles G. "Chuck" Chauncey flew 35 combat missions from Tinian with the 5th Bomb Squadron, 9th Bomb Group, 313th Bomb Wing, serving primarily as a copilot but also as an A/C. Incendiary attacks on Japanese cities often created their own violent weather systems over the target, and B-29s would be tossed around like toys while on their bomb runs:

"I would classify our fifth mission to Kobe, on March 16, 1945, as the 'roughest mission' of our 35-mission tour. It was another 15-hour-round-trip, night, single-plane, low-altitude, incendiary bombing mission to the mainland. The A/C, First Lieutenant John Fleming, and myself, decided to continue flying *Goin' Jessie* on autopilot. John controlled the heading with the turn control knob while I controlled the pitch control knob to maintain our bombing altitude. A short time later we ran into the first traces of smoke from the Kobe fires that blew smack into our faces.

"This was not the normal smelling smoke from a burning building; this had an acrid smell like an attic fire with chicken feathers or human flesh. As we continued on toward the target the ride became progressively rougher. We were whacked by alternating updrafts and downdrafts.

"I was trying my best to keep the plane level and at our prescribed bombing altitude of 6,400ft [1,951m]. This was impossible; our airspeed jumped up to 330mph [531km/h] in a downdraft and only 160mph [257km/h] in an updraft. We came out of the cloud base in a 60-degree dive looking straight down at the burning wharf area and the city of Kobe. It's still in my mind; I can picture this huge single-story warehouse building at the wharf with fires coming out of its many windows and doors . . . then all at once the whole roof collapsed consumed by the fires."

Captain Donald A. Barton was A/C with the 60th Bomb Squadron, 39th Bomb Group, 314th Bomb Wing based at North Field on Guam—his plane was *City of Spokane*. The firestorms created by the IAs produced

new and unforeseen hazards over the target area; not only did crews need to avoid enemy fighters but they also had to dodge flying debris and howling winds. Donald recalls his second mission over Japan:

"I was a pilot instructor in B-24s in Montgomery, Alabama, for over one and a half years, and then I was able to transfer to the B-29 program; I got five months of B-29 flying at Alamogordo, New Mexico. From there we went to Smokey Hill Air Base at Salina, Kansas, for combat crew training [where] we spent several months getting to know the B-29 and our respective duties. In California I picked up a new plane . . . and we departed for Guam on March 23, 1945. We flew a full tour of 25 missions including a show of air power during the surrender ceremonies aboard the battleship *USS Missouri* in September 1945.

"Our second mission, after arriving on Guam, was to drop incendiary bombs on Tokyo. The bombardier took us directly over the target point at an altitude of 6,400ft [1,951m]—we immediately went into the smoke and heat; the target area was totally engulfed in fire. We went into the

Above: *By the end of the war, Tinian had six runways and was the largest aviation complex in the world, with 11 miles (18km) of taxiways and hardstands for 450 B-29s.*

inferno at 220mph [354km/h]. I tried to maintain control, but we were hurled upward—we cut throttles clear back, put the nose down, all the while trying to maintain a level altitude and attitude, but when we came out into clear sky we found ourselves at 15,000ft [4,572m] doing 380mph [612km/h]—the updrafts were so powerful we actually saw pieces of corrugated metal from Japanese buildings flying up there with us!"

Combat to cargo

Dick Windler was one of the first B-29 pilots to fly combat missions during the war; he would go on to become one of the most experienced. Flying in both CBI (China, Burma, India) and from Tinian in the Marianas with the 58th Bomb Wing, 793rd Bomb Squadron, he racked up an impressive record: 35 combat missions and 59 flights over the Hump, for a total of 670 combat hours. Ironically, before he could fly a single combat mission he had to fly supply missions in both the B-29 and C-109 (the C-109 was the cargo/tanker version of the B-24 Liberator—he would fly 37 supply missions in this aircraft), subsequently taking part in one of the longest mine-laying missions of the war:

"Each time we made a round trip over the Hump we painted a camel on the fuselage. Between July 5 and October 26, I put 16 camels on my B-29. It had all the armament removed; in the bomb bay we had four fuel tanks, plus we carried parts and supplies. We weighed over 135,000lb [67.5 tons] on takeoff. We'd fly to China, drop off 3,000 gallons [11,355 liters] of fuel, 100 gallons [378 liters] of oil, parts and supplies, return to India and use only 6,000 gallons [22,710 liters] to accomplish this feat. The average round trip was approximately 12 hours.

"We endured horrendous weather over the Hump in addition to India's infamous monsoons. It would rain for weeks at a stretch. It got so bad that after several weeks of non-stop rain the thatch roof on our 'bashas' became saturated. We had to rig up pup tents over our beds in order to stay dry, and everything turned green with mold; leather jackets, wallets, you couldn't keep anything dry. The bamboo roof structure was also infested by termites; termite dust was everywhere. You were constantly cleaning the stuff off everything. We also had rats crawling in the roof structure just above our beds—we used to shoot at them with our Air Force issue Colt .45 caliber automatic pistols; I don't think we ever hit anything. Snakes were also a problem.

"My tour in China lasted approximately nine months. I flew nine combat missions and over 50 round trips over the Hump to China. The bombing missions averaged between 15 to 18 hours; the longest was to Singapore, a mine-laying mission in the Singapore Straits.

"Mission number five on January 25–26, 1945, was from our base in Karaghpur, India, to Singapore, landing in Ceylon [now Sri Lanka]. Singapore was heavily defended, and we were given very special instructions about how to approach it. [Singapore, now part of Malaysia, had been a British colony; it was over-run by the Japanese on February 15, 1942.] Because we were flying straight to Ceylon and not returning to base we were completely loaded with sea mines and ammo; it was

Center top: Dick Windler at the controls during the Korean War. Like many World War II B-29 pilots, Windler was recalled for duty during the Korean War.

Left: A US Navy 1,000lb (454kg) mine being loaded into the cavernous B-29 bomb bay.

Right: *The No. 51 Service
Cap was rarely worn in the hot
Pacific climate. The cap could not
be worn in flight with a headset
over it because of its stiffness.*

a mine-laying mission at the request of the British. These mines looked similar to a bomb but without tail fins to guide it down. Instead, there was a small parachute at the rear of the mine that opened after release from the bomb bay. There was also a soluble washer in the triggering mechanism that delayed its activation by as much as several weeks. If the Japanese ran mine sweepers over the area a few might explode, but the rest would remain dormant.

"The Singapore Straits were a series of rivers that were not too deep. When we arrived at the target, all of Singapore was fully lit, like nothing was happening; at around midnight we started our run. We were using radar and flying at only 2,000ft [610m]. As we approached our initial point, the opening of the bomb bay doors momentarily blocked out the radar; this caused us to miss the starting point. We had to go back and do it again. This time around all of Singapore was completely blacked out. When the first mine went all hell broke loose; it looked like the Fourth of July as flak and cannon tracers flashed by. With the last mine dropped and bomb bay doors closed, I said, 'let's get the hell out of here!' I shoved the plane almost straight down and redlined the speed at around 350mph [563km/h] in about 1,000ft [305m]. I then leveled off and went like a bat out of hell up the river.

"With all the action behind us, I pulled the yoke back and damn near went straight up past 10,000ft [3,048m] before the airspeed dropped off. I leveled out and continued my climb to 18,000ft [5,486m]. When we reached 18,000 we proceeded to readjust our engines to cruising speed; much to our dismay the number four engine rpm was stuck in the climb setting and wouldn't budge. After much discussion we decided to feather the engine.

"I had the navigator and flight engineer calculate how far from Ceylon we were and how much fuel we needed to get there. The most efficient power setting was quickly determined and the navigator suggested that by losing 50ft [15m] of altitude per minute for the rest of the way, we would make it. All of this [took place] over the Indian Ocean, the most shark-infested waters in the world.

Above right: *A ground crewman polishes* Camel Caravan *from the 468th Bomb Group.*

Left: *The 1911A1 model Colt .45 was standard for US servicemen. It shot the large .45 caliber round (shown).*

"As we approached Ceylon it was around 9 or 10am and we were squeezing it at this point. The landing was to the south and, believe me, the damn British had the battleship *Renown* anchored right off the end of the runway. We had to come in high to clear the ship, making our approach at a rather steep angle. This caused the fuel in the forward tanks to slosh forward—starving the engines. As a result, one of them stopped on final. This was way too close for comfort; I'm sure my prayers were answered on that flight."

Over the Hump

"Up we went, headed for 21,000ft [6,401m] and some sunlight. Minutes went by. Then our rate of climb and altimeter ceased to respond; we weren't getting anywhere! We stayed at a little less than 18,000ft [5,486m]. Then came the worst news: We were iced up on as much of the wings as could be seen, and we had to face it; this was going to be a low-level, high-sweat mission."—George E. Lowry, 395th Bomb Squadron, 40th Bomb Group, describing his experiences of flying over the "Hump."

When Curtis LeMay took command of the 20th Air Force in China, he described the logistics as "utterly absurd." He was right—by the end of May 1944, Superfortresses from the 58th Bomb Wing had completed 245 supply flights into China with just enough fuel and bombs to mount the first B-29 bombing raid of the war.

It took at least seven B-29 trips carrying gasoline from the US via India to support one combat takeoff from China, making it the world's longest supply line. But to get the fuel into China, pilots had to negotiate the "aluminum trail" across the Hump: the Himalayas, one of the world's most formidable mountain ranges, 1,500 miles (2,414km) long with 100 peaks over 22,000ft (6,706m).

The plan to fly B-29 missions out of China quickly proved far more challenging than anticipated, though. Army Air Force transports were already flying in supplies over the Hump for air force units already in China, but the Superfortress groups were on their own; bomber crews eager for combat were dismayed to find themselves flying cargo missions. In order to accelerate the process, 20 B-29s were stripped of armament and turned into giant gas tanks capable of carrying 9,000 gallons (34,068 liters) of fuel and 100 gallons (378 liters) of oil. In order to spare the B-29s from wearing out, more than 200 B-24 Liberators were converted to C-109 tankers, capable of ferrying 2,900 gallons (10,976 liters) of fuel. These were bolstered by cargo C-46 Commandos. On April 24, 1944, the arduous task of hauling supplies into China began; two days later the first encounter between a Japanese fighter and a B-29 occurred over the Hump: en route to Hsinching, a B-29 from the 444th Bomb Group tangled with a Ki-43 "Oscar." Tail gunner Sgt. Harold Lanahan was credited with an

Center top: A formation of B-29s climbs over the mountains and through the overcast on another re-supply mission.

Left: The Pilot's Navigation Kit. The job of navigator did not exist until the US entered the war in December 1941. Up to that point, navigation was done by rated pilots.

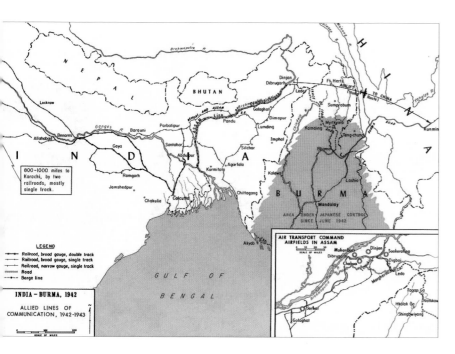

aerial victory, and the Japanese claimed one B-29 shot down; however, both aircraft made it home, with the B-29 suffering eight bullet holes.

While the Japanese did send a small number of fighters to intercept the bloated, overloaded transports, the real enemy was the weather. For the first time in history, pilots had to fly at minimum altitudes of 20,000ft (6,096m) in some of the world's worst weather conditions—forecasts were nonexistent and many pilots were forced to fly through severe thunderstorms and heavy icing.

The 40th Bomb Group's monthly newspaper later reported, "At the time, these flights were regarded as 'operational hours' for which no combat time was credited. Later, combat credit was given and George Lowry's crew received credit for the equivalent of about nine combat missions for their 34 Hump flights."

The plan to strike the Japanese mainland from China had proven to be complex and not fully thought out. Only 9 strikes of 49 were flown against Japan for the loss of 125 B-29s, 29 to enemy action, and in January 1944 all of the B-29s in China were ordered to move to their new bases in the Mariana Islands, in the Pacific.

Right: Flying Stud II. The nose markings denote both bombing and supply missions. Each camel denotes one successful supply mission flown over the Hump. The Japanese flags indicate four Japanese fighters shot down, with three "probables" beneath them.

New challenges

Lieutenant Robert E. Copeland was a member of the 500th Bomb Group, 73rd Bombardment Wing, and 881st Squadron, and was copilot for Major Robert Fitzgerald. Their B-29, *Z Square 8*, was "kamikazed" over Kobe on March 17, 1945, and crashed into a POW camp on the outskirts of Kobe. Two crew members survived, Sergeant Augunas and Lieutenant Nelson, but were beheaded. This extract from Copeland's diary tells of the first bombing raid on Tokyo, and his frustration at delays in setting out:

"November 14, 1944: There is a big mission coming up the next few days with the choicest target of all as our destination, 'Tokyo.' I hope we do a good job; this will be the first official raid on Japan by '29s.

"November 18: Maybe we'll go tomorrow, I hope. If we do, Hirohito is going to be rather upset after we cut loose with 5,000lbs [2.5 tons] of bombs from nearly 90 airplanes.

"November 19: I had expected this to be our big day but the mission was called off because the wind was blowing the wrong way. Maybe we'll go sooner or later.

"November 20: Getting up at these ungodly hours just to bomb Tokyo is getting very monotonous. We arose at 04:30 this morning and after we got all prepared they called the mission off.

"November 21: We crawled out at 05:00 this morning and had everything in the airplane before the mission was called off. I'm getting slightly bitter about this whole thing.

"November 24: This will be a day to long remember. We made the first raid over Tokyo today. It was also my first combat mission. We arrived over the target in the early afternoon soon after the first groups had bombed the primary. I could see a large pillar of smoke rising from it. Clouds covered the target when we closed in and we went to the secondary. Boren [the bombardier] said he saw his bombs working over docks so I guess we may have done some good.

"The flak was from meager to moderate, and most of it was accurate as far as altitude was concerned. We didn't lose a ship

Right: *My Girl, a North American P-51, about to take off from Iwo Jima. Equipped with two 220 gallon (833 liter) drop tanks, Mustangs were able to escort B-29s all the way to Japan and back.*

from our group. A ship from one of the other groups was reported to have ditched just off the coast of Japan. One tail gunner died of anoxia [oxygen starvation] and a bombardier was shot in the leg, so we had very few casualties.

"We had a few shots at fighters; [one] came in at 11 o'clock low. Another came in from the front, but no one got a shot at him. Another came in at 7 o'clock high, but no one got him either. Ten to 15 sat out of range but never came in."

The North American P-51 Mustang was the premier escort fighter of the war, and in late 1945 these fighters began escorting B-29s from Iwo, Burma, and attacking targets on the Japanese homeland. Because most of the flight to Japan was over water, the Mustang pilots needed a guiding hand; to help them on their way, B-29s were used as escort ships. Aircraft Commander Nelson Sanders and his crew of the 58th Bomb Wing were given the task of escort for the "escorts:"

"On June 6, Bill Kingsbury, C/O of the 25th, assigned us to temporary duty providing navigational escort for P-51s. We would usually navigate a group of 70 to 90 P-51s. We would take off first and, once airborne, we would circle at 5,000 to 8,000ft [1,524 to 2,438m] and wait until all of the P-51s were in formation. We then headed to our targets at approximately 8,000ft [2,438m] and indicated air speed of 210mph [338km/h]. The flight to Japan was approximately 650 miles [1,046km] one way, and the missions normally lasted eight to ten hours. The P-51s had problems flying on instruments in bad weather and especially through fronts; we were advised to abort if we encountered severe weather. Fortunately, we were never forced to.

"Upon reaching Honshu, the P-51s would have an hour of combat over Japan. The B-29s would circle over the ocean about 5 miles [8km] from the coast. The majority of the fighter[s] would usually return to the rendezvous point within five to eight minutes of each other. One of the B-29s would lead the first pack of fighters back to Iwo Jima in a loose formation. Most of the other P-51s would appear within ten minutes or so; our job was to wait for any stragglers."

Above: *This POW camp was located in Kobe, Japan. It was just one of the 154 camps known to exist in Japan, Korea, and China shortly after the war ended. B-29s were quickly modified to carry maximum loads of provisions and air drops soon followed.*

On Sunday June 25, 1950, the Korean War began, and the B-29 would encounter a new and deadly enemy over the skies of Korea. A/C William "Bill" Reeter and his crew, from the 371st Bomb Squadron, were savaged over the target by the world's newest jet fighter—the Russian MiG-15:

"As we were approaching the target, CAP radioed that MiGs were inbound. The MiGs attacked just as they rolled out of the turn. I was too busy maintaining formation to look around much. I only saw two: one was making a head-on pass; then one came in from behind. I could hear fire control talking about it. Then there was an explosion and the cabin depressurized.

"My tail gunner was wounded; he had a slug sticking out the bottom of his foot. The radio operator and another gunner were hurt pretty bad. Most of the injuries (up front) were from the exploding shell. Pieces of plastic (from the navigator's window) were embedded in the squadron commander's leg. I didn't know I was hurt until I felt something wet on my neck; when I reached up I felt something sticking out of my jaw. I pulled it out. It was a blue piece of tubing, probably part of the oxygen system.

"Edwards [the navigator] was the worst off; my copilot went to check on him. He was slumped forward, face down on the navigation table. He was alive but his left eye was lying on his cheek, a piece of his skull was flipped back and you could see his brain.

"As we approached Kimpo and slowed down, it got a lot harder to control the airplane. I told the crew that they could bail out, but they didn't want to—I had two guys who couldn't bail out, so I had to land the airplane."

Reeter was awarded the Silver Star for his actions. Part of the official citation read: "While on the bomb run the formation was attacked by approximately 150 enemy MiG-15 jet fighters. In the ensuing battle, Lieutenant Reeter's aircraft was severely damaged and he and seven crewmembers were injured. Three separate fires developed in the aircraft, but with Lieutenant Reeter's aid and supervision, they were extinguished."

[After the war, Bill transitioned to B-47s. In 1956, his crew became Strategic Air Command's "Crew of the Year."]

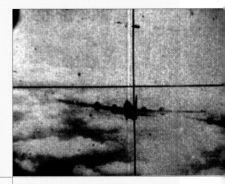

Above: *A MiG-15 gun camera frame taken by Kapetan Ivan Suckhov on April 12, 1951, while attacking a formation of B-29s. Fifty F-84 Thunderjets flew escort, but were unable to prevent the Soviet pilots from getting through.*

Left: *A/C William Reeter addresses his crew prior to flying a new mission. Reeter was assigned to the 371st Bomb Squadron, 307th Bomb Group based at Kadena Air Base, Okinawa. The 307th BG was part of Strategic Air Command's contribution to the Korean War.*

The Bombardier

"We were to drop two 500lb [227kg] fire-bomb clusters on the island of Rota. One of the majors aboard wanted to drop the bombs, so I showed him the whole procedure from pulling the pins on the bombs, calculating all data, setting information in the bombsight—then after starting the bomb run let him take over: results were good."

—First Lieutenant Leonard A. Kuther, bombardier, 62nd BS (VH), 39th BG (VH), Guam

The bomber and its crew were created to deliver bombs to a target; it was the bombardier's job to ensure that those bombs actually hit the target. The bomb run itself—the time between reaching the Initial Point (IP) and "bombs away"—rarely took more than a few minutes of a 12-hour mission, but any error in that time could leave the target intact, forcing the bombers to return on another mission on another date. By the time of the B-29's combat debut, USAAF doctrine had a lead bomber sighting the target for each squadron. Bombardiers in the other aircraft were trained to drop on a precise interval after the leader (a practice known as "toggling," after the toggle switch used to release the bombs), ensuring a tight bomb pattern on the ground and obliteration of the target. In the event of a problem with the lead aircraft, each bombardier was trained to take the lead. The preferred sighting method was visual, with the lead bombardier relying on the legendary Norden bomb sight to get his bombs onto the target. If the target was obscured, every B-29 was equipped with radar; this was an enormous increase in a formation's capabilities when compared to the USAAF in Europe,

Left: Centered on the Norden bomb sight, the bombardier's position offered great visibility and easy access to all his instruments and controls.

where only one or two BTO (Bomb Through Overcast—see page 62) aircraft would be assigned to each B-17 or B-24 group. Still, the radar was not linked directly to the bomb sight; instead, the B-29 radar operator fed data to the bombardier, who manually entered it into the sight, toggling the bombs at the appropriate time. The least desirable sighting method was DR (Dead Reckoning) bombing. Without a visual or radar fix on the target, the bombardier would search for a known landmark, compute the bearing and distance to the target, set the aircraft on that course, and, with the aid of a stopwatch, release the bombs at the instant calculated to be the proper distance and angle from the target. Whenever possible, a formation could divert to an alternate target, but if fuel was low, DR bombing was preferable to bringing the payload home.

Of course, the bombardier's job carried many more responsibilities than those few minutes on the bomb run. Before each mission, he checked the bombs, shackles, and fuses, monitoring the armorers as they filled the bomb bays. There were other systems checks to perform before takeoff, and with the "best seat in the house"—forward of the pilots, with a perfect view of everything ahead—the bombardier was trained to watch for other aircraft as the formation assembled over home base. With the aircraft above 5,000ft (1,524m), the bombardier moved aft to remove the safety wires and arm the bomb load.

As the only gunner with an officer's commission, the bombardier was also responsible for training and organizing the B-29's other four gunners. With an estimated 45 per cent of Japanese fighter attacks being made from head-on, the bombardier had primary control of both forward gun turrets though, when necessary, he could release control of either, or both, forward turrets to the gunners in the aft fuselage. (The Central Fire Control system [see page 96] meant that B-29 gunners needed to operate as part of a gunnery team, and most Superfortress bombardiers were assigned to a 12- or 6-week course, training as part of a five-man gunnery crew.)

Each B-29 also carried a strike camera to document bombing results, with the bombardier ensuring that the camera was working properly as the bombs reached their targets. If the navigator was injured, the bombardier was expected to assume the navigator's duties "accurately and confidently." Even on routine missions, the bombardier assisted with navigation, taking drift readings and using his bomb sight to help calibrate ground speed.

But, for all their training, B-29 bombardiers hardly ever delivered accuracy on high-altitude precision bombing missions over Japan; targets were often obscured by cloud, haze, or smoke, and radar was proving less reliable than originally projected. Even with perfect visibility, the jet stream winds over Japan were difficult to adjust for with the Norden bomb sight. Needing results in the Twentieth Air Force's strategic air war, in early 1945 General LeMay decided to switch from a daylight precision bombing campaign to a night area bombing one. Using a lesson from the RAF's Bomber Command, LeMay sent pathfinder aircraft out to mark the targets with fire bombs. Arriving over the target in individual aircraft, rather than in squadron or group formations, each bombardier simply sighted on a dark area below, certain that he was aiming at an area not already on fire. The results of these firebombing raids were devastating to the Japanese; the attacks destroyed not only the factories, but the smaller supporting shops, as well as the workers, their homes, their families, and their neighbors. The B-29 bombardiers were hitting their targets, as ghastly and merciless as the task had become, and Japan's willingness and ability to wage war began

to waiver. The decisive acts fell to two bombardiers in August 1945: Major Tom Ferebee would drop the world's first atomic weapon on Hiroshima, followed a few days later by Captain Kermit Beahan, who dropped the second atomic bomb on Nagasaki.

Page right, clockwise from top left: *Gun sight; bombardier in position; his instrument panel; gun control panel; the bombardier's datatable; and the base of the stowed gunsight.*

The Norden Bomb Sight

Touted for its fabled ability to put a bomb into a pickle barrel from 10,000ft (3,000m), the Norden bomb sight was the most accurate bomb-aiming device of World War II. The sight automatically compensated for drift, altitude, and ground speed, allowed the bombardier to adjust the aircraft's course, and automatically salvoed the bombs at the calculated release point. But the jet stream over Japan accelerated B-29s to ground speeds over 445mph (716km/h), well beyond the Norden's computational abilities. Accuracy was further eroded by dramatic variations in lower-altitude wind speeds and directions. Above 30,000ft (9,000m), no bomb sight could put the B-29s' bombs on their targets, and missions were thus moved to lower altitudes and area bombing attacks.

RESTRICTED   MARCH, 1945 BIF 6-1-1

NOMENCLATURE
AND
OPERATION

1. LEVELING KNOBS
2. CAGING KNOB
3. EYEPIECE
4. INDEX WINDOW
5. TRAIL ARM AND TRAIL PLATE
6. EXTENDED VISION KNOB
7. RATE MOTOR SWITCH
8. DISC SPEED GEAR SHIFT
9. RATE AND DISPLACEMENT KNOBS
10. MIRROR DRIVE CLUTCH
11. SEARCH KNOB
12. DISC SPEED DRUM
13. TURN AND DRIFT KNOBS
14. TACHOMETER ADAPTER
15. RELEASE LEVER
16. CROSSHAIR RHEOSTAT
17. DRIFT SCALE
18. PDI BRUSH AND COIL
19. AUTOPILOT CLUTCH ENGAGING KNOB
20. AUTOPILOT CLUTCH
21. BOMBSIGHT CLUTCH ENGAGING LEVER
22. BOMBSIGHT CLUTCH
23. BOMBSIGHT CONNECTING ROD
24. AUTOPILOT CONNECTING ROD

The bombsight has 2 main parts, **sighthead** and **stabilizer**. The sighthead pivots on the stabilizer and is locked to it by the dovetail locking pin. The sighthead is connected to the directional gyro in the stabilizer through the **bombsight connecting rod** and the **bombsight clutch**.

RESTRICTED

Seconds to spare

One of the worst things that bombardiers could encounter over the target was cloud. It took them out of the game and gave the radar operator the job of bomb aimer. On September 26, 1944, while on their way to bomb the coke ovens at Anshan (in northeast China and under Japanese occupation since 1931; Anshan was one of the largest producers of iron and steel in Asia), bombardier Frank W. McKinney and his crew found the target socked in by cloud. The secondary target was also covered in cloud; and to make matters worse, the radar malfunctioned. With seconds to spare, McKinney found a break in the clouds and made the drop:

Above: A 498th Bomb Group B-29 encounters overcast skies. Precision daylight bombing required clear weather; unfortunately the weather rarely cooperated, forcing the majority of bomb runs to be made by radar.

"I felt a great disappointment not being able to bomb Anshan, but when we made the decision to go for the secondary target at Dairen, my enthusiasm returned and the adrenaline started to flow; but as it turned out this wasn't a good day for bombing.

"As we approached Dairen we were disappointed to see further cloud cover. As we approached the target area, I had a sinking feeling that we would have to bomb by radar. Then our radar equipment malfunctioned and the radar operator couldn't identify the target. I was frustrated. Even though we had to get rid of the bombs, I was determined to do something with them and not drop them at random. Fortunately, the radar had lined

us up effectively with the target. I kept searching ahead hoping for a break in the cloud cover while keeping the bombsight ready in case the target showed itself. Operating the Norden bomb sight required a lengthy sighting procedure in order for the mechanism to adjust for ground speed, trajectory, etc. Time was getting short as I anxiously looked ahead, searching for an opening in the clouds.

"Suddenly, as I looked down, the target appeared. I had a few scant seconds to make a decision. Drop the bombs manually or salvo? Since part of the nose was iced up, I used the cross brace in the Plexiglas nose as an aiming device. I made a guess as to when to salvo the bombs. And miracle of miracles, the side gunners reported the target had been hit; later strike photos confirmed that the target had indeed been hit.

"We had no idea how important the target was to the Japanese, but I suppose our intelligence must have known. Luckily for us, even with the weather and mechanical problems, we hit the target and didn't drop our bombs just to get rid of them."

By late 1944, Japanese fighters were armed with two or four 20mm cannons. These weapons fired explosive shells that—once they pierced the aircraft's skin—would explode inside the aircraft, causing further damage. Bombardier Fritz Kulicka with the 58th Bomb Wing, 40th Bomb Group, dueled with a Japanese fighter over Takao on October 17, 1944. He describes the brief encounter:

"There was that fighter about two o'clock high. He was looking us over when I gave him a short burst from our twin .50s. The tracers bounded off his aircraft, and he must have been displeased because he dipped his wings and came at us. I could see bright flashes coming from his guns so, apparently, we were shooting at each other. After a brief

Above: This 73rd Bomb Wing B-29 was damaged by a Japanese fighter, probably due to a single 20mm cannon shell.

moment there was a loud explosion in our cockpit. Bob Moss sensed an explosive decompression and called on the intercom for us to immediately put on our oxygen masks.

"We were still in formation. After all the hell broke loose, we settled down to survey the damage. It appeared that we were hit with a 20mm explosive shell just inches above Carter's head and right in Ed Haggerty's flight engineer's position. Ralph Weinberg was sprayed with shrapnel as was Royal Klaver. Joe Duemig informed us on the intercom that our right side blister had blown away, and Sergeant Hornyia was parachuting down. Royal Klaver radioed lifeguard submarines of our predicament, but Hornyia was never found.

"We continued our flight to Luichow and landed there. About sunset, we were called for a meeting with an Associated Press news reporter named White. In retrospect, I think it was Teddy White, the China correspondent for *Time* magazine. We were briefed not to mention our names because Tokyo Rose would pick it up and make an issue of it in her broadcasts; this did not concern us so we gave names anyway. The story was filed, and our names made all the newspapers the following day. My hometown newspaper—the *Delta Democrat Times* in Greenville, Mississippi—carried the story."

It was a court martial offense, but bombardier Ray Ebert of the 497th Bomb Group kept an account of his first mission to Tokyo in his diary. Below is a small but revealing portion that describes the beginning of that raid in November of 1944:

"Hell we are now over the Blue Pacific. Tokyo bound. Have to excuse the penmanship; the air is terrifically rough. Because of our delay in takeoff, our group will be the last ones over the target. It is not an enviable position . . . temperature outside is 30 Celsius [86°F] at 1,000ft [305m] we are practically melting inside the ship . . . the entire distance thus far has been a series of thunderstorms, sure hope the target is clear . . . we also have our bombs all autographed [by ground crew] . . . Mikie, Eve, Dotty, Roselle, Bunny . . . the crewmembers are saving the safety pins from this first load . . . well we're getting nearer to the Jap homeland on the greatest history-making flight of the war (first Tokyo mission); just hope we don't become part of it. We have been joking and having a lot of fun in the plane but confidentially I think I'll be a wee bit scared. Major Morgan's outfit should be hitting the target in about one hour. We are keeping the radio tuned in hopes of hearing their results.

"Wonder with what feeling Myra will receive the bombing news. It will reach her by radio long before I am ever able to mention it in letters." [In this attack, only 63 B-29s bombed the primary target, most by radar due to heavy cloud cover. The Mitsubishi engine works at Nagoya did receive

Left: A fountain pen rests on top of a manual that was developed to standardize B-29 bombardier procedures and provide a handy guide for the combat crew.

some damage, but production was suspended by only ten days.]

On another 1944 mission, Ray was flying as bombardier in the 497th's *Ponderous Peg*:

"07:30: Here is your little reporter again with on the spot coverage. 07:36: Started engines. 07:39: Taxing. 07:57: Ready for takeoff. 07:59: Airborne. 08:30: Test-fired the guns, let's hope that's all we'll need fire from them. 09:37: Just saw Pilot's Halo [a rarely seen circular rainbow around a plane] ahead of us—we should have good luck. 12:30: Well we are in our climb and will be at the target in about two hours. 13:00 and 14:04: Two ships abort. Now we are six. 14:15: Now there are only five of us left, the Japs will have a chance to shoot the shit out of us. 14:30: Just test-fired our guns and three turrets are jammed. Frankly, I'm getting scared. 15:45: Can see the coast of Japan. 16:30: That's finished again, no casualties in our ship . . . had a chance to shoot today but I'm afraid I missed. Our bombs hit the target dead center . . . "

Above: A bomb tag "diary." Before reaching the target, each bomb would be armed by removing a pin designed to keep the fuse from arming itself while in flight. This pin would have a tag attached. This collection includes dates and targets hit.

Nights of fire

During the nights of May 24 and 26, 1945, Tokyo was bombed by more than 500 B-29s. The firestorm burned out 22 sq miles (57 sq km). The Japanese threw everything they had at the B-29s, including heavy flak, night fighters, and, unconfirmed, "Bakas." Forty-three B-29s were lost, with 86 per cent of the target destroyed. Hibbard A. Smith, a bombardier with the 45th Squadron, describes one of those harrowing nights:

Left: The "Baka" bomb was in fact the Yokosuka MXY7 Ohka; powered by three rocket engines, this was an air-launched piloted weapon armed with a 2,646lb (1,200kg) warhead.

"I flew both missions in #555 with Maj. Glen Landreth as pilot. The Tokyo missions were the 4th and 5th I flew in May, but my recollection is hazy. Because there was a shortage of bombardiers (Plexiglas is lousy armor plate), I flew several times with Maj. Landreth as check pilot with new crews [a check pilot flew with a new crew to make sure they were OK]. However, on both Tokyo missions I believe I flew with his regular crew, but I am not sure. Both missions were similar in plan. A series of four or five aiming points on a north/south line. Approach was from the southwest, with breakaway over the bay. As I recall, the aiming points were shifted to south on the second mission to take in the undamaged areas.

"The sight of Tokyo in the midst of a fire raid was awesome. As a bombardier I had a view like no one else . . . There was fire on the ground, fire in the sky, with no line of separation. The defenses included some sort of pale green pyrotechnics on the ground to light up the sky, but they also lit up the target.

"The 45th must have been one of the last groups over the target on both nights. The area was engulfed in flames as we came in. I could see B-29s ahead silhouetted against the burning city. I could only hope there were no stragglers under or above us . . . Aiming was visual, and I picked out an area not yet burning heavily. Later study of detailed target charts told me we had bombed in the general vicinity of the American Embassy.

"The May 26 mission was almost a replay of May 24; again B-29s to left and right of us were caught in searchlights as we tried to

Left: A B-29 from the 504th Bomb Group being serviced. The black/yellow stripes indicate that this was a "lead crew" ship.

sneak through; this time they weren't fooled. A beam pulled off the main cones and locked on to us—being in searchlight [is] a most helpless feeling; you can't see beyond the surface of your window. I assume the pilots went to instruments. Maj. Landreth took violent evasive action, and shook off the lights. I do not recall if the radar op released or I salvoed, but the bombs did go. [The] tail gunner reported a suspected Baka bomb behind us, but a relatively gentle turn to the right settled that problem, and we were on our way back to Tinian."

Bombardier Jim O'Keefe, also with the 45th Squadron, flew on both missions. He recalls being briefed on the Baka, and a mysterious light that would follow them all the way home:

"Our intelligence officers . . . came up with details of a crude, small aircraft captured on Okinawa. It was the Baka bomb, a suicide plane which could be air-launched from the belly of an aircraft such as the Betty, your standard Japanese medium bomber. Aside from the demented suicide pilot, the Baka carried a warhead weighing close to a ton; it was rocket-powered with sufficient fuel . . . for half an hour.

"The following evening we took off, once more heading for Tokyo with the diagrams and pictures of the crude but deadly Baka.

" . . . The moment we hit the IP we were picked up by a searchlight and subjected to intense flak. We were passed from searchlight to searchlight, [and] we suffered at least ten direct hits . . . Several minutes from the aiming point, the radio operator reported the incendiaries in our forward bomb bay were on fire. Then, one of the gunners told us the incendiaries in the rear bomb bay were also ablaze.

Double trouble—for Japs

Bombs are away . . . bomb-bay doors are closing on those empty twin caverns in the big ship's maw. In 40 seconds a shattering explosion will occur in a Japanese factory, 25,000 feet below. . . . "Mission accomplished."

The Boeing B-29 Superfortress is designed for a vital purpose: to carry a larger load of explosives farther and faster, with the ability to fly at higher altitudes, than any other bomber in the world.

The huge, double bomb-bays are the B-29's reason for being. Around them Boeing engineers have built

a great airplane. But the superb, aerodynamically clean wing and body, the turbo-supercharged engines, the pressurized cabins, the remote-control guns all serve one goal — to deliver the bombs.

Today Superfortresses of the 20th Air Force are pounding enemy industry with steadily mounting fury. In a single day the big planes have roared in over several different targets, from Singapore to Nagoya, and let go tons of destruction.

Manning the B-29 squadrons are picked crews — skilful, cool-headed and courageous — as fine a body

of flying fighters as can be found on earth or in air. The Superfortresses, like the Flying Fortresses, represent Boeing's effort to give American airmen the best possible weapons for accomplishing their difficult and hazardous missions.

When final victory is achieved, Boeing's broad experience in research, design, engineering and manufacture will once more be applied to peacetime aircraft. Of any such product you can be certain . . . if it's "Built by Boeing" it will lead the way.

DESIGNERS OF THE B-29 SUPERFORTRESS • THE FLYING FORTRESS • THE NEW STRATOCRUISER
THE KAYDET TRAINER • THE STRATOLINER • PAN AMERICAN CLIPPERS **BOEING**

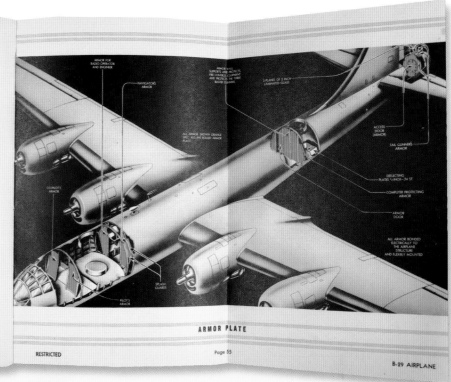

Above: *This manual foldout illustrates the placement of the B-29's armor, designed to protect the crew from rear attacks.*

Above left: *This Boeing ad highlights the B-29's enormous bomb bays. It could accommodate a 4,000lb (1,814kg) bomb.*

Left: *A/C, Bob Peckham, and bombardier, Warren Meek, prepare for a mission during the Korean War.*

we took the searchlights and flak for several long tense minutes—I was almost certain were we finished.

"Rod Wriston, as cool and able a pilot as ever I flew with, banked the battered plane slowly and carefully away from the burning city, the searchlights, and antiaircraft guns. We caught our collective breaths only to gasp in sudden shock and alarm at the bright light which appeared above and in front of us; was it a Japanese plane's searchlights probing for us? I swung my gun sight to cover the light and brought the four .50 caliber machine guns to bear on it. We staggered on, the light neither gaining on us nor fading away . . . visible until the sun came up.

"I didn't report the 'Great Searchlight' in the sky. But rumors had circulated over at interrogation. Several gunners and bombardiers on other crews had seen the light and fired on it without hesitation. The .50 caliber slug would have sped unerringly toward the target. I got up and poked through my footlocker and found some notes from navigation school: given the muzzle velocity . . . and the distance to travel, and the slugs would have landed on Venus about 12 months later."

" . . . I, as bombardier, could have immediately salvoed all bombs and told Rod to get the hell out of there; I didn't. I held those bombs to the aiming point (which resulted in our taking more flak) and put them in the target area. Rod [the pilot] could have ordered me to salvo the burning bombs, but he said nothing; as A/C his orders would have prevailed. So

Near misses

Bombardiers were also trained as gunners, whose job was to control the front top turret armed with four .50 caliber machine guns. Japanese fighter defenses had proven anemic, but when the target was Tokyo the response was at times extremely vicious. Bombardier Raleigh Phelps from the 870th Bomb Squadron recalls a particularly heavy and determined attack by multiple Japanese fighters while flying over Tokyo in early 1945:

"They were waiting for us. We figured out that more than one hundred passes were made at *Thumper*—I counted 57 from the nose alone. They barreled in without let up, usually alone, but sometime in bunches. Some bored in to within 400 yards [366m] and then turned off. But others really pressed the attack, clearing us by inches. They went down in droves, but the rest kept coming. We downed six and damaged at least a dozen."

[*Thumper* made it out of the target area, with one engine out and her aft turrets empty. A lone Tony (Ki 61) tried many times to clip the tail of the B-29 with his propeller, but with each pass the blister gunners would report the Tony's movements and give the pilot ample time for evasive maneuvers. Damaged from the fight, *Thumper* managed to limp home.]

Below: A bombardier poses with his front gun sight. From here, he could protect the aircraft from head-on attacks. At his command were six .50 caliber machine guns in the top and bottom front turrets.

Above: There were two B-29s called Thumper. *One belonged to the 73rd Bomb Wing, 497th Bomb Group, 870th Squadron; the other one, which is pictured above, flew with the 313th Bomb Wing, 504th Bomb Group.*

The end of the war in the Pacific did not mean the end of operations. POW camps across Japan and the occupied territories contained thousands of prisoners, many of whom were at death's door due to the appalling conditions they had been living under. From August 27 through September 20, 1945, there were 1,066 B-29 takeoffs on mercy missions, which dropped more than 4,400 tons of supplies to 154 different POW camps housing an estimated 63,400 prisoners. Tragically, eight B-29s and 77 crewmembers were lost on these missions. Delmar Johnson, a bombardier with the 58th Bomb Wing, describes one such mission in which they survived and, tragically, another crew did not:

"At the end of hostilities, volunteers were requested to fly POW supply runs. I was fortunate to fly two such missions. The second to Yawata, Japan, was the most memorable and tragic. This was the mission on which . . . John Cornwell, our original

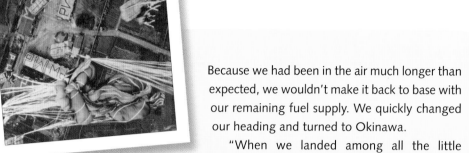

Right: *POW supply bundles tumble to earth. The buildings below have been clearly marked with "PW." Some 12,000 bundles were dropped in the first phase after the surrender; a standard package contained three days' food, plus clothing and medical kits.*

Command Pilot, flew another aircraft. Knowing some of the other crewmembers from various aircraft, I had my choice of aircraft and crew. Since I had flown once before with Aircraft Commander Ken Dothage, I chose his aircraft; it turned out to be our good fortune.

"The flight was long and uneventful but as we approached the Islands, they were completely socked in [by cloud]; we stayed on top in the clear weather searching for openings. To drop our supplies we had to drop down to an altitude of 800ft [244m]. After a couple of hours circling the target area, we didn't find any breaks in the cloud; we decided to go out over the water. Our plan was [to] get down under the heavy clouds, head into the harbor, make our drop, and climb out immediately. If my memory serves me correctly, our maps showed hills not more than 600 to 650ft [183 to 198m] in height but close to the heading we were on. There was absolutely no visibility above our approximate altitude of 600 to 800ft [183 to 244m]. We made our drop and as we began slowly climbing the radar observer screamed, 'pull up and turn right!' Ken reacted immediately, pushing the throttles to the limit. Thankfully our radar operator [had] spotted a dark patch on the left side of his screen.

"A few seconds later I remember looking off to the right. We were about 1,300 to 1,350ft [396 to 411m] altitude when, for a brief second, the clouds opened up. There off our right wing, just as we cleared the top of the hill, were trees not more than 20 or 30ft [6 or 9m] away. Ken Dothage, John Laxton and I had seen what, in all probability, John Cornwell and his crew did not. They were a couple of minutes behind us and unfortunately they didn't see the hill and crashed; they were all killed. This was not, however, to be the last of our worries.

Because we had been in the air much longer than expected, we wouldn't make it back to base with our remaining fuel supply. We quickly changed our heading and turned to Okinawa.

"When we landed among all the little potholes on the runway, it was on fumes and not fuel. It was verified later [that] we had no more than 25 gallons [95 liters] of gas in each of our tanks. That night we slept under the plane; through the night we heard gunfire that seemed to be very close. The next morning we were refueled, but only partially. I was told it was because of the short runway on Okinawa. We needed to be as light as possible. We took off and barely cleared the numerous ships' masts in the harbor below."

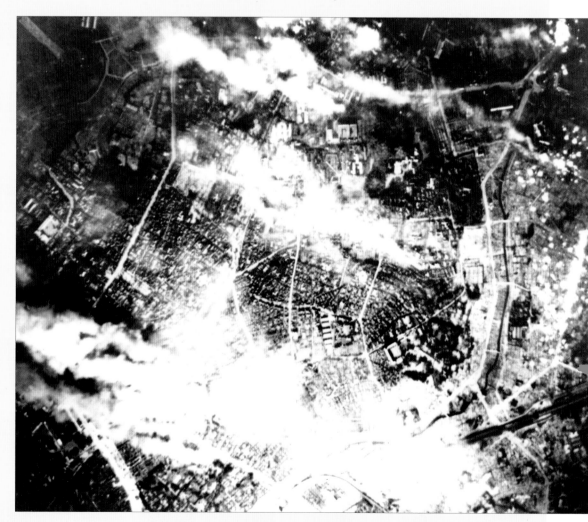

Above: *By the end of May 1945, 51 per cent of Tokyo had been destroyed by B-29 raids. During 1945, it was bombed more than 15 times. This photo shows the May 26 raid during which 464 B-29s bombed urban areas to the south of the Imperial Palace.*

Fire from the Sky

Long before the first incendiary bomb was dropped on a Japanese city, the Americans knew these urban centers could easily be destroyed by fire. In September 1940, the US naval attaché in Tokyo, Lieutenant Commander Henri Smith-Hutton, reported that "fire-fighting facilities are woefully inadequate. Incendiary bombs sowed widely over an area of

Left: This triangular patch was issued to those who successfully graduated from Armament School; the bomb denotes their title as Armorer.

Japanese cities would result in the destruction of the major portions of the cities." The fact that Tokyo's buildings were largely made of wood (90 per cent) made Japanese cities ideal targets for incendiary attacks.

The primary weapon used by the B-29 in the early stages of the war was the high-explosive bomb, generally of 500 or 1,000lbs (227 or 454kg). During operations from China, more than two-thirds of the bombs dropped were high explosives—even in the first three months of operations from the Marianas, the figures held steady. However, there was a major problem; bombing results were poor. The culprit was the weather, which was beyond anyone's control: Pacific currents and frigid winter winds from the Asian landmass created almost continuous cloud cover over Japan. Bombardiers could not hit what they could not see, but what proved even more insurmountable was the jet stream, which scattered bombs far and wide.

Analysts calculated that it would take 400 B-29s to destroy a single industrial target via high-altitude bombing. Unfortunately, in early 1945 the Marianas-based B-29s had been unable to launch 200. And daylight "precision bombing" was more myth than reality; in January and February 1944 six raids were launched, with mixed results; just one in three bombers attacked the primary target. Clearly a new method had to be found.

The idea of firebombing Japan was first put forward by Billy Mitchell in 1920. Curtis LeMay, by then commander in the Marianas,

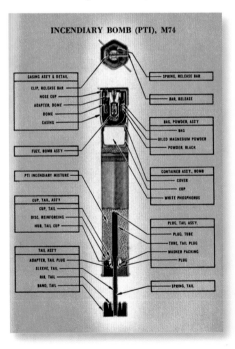

INCENDIARY BOMB (PTI), M74

Left: A 39th Bomb Group 314th Bomb Wing B-29 unleashes its load of incendiaries on the city of Hiratuska, Japan, on July 16, 1945. The 314th Bomb Wing's 132 B-29s dropped 1,163 tons of incendiaries on the target that day.

Above right: The M74 incendiary bomb was just one of 38 that formed a single 500lb (227kg) unit. This type was used in the Korean War. Like the M69, upon igniting, the M74 would spew a burning stream of jellied gasoline up to 180ft (55m).

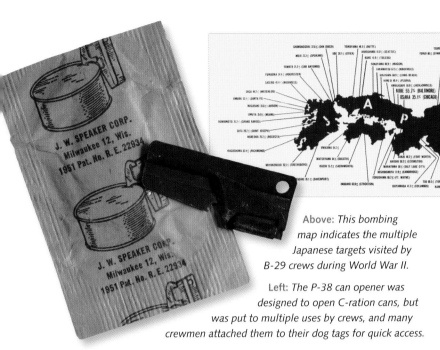

Above: *This bombing map indicates the multiple Japanese targets visited by B-29 crews during World War II.*

Left: *The P-38 can opener was designed to open C-ration cans, but was put to multiple uses by crews, and many crewmen attached them to their dog tags for quick access.*

Right: *The Mitsubishi A6M Zero was the mainstay of the Japanese Navy Air Force throughout World War II. Originally designed as a carrier-based fighter, it did not fare well against the B-29.*

Below: *500lb (227kg) bombs are hoisted from a specially equipped Dodge truck. These bombs are not ready for loading; fins and fuses have yet to be fitted.*

approved a new and controversial change in tactics: the B-29s would now fly low-altitude night missions. The switch from high-explosive bombs to incendiaries also meant a change in the choice of target; the Japanese aircraft industry was moved farther down the list, with urban areas and cities now taking top priority.

Fire now became the main weapon against Japanese cities, and the most effective weapon in the incendiary armory was the lightweight M69 bomb. About 20in (51cm) long and 3in (7.6cm) in diameter, it looked just

like a length of pipe. On impact, the M69's cargo of napalm (gasoline in a gel form) would ignite, producing a hellish jet of flame. But dropping these small bombs in loose packets produced poor results, so an "amiable cluster" was developed, which contained 38 M69s wrapped together with a finned tail and nose shroud. When dropped, the unit would break apart at about 2,000ft (610m), spewing its submunitions over a wide area.

Tokyo would be the first Japanese city to experience the full effect of these dedicated incendiary attacks. Mission 40 was code-named "Meetinghouse," and on March 9, 1944, 325 B-29s unloaded 1,665 tons of incendiaries on the fragile city. The firestorm that followed would be unstoppable. Sixteen square miles (41 sq km) of Tokyo were turned to ash, and 84,000 people were killed and 40,000 injured.

The sudden switch to low-level incendiary attacks had changed the nature of the air campaign. It also changed the job of the bombardier; in the coming raids the radar operator would play a more prominent role. Nevertheless, when the aiming was visual, the bombardier would simply pick an area that was not yet burning and drop his bombs.

Ordinary men; heroic deeds

B-29 missions involved long flights over water, and a return trip to Japan and back was 3,000 miles (4,828km). Add to this that battle damage or other malfunctions could seriously affect an aircraft's performance and, hence, range. Bombardier Carl Routh of the 768th Bomb Squadron, 462nd Bomb Group, relates how he and a crewmate, with no parachutes, no oxygen, and no safety line, saved their B-29 from ditching in the sea during a mission in the late spring of 1945:

"I was a lieutenant bombardier in the original B-29 group of 18 crews that arrived in India in 1944. Our home base was Paridoba, with an advance base in Chengtu, China. After six months, we left India and were based on Tinian . . . part of the Northern Marianas, which also included Saipan and Rota. Our 11-man crew flew 50 missions without a scratch.

"We had a lot of adventures, some dangerous and some just fun, but there was one particular mission that proved extremely dangerous. We had just finished bombing a major city in Japan; after 'bombs away,' I waited for the gunners in the rear of the plane to give me the okay the bomb doors had been closed; I never got the call—a malfunction in the doors caused them to stay open. Flying back to Tinian, which was about 1,500 miles [2,414km] away, required all the fuel we had. The drag of the open bomb bays would cause us to burn too much fuel and that meant we would have to ditch before we reached home base.

"Arvin Rivers, our Flight Engineer, and I realized there might be a solution. We had equipment in the bomb bay that was used to haul bombs up and station them on the racks. By getting the chain with the hook on the doors, we could pull them shut; the question was how to get back into the bomb bay and hook the chain onto the doors. At 17,000ft [5,182m] with no oxygen or parachute I held on to a bomb rack with one arm. With the other I held

Above: 500lb (227kg) bombs ready for loading on to Silver Lady. The B-29 was capable of carrying 40 500lb (227kg) bombs, but rarely did. The 500 "pounder" was filled with TNT with an explosive weight of 225lbs (102kg). Two fuses would be fitted, one in the nose, the other at the rear enclosed by the tail fin. This was the most widely used bomb in the CBI (China, Burma, India) theater.

Left: A stopwatch issued to bombardiers for calibration and adjustments on the bomb sight. This particular stopwatch flew in B-29s during 52 missions over Korea during the Korean War.

on to Rivers, who, with one arm dangling into the slipstream, managed to hook the doors and close them shut. Several days after, the squadron bombardier confronted me about what had happened. I am sorry I didn't seek the recognition Rivers should have received. He did, after all, save the lives of 11 men."

During the two atomic bomb attacks, Allied air attacks against Japan continued around the clock, including raids by B-29s. When there were hints the Japanese might be close to a surrender settlement, some missions were initially canceled, but on August 14 the 315th Bomb Wing was told to prepare for a maximum-effort, 143-aircraft mission. This was to be the last B-29 mission of the war and the longest ever attempted. The target was the Nippon Oil Company Oil Refinery, 275 miles (443km) northwest of Tokyo. The briefing officer explained that the word "Apple" would be transmitted in the event of a Japanese surrender, which would effectively scrub the mission. Bombardier Dick Marshall, aboard *The Boomerang*, describes what had to be an agonizing wait for takeoff under the constant hope that the mission would be canceled:

"Some time passed; I don't recall how long, but then the order came through to start engines. We were idling for a while and nothing was moving. The thought went through my mind that those suckers out there are really consuming a hell of a lot of fuel, so let's do it or get off the pot. About the same time an order came through to stop engines. We were all thinking the mission had been scrubbed.

"Soon after, we got the order to start engines again. This time when those engines kicked over they were really laying down a smoke screen having idled for so long, but everything was checking out fine. This time it was for real."

Top right: *The "Bombardier's Check List" for the Norden bomb sight. The much vaunted accuracy of the Norden sight was more myth than reality.*

Below: *The shadow of a B-29 as it takes off for another mission. This would be the last patch of friendly land the crew would see before Japan.*

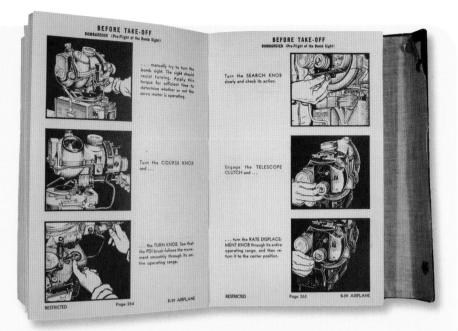

Now 200 miles (322km) from the target, the crew of *The Boomerang* waited anxiously for the abort code word—"Apple"—but there was nothing forthcoming. As Marshall's aircraft approached Kodama at midnight, just west/northwest of Tokyo, the JAAF's 27th Sentai responded with a surprisingly large force of 36 fighters; shortly afterward, the bombers found their target. Marshall recalls the run up to the target:

"I went back into the bomb bay to arm the bombs. I crawled out on to the catwalk and proceeded to pull the cotter pins from the detonating fuse on each bomb. When I finished, I returned to my bomb sight in the nose of the aeroplane, and prepared it with the data I was going to use on this run. Once we crossed the coastline at the predetermined point, we would have about 100 miles [161km] or roughly 20 minutes to target.

"An actual bomb run would be around three minutes, but prior to the run the exact altitude and the exact air speed had to be maintained. Once the pilot had that, he would tell me when it was all mine. That was my signal to engage the bomb sight. From that moment on, any correction in the sight I would make would also correct the flight path of the plane. As the target would pass through the cross hairs of the optical sight, the bombs would automatically release. I also had a manual switch in case of malfunction. The bomb bay doors were open, and the pilot told me to go ahead."

[It was around 1:18am local time, roughly two and a quarter hours after the Allies had received Japan's acceptance of peace.]

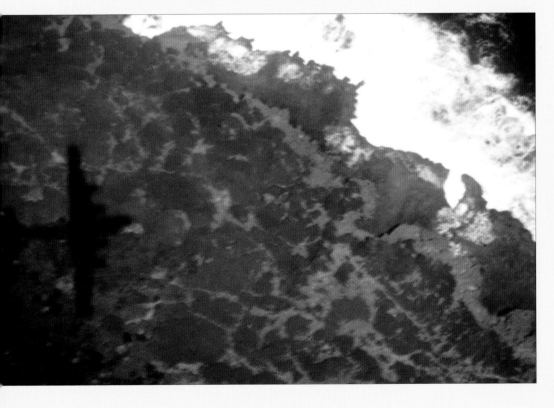

The Navigator

"I got nervous as we approached the Japanese coast; 'were we on course?' I asked myself. This was particularly critical on the couple of Pathfinder missions we flew; an error here by yours truly might ruin the entire mission . . . "

—1/Lt. Alexander "Sandy" Amell, 314th BW (VH), 29th BG (VH),
6th BS (VH), North Field, Guam

Compared with earlier B-17 and B-24 sorties, the very-long-range nature of most B-29 missions increased the demands on all crewmembers, but the navigator's duties were expanded exponentially. By comparison, a round-trip mission from the UK to Schweinfurt, Germany, would take more than eight hours, covering over 800 miles (1,287km); and Schweinfurt was one of the Eighth Air Force's furthest targets. Every B-29 mission from China or the Marianas to Japan covered more than 3,000 miles (4,828km) and lasted more than 15 hours. Remarkably, as recently as 1942, the US Navy had been openly critical of the army's inability to navigate accurately over open water. Safety concerns had limited most prewar army training flights to within a few hundred miles of shore. Some experience was gained through long-range goodwill flights to South America, and much publicity was generated when B-17s intercepted the Italian ocean liner *Rex* some 300 miles (483km) out in the Atlantic (more than 700 miles [1,126km] from New York). By late 1941, the army was flying a few B-17s to Hawaii and the Philippines. When the war began, safety concerns became secondary to tactical necessities, and USAAF navigators were soon guiding their bombers to targets throughout

Left: *Wartime and later advances in navigation meant that navigators' stations varied widely between aircraft. In* Bockscar *(left), the navigator sat aft of his work table, the original arrangement in most B-29s. Note the navigator's radar screen beneath the overhead rack.*

Europe, Africa, and the Pacific. By the time the first B-29 units were forming in 1944, the army could draw navigators from a deep pool of experienced officers.

The B-29 navigator relied on the standard navigation tools developed between the wars: drift sights to measure wind drift, flight instruments for dead reckoning, a sextant for celestial navigation, with bearings on stars or the sun, radio direction finding (RDF) to take bearings on known radio stations, and visual sightings for taking bearings on any landmarks. Although the outdated and inaccurate maps available early in the war added to any confusion, the army and navy moved quickly to develop and print replacements. Over the Pacific, the Army Airways Communications Service (AACS) established LORAN (Long Range Navigation) transmitters on several island bases; if an aircraft was within 700 miles (1,126km) of two transmitters (or 1,400 miles [2,253km] at night), LORAN was an often-effective tool. If conditions allowed, a sextant could help with sun or star fixes taken from the navigator's astrodome behind the forward dorsal turret.

But a navigator over the Pacific was at the mercy of a host of variables. As mentioned previously, maps were often full of errors. The navigator's instruments for measuring airspeed and altitude were subject to variations from air pressure, dirt and dust in sensors, and imprecise dials. His compasses could not be read within a half a degree; the gyro compass could be affected by unsteady gyros, and the magnetic compass could be deflected by electrical fields created by the aircraft's generators and electrical equipment. It was also subject to variations in the earth's magnetic field. Wind speeds and directions varied widely, and at different altitudes; minor changes in the flight engineer's engine settings or the pilot's course could throw off the navigator's computations; major changes could leave an inexperienced navigator totally lost.

If the navigator was lost, the crew was lost, and the most effective crews worked together: if any island-based High Frequency Direction Finder (HF/DF) ground stations were in range, radio operators could provide bearings. All crewmembers watched for any islands; such sightings could confirm a course or help correct it. At night or above an undercast, the radar operator could pick up features. Bombardiers helped with drift measurements, establishing changes in wind speed and direction. (Navigators were also trained as bombardiers, and were required to take over the bomb run if a bombardier was incapacitated.)

Navigation during the Korean War was more reliable. For one thing, missions were shorter, flown a few hundred miles from Japan to the Korean Peninsula and back.

Ground-based beacons in Japan and Korea helped provide positions, and weather ships and aircraft removed most meteorological surprises. But once the strategic phase of the war was over, B-29s moved to tactical missions, which often meant guiding the aircraft to one mountainous area, visually navigating with topographical maps. Newer and improved navigational aids became a hallmark of the postwar era, meeting the demands of Cold War military readiness and civilian airways. Most of those advantages would be introduced in newer generations of bombers and airliners, but the men who helped keep those aircraft on course were often the same men who had proved their worth guiding Superfortresses to Japan and back.

Page right, clockwise from top left: The navigator's Loran receiver; the floor-mounted forward ventral turret (not installed on Bockscar) meant the navigator's seat was placed behind the work table; the navigator's flight instruments were mounted at the opposite end of his table (his breathing oxygen control panel can be seen above the headphones); unused maps were stored in the tubular mapcase above the work table.

The "Whiz Wheel"

Despite the somewhat sinister sound of the name "Dead Reckoning Computer," the E-6B was the most popular of a series of analog navigational aids used for deductive ("ded") reckoning. Known to navigators as the "Whiz Wheel," the E-6B was first produced in 1940 and is still produced today. A highly specialized form of circular slide rule, the device proved useful in correcting courses for wind variations and computing true ground speeds.

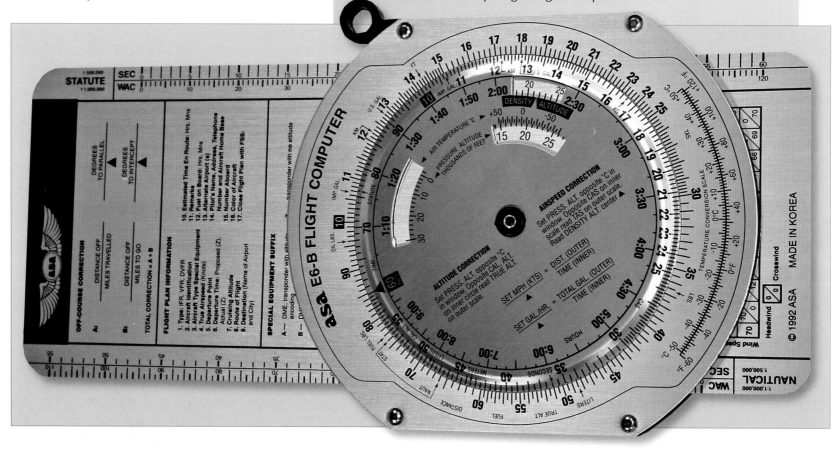

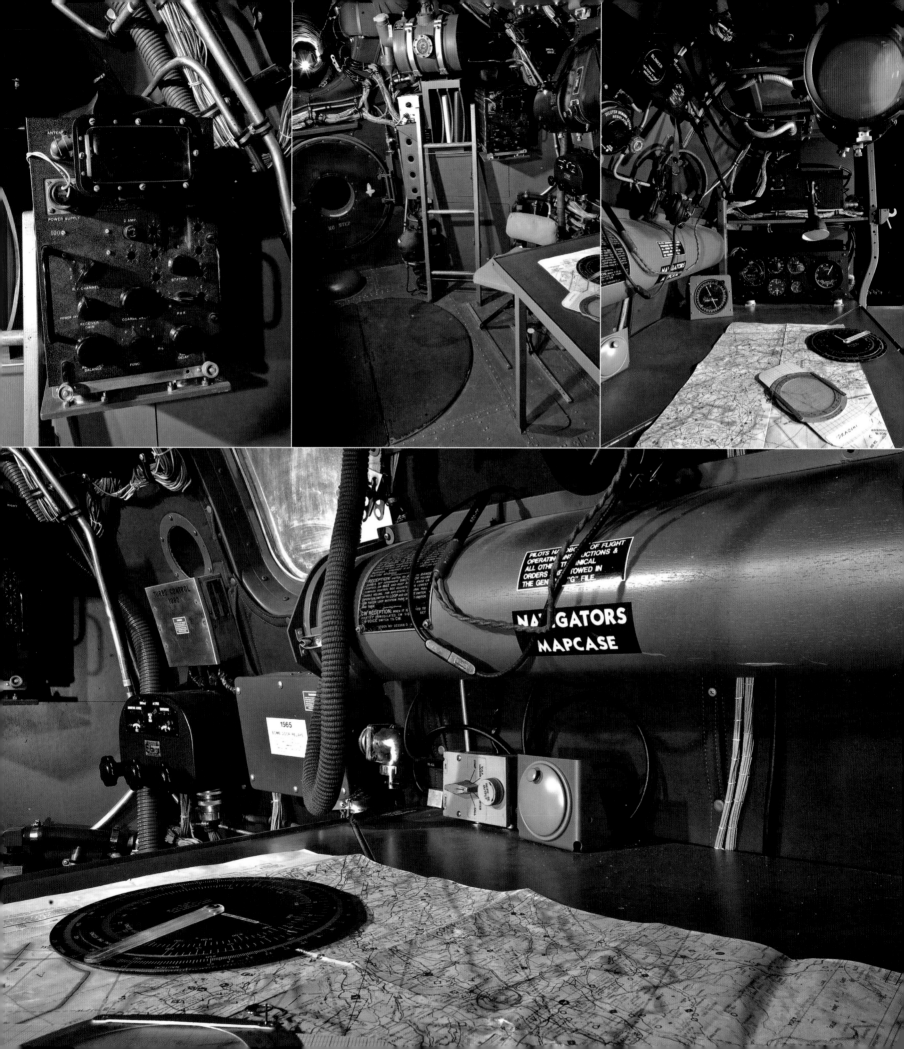

Maritime bomber

Operating from Guam, the 313th Bomb Wing began mining operations on April 1, 1944. Such missions meant a 3,200 mile (5,150km) round trip with twelve 1,000lb (454kg) mines or six 2,000-pounders (907kg). From late March to mid-August, B-29 mines sank 293 ships. Navigator Ed Perry of the 462nd Bomb Squadron describes his role:

"Tall trees along the river really highlighted the water's surface, with the trees quite dark and the river surface shimmering from the rays of the moon. I moved to the front of the cockpit and sat piggyback on Red Ball, the bombardier, with my legs each side of him. From this position I could reach the release button if it became necessary for him to man the forward gun sight and [I] could also help in the direction of the aircraft along the river.

"Red and the gunners did some low-level strafing of boats along the river as we went upstream to our release points. Since we were the first aircraft, we had the element of surprise in our favor. The tail gunner did report some ground fire at us after we had passed the ground positions.

"As we approached the scheduled release point we saw a large ship, presumably a tanker, in the channel. Before we reached the ship, Red released one mine and strafed it as we passed overhead at no more than 350ft [107m]. A second mine was dropped shortly after flying over the tanker. The tail gunner reported both mines entered the channel."

Above: US Navy 1,000 and 2,000lb (454 and 907kg) mines being prepared for a mission. Several mine types were dropped by B-29s in Japanese waters by parachute.

Not all missions ended in success. Newly trained and ready for action, navigator Dick Steiner of the 40th Bomb Group and his crew were forced to ditch on their way to India (from the US via Africa) in May 1944:

"There was some excitement, and apprehension, as Capt. Clark opened and read the orders to the crew over the inter-phone. It was finally

Left: A standard magnetic compass. For new cadets, emphasis was placed on precision dead reckoning navigation with basic proficiency in pilotage, radio, and celestial navigation.

confirmed—we were going to India! Our trip south to Atkinson Field, British Guiana [now known as Guyana], and our landing, was without incident. We spent one night [there] and took off for Natal [South Africa] early the next morning; all went well to Natal and, from there, we departed late in the afternoon for Accra, West Africa [Ghana].

"Our briefed route to Accra was direct to landfall at Cape Palmas [the southwesterly point on the 'hump' of Africa], then southeastward along the coast to Accra. We battled equatorial squalls along the route all night, but our major concern was with the fuel-transfer system. About halfway between Cape Palmas and Accra we became aware of the dangerously low fuel levels; for some reason we couldn't transfer any fuel from the aircraft's

other tanks. We made a decision to return to the emergency strip at Cape Palmas. As we made the turn, both outboard motors quit—suddenly we were a twin-engine B-29 and losing altitude. Capt. Clark ordered us to ditching positions. After the initial shock and deceleration we were soon under water; the escape route out of the aircraft was through the armored door at the rear of the gunners' section, but it was jammed shut [and] the water level was rising. I tried using my .45 pistol by shooting out the top blister. I nearly hit Edsel Clark, who was on top of the fuselage trying to help us out. With the weapon still fully cocked I tried using the butt to knock out the Plexiglas; it was useless. In desperation all five of us went through the tunnel to the front cockpit and out

the pilot's window. When I finally got out . . . I still had my loaded and cocked .45 automatic in my right hand; I was so startled I threw it away . . .

"Fortunately, no one was seriously hurt in the ditching. Although we could see the coast before we ditched . . . on the surface we couldn't see a thing. Attempts to get our life rafts out were futile, as the over-wing sections of the skin were buckled, jamming the raft compartments. We tied ourselves together and just floated there in our Mae Wests for several hours until, eventually, the surf took us into [the] beach."

Left: During the Korean War, crewmen were issued with their own baseball caps. Each had the same design with the crew position clearly illustrated.

Above and left: Sperry, Bendix, and the Fisher Body division of General Motors produced instruments for military aircraft.

Right: The 9th Bomb Group drops an aerial mine. Japanese officials interrogated after the war testified that the economic effects of mining had been as serious as those of bombing.

Difficult missions

Early B-29 operations were fraught with mechanical problems, causing many aircraft to return to base. During a mission to Yawata on August 20, 1944, Donald Starkey, squadron navigator with the 44th Squadron, describes a deadly situation in which an overeager flight engineer gave a whole new meaning to the phrase "running on fumes:"

"We reached the China coast and headed out over the Yellow Sea. I shot a quick fix which showed us to be 15 to 20 miles [24 to 32km] north and off course; I gave the pilot a new heading. Just after the course change, the flight engineer said, 'I don't think we have enough fuel remaining to make it to the target and back.' 'Are you sure?' the pilot asked skeptically; he then asked the engineer to recheck his calculations. I sat just opposite the flight engineer's station and I couldn't help but notice his meticulous attention to detail; I suspected this was his first combat mission.

"Eager to check his calculations, the flight engineer released the cabin pressure, stepped to the rear of the compartment and opened the forward bomb bay hatch. (The forward bomb bay contained two auxiliary gasoline tanks, one atop the other.) Convinced that the bottom tank was essentially empty, the engineer removed the access cap and inserted his arm to check the fuel content; he didn't feel anything. Leaving the cap off, he returned to his station and tripped the switch to transfer fuel from the upper to the lower tank. Suddenly the highly volatile fuel gushed out of the opening and ran down into the ribs of the bomb bay doors. Rushing back he quickly replaced the cap. By this time gasoline was now spraying out in all directions and into the forward cabin. In the process, the engineer was drenched from head to toe. He was chilled to the bone, suffocating from the fumes. He managed to crawl back to his flight station only to fall unconscious; Winn Cox, the radio operator, immediately strapped an oxygen mask onto his face.

"The cockpit windows were now open, but . . . the fumes were now being sucked up through the plane's interior. We had to open the bomb bay doors and dump the gasoline. The pilot ordered the bombardier to open the bomb bay doors manually; the bombardier tripped the control lever, but nothing happened; he tried again—the system wasn't working. There was no alternative now but to use the electrical mode and pray it didn't set off a spark and a catastrophic explosion. We waited while the bombardier threw the toggle switch. The doors opened, dumping the fuel.

"The engineer regained consciousness and . . . his first words to the pilot were something like, 'We have enough fuel to make it, Colonel. I apparently miscalculated.' It fell to the pilot to tell him that we were returning to base. The aborted mission had taken exactly 12 hours."

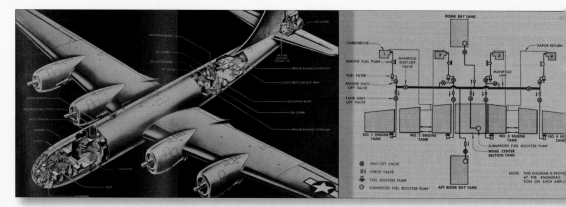

Above: *Crew position and manifold fuel system diagrams from the B-29* Flight and Operation Manual.

Below: *A B-29 departs the Marianas for a 14-hour mission to Japan. Time spent over Japan could be as little as one hour, with actual combat being measured in minutes.*

On October 17, 1944, Ralph Weinberg of the 45th Bomb Squadron and his crew were assigned to bomb Takao harbor on Formosa (now Taiwan) and assist in the invasion of the Philippines. Unfortunately, Takao was home to a major fighter base. Weinberg's aircraft was damaged during the mission, resulting in several wounded crew members and the loss of one gunner, who was blown out due to rapid decompression. Weinberg describes the events:

"On the return home, we were at least a mile behind on the left side of the formation. I looked out and saw a Japanese fighter flying level and parallel with us, but out of gun range. Just as I realized he must be transmitting to the fighters above, a shell came through the top of the plane and exploded behind Carter McGregor [copilot]. The concussion knocked Carter's helmet off and blew out the right gunner's blister.

"I was knocked off my seat and ended up with a shell fragment in my right foot and calf. After the shock had worn off I soon realized [that] with the amount of oxygen and fuel left on board we couldn't make it back to Chengtu. We had to head for the nearest American air base in unoccupied China.

"I checked with the lead formation navigator to make sure I had the right position before giving a heading to the base. About ten minutes before my ETA was up, Moss [the pilot] started circling. I asked him what he thought he was doing; he said he was trying some dead reckoning. Just then two Black Widows [P-61s] came up and escorted us back to the base.

"After receiving some first aid from the flight surgeon, Royal Klaver and I were lying under the wing of the plane when this jeep pulls up. A sharp-looking young lieutenant jumps out. He looks at me, says, 'You're Weinberg, aren't you?' I said, 'That's right.' He said, 'You don't remember me, but I have to salute you now.' And he threw me a highball.

Left: The Type A-14 Demand oxygen mask was standardized for USAAF use in July 1943. It was used during emergency depressurization only aboard the B-29.

Below: The Kawanishi N1K2-J Shiden Kais were based on Miyazaki Air Field. They boasted armor that was superior to the Zero, and US pilots noted that it was much more difficult to set one on fire.

Above: Designed as a strategic bomber, the B-29 was also employed in a tactical role. Here, bombs burst on the Miyazaki Air Field on Okinawa during a B-29 raid in April 1945. This was followed at the end of the month by two more raids.

He said, 'I was in the first class of bombardiers sent to navigation school, and you were our head instructor. We thought you were the most iron-assed SOB that God ever sent to this earth. We all hated your guts, but I want to tell you, I thank you for what you did because you made it possible for me to perform my duties and stay alive up to this time.' You know, that helped ease the discomfort quite a bit. We then proceeded to Chengtu without any problems. I was kept there for two months. The small shell fragment they took out of my foot had lodged itself in a very sensitive area and required some time to heal."

A familiar face

Norman Larsen was a navigator with the 25th Squadron, 40th Bomb Group. Shot down over Rangoon in December 1944 and made a prisoner of war, he had the unusual experience of being interrogated by a fellow alumnus from the University of New York:

"It was late in the morning on December 14, 1944; I found myself with my hands tied securely behind my back and being transported by a Japanese soldier to the New Laws Court jail in downtown Rangoon. I was soaking wet after parachuting into the Rangoon River. I was questioned briefly, actually no more than name and rank, and then brought to a room which had a shower.

"After the rinse, I was marched, naked, to a cell on the ground floor; it was a large cell with a tiny lightbulb in the ceiling which burned continuously. The only object in my new home was a small, tin-lined British ammunition box called the 'binjo.' This would be my toilet. Pasted on the back wall was a piece of paper. It read 'Rules for Prisoners.' I recall the eighth or ninth rule was: 'THOSE [sic] WILL BE CLEANLINESS EVERYWHERE.' I was alone, scared, and down in the dumps. I didn't know if any of my crewmates had made it.

Below: Takeoff was the most dangerous time for all B-29 crewmen. This was when the aircraft was fully loaded, often beyond prescribed limits, and even a slight loss of engine power could result in disaster. This 40th Bomb Group Superfortress begins its takeoff run from Chakulia, India.

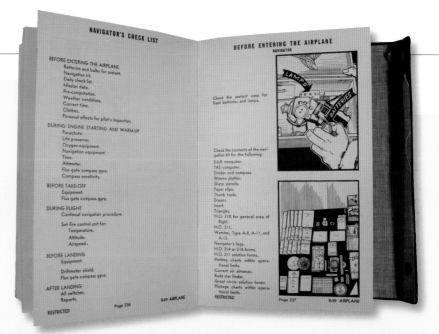

Above: Navigator's Check List as found in the B-29 Flight and Operational Manual. When B-29s flew formation missions, a lead navigator would be assigned. He was usually the most experienced in the group and his job was to lead the entire formation to and from the target.

"That night when the jail quieted down, I tried to get some sleep. I lay down on the bare wooden floor, but sleep was out of the question. It was cold, and worst of all I was being eaten alive by a swarm of mosquitoes; I've never been so miserable in all my life. The next morning I had the first of many interrogations over the next two days. I refused to go beyond name, rank and serial number and tried to invoke the Geneva Rules of War. The Japanese replied, 'Here in Rangoon we go by the Japanese Rules of War.' The fact that I had bailed out of an American bomber, was wearing a khaki uniform and [had] dog tags on didn't count. I refused to give any information and was given quite a hard time during the interrogations.

"I remember one interrogation that I enjoyed. The interrogator was a young Japanese who had been brought up in the United States. He told me he had been back in Japan when the war started and was drafted. I asked for, and he gave me, the first cigarette I had smoked since being captured. We both learned that we had been students at New York University. He attended during the day, me at night. It was an interesting session; he pleaded with me to give him any kind of information, even if it was meaningless, so he could show his superiors that he was doing his job. He said he didn't think these superiors really trusted him. I regretfully declined but did thank him for the cigarette and said I hoped we could get together sometime in New York."

While en route to bombing the Japanese aircraft factory at Hamamatsu, navigator Vince Ford's aircraft began to suffer an oil leak in their number two engine. Soon after "bombs away" the leak became worse, forcing the flight engineer to feather the prop. Vince gives his version of their forced bailout over Iwo Jima in June 1945:

"Joe Phalon [1/Lt.] figured the engine had blown the top two cylinders, carrying the propeller feathering lines with them. This caused the prop to windmill freely while pumping out precious oil. The only control Maj. Roberts had was to reduce air speed.

"As the navigator, I knew accurate position coordinates were crucial in the event we had to ditch. Howard Anderson [radio] sent my coordinates to our closest Life Guard sub and received the following response: 'These seas are so damn rough I can't get up on top of them. Try to make it to the next one in line.' Along with navigating, I kept a watchful eye on number two engine. The prop shaft went from red hot to white hot. Maj. Roberts suggested I leave my station and come up to the cockpit.

Above: *Not only were the B-29s bombing Japan, but the US Navy, with its large carrier task forces, was also pounding harbors and all remaining Japanese naval forces. Here, a Grumman Hellcat forms up on a B-29.*

"The fighter escorts joined us; they looked us over and we heard via radio: 'I don't see anything wrong with this plane except an oil leak.' Just about then, the prop came off, and the fighters went into instant evasive action to avoid the four . . . prop blades.

"The prop tore through the fuselage cutting out a large section and severing several key flight controls. The aircraft was damaged, but Roberts and Harvell [pilot, copilot] realized the aircraft was still flyable; they were able to maintain level flight and make wide turns by using the three good engines. As luck would have it, we were flying in relatively smooth air. Any heavy turbulence could have broken the plane in two.

"As we neared Iwo, Maj. Roberts agreed the plane could not be landed safely; bailout preparations were made. With communications cut off to the rear compartment I threw instructions through the crew tunnel. These simply stated to follow me when they saw me leave the plane. Standing in the wheel well, ready to let go, was an experience I'll never forget. There I was, holding on to a very solid airplane and looking down at nothing but space and ocean. I paused long enough to get in a better drop position. I let go, counted to six, pulled the rip cord and looked down with relief.

"Ambulances and personnel were running around ready to help us. I landed about two or three yards up on a beach. All but the pilot and copilot jumped on the first pass; they then made a wide turn coming back for their jump. Of the eleven crew members, five were uninjured. Those who were injured sustained [their injuries] when 'chutes dragged them through patches of stubbed roots."

Above: *Smoke rises from the volcano on Iwo Jima. The airfield on Iwo served two purposes: as an emergency airfield for damaged B-29s returning from Japan, and home to the various P-51 and P-47 long-range escort groups, including the new P-47N version of the Thunderbolt that was specifically designed for the Pacific theater.*

Through the Ether

"Those of us who were second lieutenants fresh from training school were surprised to find so many high-ranking officers at Pratt, Kansas. We learned the reason: the 40th Group and three other B-29 groups comprising the 58th Wing had a special mission—we would be the first to take B-29s into combat."—Navigator Jim O'Keefe.

Men like Jim O'Keefe and those who followed him made what had seemed impossible just a few short years earlier almost routine. While B-17s and B-24s were flying long-range missions in Germany, B-29 operations in China and the Pacific were doing something that had never been done before—transoceanic combat missions. It was a first, and the young crews who flew those missions were making the rules. The distances were incredible: 1,500 miles (2,414km) one-way from the Marianas to Japan, a 15-hour round trip. These VLRs (Very Long Range) missions had never been attempted or even contemplated at the time of the outbreak of war in 1939. Navigation over 3,000 miles (4,828km) of featureless ocean was

"NAVIGATOR GOONEY" THOUGHT HE KNEW HIS D. R.
WAS SURE THAT *HE* WOULD NEVER GO TOO FAR
BUT ALAS FOR GOONEY WHEN THE FUEL RAN OUT
THERE WAS NOTHING BUT OCEAN ROUNDABOUT.

RADIUS OF ACTION IS NAVIGATOR'S PROBLEM

Left: Despite the many challenges and difficulties of a 3,000 mile (4,828km) flight, navigators generally bore the responsibility for their aircraft becoming lost or running out of fuel, as this crew training poster colorfully illustrates.

both a skill and an art; crews literally entrusted their lives to their navigators. How many B-29s were lost due to poor navigation will never be known—the worry of getting lost or running out of fuel was a constant, and rescue was very far from certain. Fuel consumption and good navigation went hand in hand; how far one had to go, and how much fuel was on board, were hard numbers. About the work of B-29 navigators, a fuel consumption expert remarked, "Analysis of flight logs to date show[s] that increased navigation proficiency will do much to reduce the variation in fuel consumption. Every possible means should be used to impress the navigator with the effect his errors have on fuel consumption."

But with General LeMay's change of tactics to night bombing operations, nocturnal navigation proved more efficient and reliable; at night, weather permitting, a navigator could take a star shot with his sextant that was more accurate than sun angles. He also had electronic aids that had not existed or even been dreamed of just a few years earlier. Radio aids also worked better at night; better atmospherics gave LORAN (Long Range Navigation) beams a range of up to 1,400 miles (2,253km) at night (or 700 miles [1,127km] during the day), a considerable advantage when flying over cloud.

The navigator also had access to the Liaison Radio, the VHF Command Set, Radio Compass, IFF (Identification Friend or Foe), and one of the newest scientific developments in World War II—radar. Ground-mapping radar, such as the APQ-13, gave the navigator the ability to see islands and coastlines. "The coastline features of Japan are such that it is highly improbable that any navigator will fail to recognize the coastal features where landfall will be

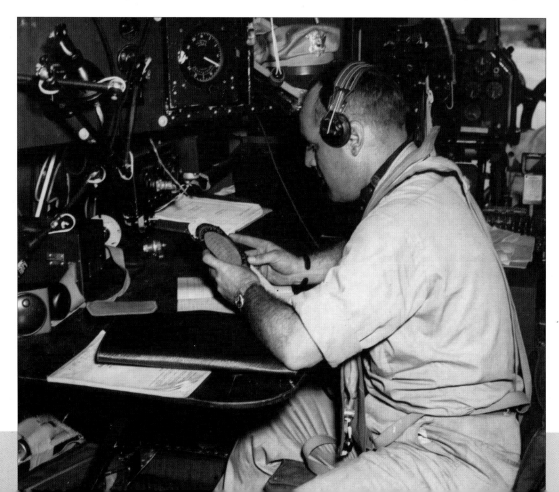

Left: With the removal of most of the gun turrets, some B-29s housed a redesigned navigator's station, with the seat moved to the center aisle. Note the dial for the gyro-stabilized fluxgate compass beside the hat.

Above: *The Air Training Command's manuals were designed to educate new crews and maintain their proficiency in the field of combat.*

The Tunnel

The pressurized front and rear crew compartments were connected by a 33ft (10m) long communications tunnel, mounted along the spine of the fuselage over the bomb bay. The tunnel, which allowed crewmembers to crawl between compartments when necessary, had no hatches and could not be closed off. As a result, in an emergency, the decompression of one compartment resulted in the decompression of both, which was in actuality an advantage; with no hatch to be "locked" by a pressure differential, crewmen could move with relative ease between compartments when circumstances most demanded. (When approaching a target, the cabins were normally depressurized to avoid an explosive decompression if the aircraft was hit by enemy fire.)

Right: *Crew rest was important on very-long-range missions. Four bunks were originally provided for this purpose in the aft cockpit, though the number was soon cut to two to make room for other equipment. The tunnel could also double as a crew rest area on long missions.*

Below: *The forward end of the tunnel also provided access to the navigator's astrodome, the base of which can be seen just beyond the quilting in this photograph. A web strap helped brace the navigator as he took celestial bearings with his sextant.*

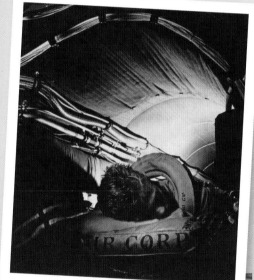

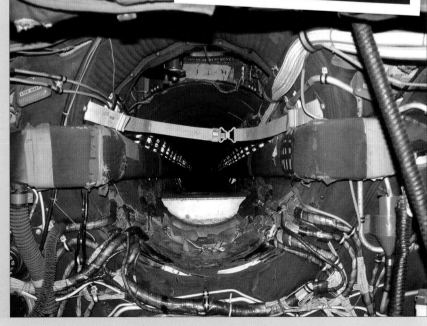

made if he has studied the terrain feature to be expected," reports the 1945 manual *How to Fly the Superfortress*.

Strangely, even though navigation was a vitally important component of a crew's success, navigators remained second-class citizens in some pilot's eyes: ". . . right from the start of this flight, it became obvious the Colonel wasn't taking directions from any First Lieutenant pencil-pushing navigator," recalls navigator Donald Starkey, of the 40th Bomb Group.

Nevertheless, cooperation between the pilot, flight engineer, and navigator was vital to ensuring success and survival. As the Navigator's Manual states, "You have to be right the first time. The necessary combat and flying odds against a successful mission are sufficient without adding further uncertainty from equipment trouble and lack of knowledge, technique, and cooperation."

Costly mistakes

Good navigation was crucial to the success of every B-29 mission. The crews literally entrusted their lives to their navigators; just one degree off course could send them out over the Pacific Ocean, never to be seen again. Gerard Rau of the 497th Bomb Group was a skilled navigator who saw his share of snafus. During his tour, in July 1945, Rau survived passing out during one mission and a wayward bomb that flew back up into the bomb bay instead of falling out of it and on to the target below:

"We had dropped our bombs and I gave the pilot the heading home. I always gave him the return heading before we took off; if something happened to me, he would know which way to point the airplane. We were not too far off the coast of Japan when I looked over at the flight engineer and saw him slouched over a little bit; his skin had a bluish tint. I knew he was suffering from a lack of oxygen. I told the pilot, [and] he told me to take the portable oxygen tank and help him out; that's the last thing I remember. Either I didn't put my oxygen on properly or it didn't work—I passed out, [and] when I woke up I didn't know where I was. It took a while to get everything straightened out; the bombardier or the copilot came back to help us out. While this was going on I wasn't navigating; we didn't know where the airplane was. If this had been a night mission I would have taken a celestial fix; unfortunately there was nothing but cloud beneath us.

"At that point it began to look hopeless—all we had was the heading I had given the pilot prior to the mission. Then all of a sudden, the left gunner shouts, 'There's an island.' There's only one island in the whole Pacific that looks like a cigar sticking out of the ocean. It was Sofu Gan, 100 miles [161km] off the coast of Japan. Once I knew where we were I had no problem setting a course for home—and just as quickly as the island appeared the clouds closed in and it was gone.

"General Curtis LeMay came up with the idea of bombing Japanese cities at night and very low altitude; so the blitz started. When you're one of the first planes over the target, the fires below are small and few in number, but after that the fire and heat begin to build, creating violent thermo air currents. On this particular mission we had just dropped our bombs when we were suddenly caught in a violent

Above: Two B-29s from the 98th Bomb Group, 344th Bomb Squadron, based at Yokota, Japan. The B-29 closest to the camera has been painted black on the underside of the aircraft for night bombing camouflage.

downdraft. Incredibly, we were now falling faster than the bombs we had just dropped! One of them actually flew back into the bomb bay and got stuck; the bombardier had the unenviable job of crawling back into the bay to try and dislodge the damn thing."

Navigator Ralph Livengood was one of the many crewmen called back to active duty during the Korean War as part of 93rd Bomb Squadron. After flying and surviving 30 missions over Germany during World War II and a short six-month refresher course, Ralph was once again flying combat missions. He talks of his apprehension in September 1950:

"We were right on schedule and my first mission over Korea was about to begin. With my immediate duties completed I had a few minutes to reflect on my feelings and thoughts about the mission ahead. There was some apprehension concerning the

Below: Navigators kept precise logs, which were constantly updated—vital in case of ditching or bailing out.

Above: The last landmark before sighting Japan. The small islands off the Japanese coast were used by all B-29 navigators to confirm their position.

Navigator Vern Piotter of the 92nd Bomb Wing remembers his first mission over Korea and dropping leftover bombs from World War II:
"Our first mission to Korea was disastrous. At the assembly point over the Sea of Japan, our flight commander got a call that one of the aircraft had lost an engine. The commander told him to leave the formation and head back, and to jettison his bombs after leaving the formation.

Left: A 19th Bomb Group B-29 drops its load of 1,000lb (454kg) demolition bombs on a target in Korea. The cloud cover would indicate a radar bomb run, requiring precise coordination between the radar operator and bombardier.

Center: This is a leather patch worn by the 462nd BG (VH) Hellbirds of the 58th BW (VH) based in India, then the 73rd BW (VH) at West Field, Tinian.

Below: The crew of Command Decision *prior to another mission. The aircraft was officially credited with five MiG-15s shot down.*

flight, as with any new job, but that passed as the time for takeoff neared. Fortunately, the job ahead was enough to keep my mind occupied and left me little time to think of the hazards. The possibilities for disaster were almost endless and could cause a lot of stress. Engine failure, either on takeoff or while airborne, enemy fighter attack or AA fire could cause the plane to crash. Mechanical failure, running out of fuel, weather and the all-too-real possibility of human error could be catastrophic. I couldn't afford to let emotion or thoughts of personal welfare cloud my thinking; I was responsible for guiding the aircraft and its crew to the target and back.

"I had 'been there, done that' in World War II and survived, but I also believed that my 'number' could be called at any moment. I was scared to death about returning to combat and had told my wife how I felt. I really didn't expect to return alive from another combat assignment. The odds were simply not in my favor. The sound of the engines starting brought me back to the job at hand and signaled the beginning of a long day in cramped quarters with the constant roar of the engines ringing in my ears."

[Sadly, this mission was not a success, with no bombs hitting the target. But there were no losses, and Livengood's crew returned to base.]

"The pilot acknowledged [but] . . . in a few seconds he reported that some of the bombs had hung up, and they were going to try again for release using the intervalometer [for automatic time release in succession]. They were still hung up after he tried that, and so he called again to say that he would hit the salvo switch. As the bombs left the bomb bay, two of them hit together and blew up the airplane. We were still using bombs left over from World War II, and the RDX [Research Department Explosive] explosive was unstable after five years . . . "

The Flight Engineer

"As I was finishing up my training, I found myself with a flight engineer rating and on my way to combat crew training. These were experiences I'll never forget, but nothing like what was forthcoming in India and China."

—1/Lt. James J. Whamba, 58th BW (VH), 444th BG (VH),
678th BS (VH), India, then West Field on Tinian

The role of the B-29 flight engineer was unique in the USAAF—this dedicated position existed in no other operational USAAF combat aircraft. Earlier aircraft, such as the B-17 and B-24, carried crewmen known as flight engineers, but these enlisted gunners acted mainly as extra eyes and hands for the pilots. By comparison, the B-29 flight engineer was trained specifically to manage the aircraft's many systems from takeoff to landing; his was a full-time job, essential to every B-29 flight. Boeing's design staff had first introduced the full-time flight engineer position to the company's long-range commercial aircraft, where a "third pilot" had proven critical. On the trans-Pacific flights of the Model 314 Clipper flying boat, the flight engineer was primarily responsible for "cruise control:" calculating and adjusting the most efficient fuel/air mixture, cooling flap settings, prop pitch, engine speed, and temperature for the aircraft's altitude, making efficient use of the aircraft's fuel. The flight engineer also performed these duties on board the high-altitude Model 307 Stratoliner, where additionally he controlled the "cabin supercharger," the system that pressurized the crew and passenger compartments.

Left: The flight engineer managed an array of instruments and controls. Seen to the right of this panel are the circular floor access to the lower forward gun turret, the pressurized hatch leading to the bomb bay, the open tunnel leading to the aft fuselage, and the base of the access to the upper forward fuselage turret.

The B-29 flight engineer thus monitored and controlled that aircraft's numerous and complex systems, while assisting the navigator and pilots in their duties. He worked with ground crews on maintenance between missions, and performed preflight checks; responsibilities that the pilots normally carried out on B-17s and B-24s.

The flight engineer sat behind the copilot, facing aft, at a panel that included nearly all of the aircraft's engine instruments and controls; each pilot had his own throttle quadrant and could override the flight engineer's power controls, but for much of the mission it was the flight engineer who managed the aircraft's power settings and cruise control, providing the navigator with regular updates on the aircraft's projected endurance, and ensuring that there was sufficient fuel for the round trip. His panel also controlled electrical, hydraulic, fuel, lubrication, oxygen, and pressurization systems.

The first crop of B-29 flight engineers began as officer graduates of the USAAF's sophisticated maintenance engineering courses; they were supplemented by a handful of experienced mechanics. But the numbers of aircrew needed quickly exceeded the supply of qualified officers; the engineering prerequisites were relaxed, and a number of promising enlisted mechanics were brought into the program. The USAAF even cross-trained some of their rated pilots, though the change in duties proved an unpopular one, particularly for those who had trained as fighter pilots.

In early 1945, the army began accepting qualified civilian applicants through its aviation cadet and aviation student programs. Starting with nothing, the army would produce some 7,800 qualified flight engineers by the war's end.

Most of the kinks had been worked out of the training syllabus by 1945; by that time, the program that trained flight engineers began with one of the army's aircrew preflight schools, then moved to a 19-week basic course at Amarillo Army Air Field, Texas. Students learned 1st and 2nd echelon Superfortress maintenance, B-29 flight characteristics and procedures, and engine operation, with emphasis on efficient power settings and management of fuel consumption. The basic course, which included only eight days of flying, was followed by a ten-week advanced course at Hondo Army Air Field, Texas. Again, there was a heavy emphasis on mechanics and B-29 cruise control, all of which included four weeks of flight experience. The shortage of B-29s meant that many of the training flights used modified B-24s with several flight engineer stations.

The need for cooperation between the B-29 primary flight crew sent pilots, copilots, and flight engineers to a transition school, where they learned to work as an interdependent team before combat crew training. The complexities of the B-29 meant that no crewman could do his job alone.

Flight engineer training for the Korean War was much the same as that developed during World War II; however, by 1950 there was a pool of trained and experienced flight engineers, many of them with hundreds of hours of flight time. The increasing complexity of aircraft systems also meant that the post-World-War-II air force could transition its B-29 flight engineers into many of its next generation of heavy aircraft. As the B-29 dropped back from the vanguard of strategic aircraft, many Superfortresses were assigned to instructional duties to help train the Cold War flight engineers who would fly newer bombers and heavy transports.

Page right, clockwise from top left: Throttles; engines were numbered from the left outboard. White-capped levers controlled cabin pressure, with the black-capped lever switching vacuum pumps (needed to operate instrument dials). The four mixture control levers regulated the fuel and air mixture for each engine's carburetor; a fifth lever locked the other four. The flight engineer controlled the B-29's seven generators, flipping this black switch to check the voltage output of each.

Cyclone Powered

A 73rd Bomb Wing B-29 undergoing engine maintenance on Saipan. The flight engineer's job centered on the B-29's Wright R-3350 Cyclones, which—still under development as the first B-29s entered combat—suffered from teething troubles, and an often fatal tendency to quit on takeoff. While engine maintenance was the ground crew's purview, flight engineers were involved throughout the process.

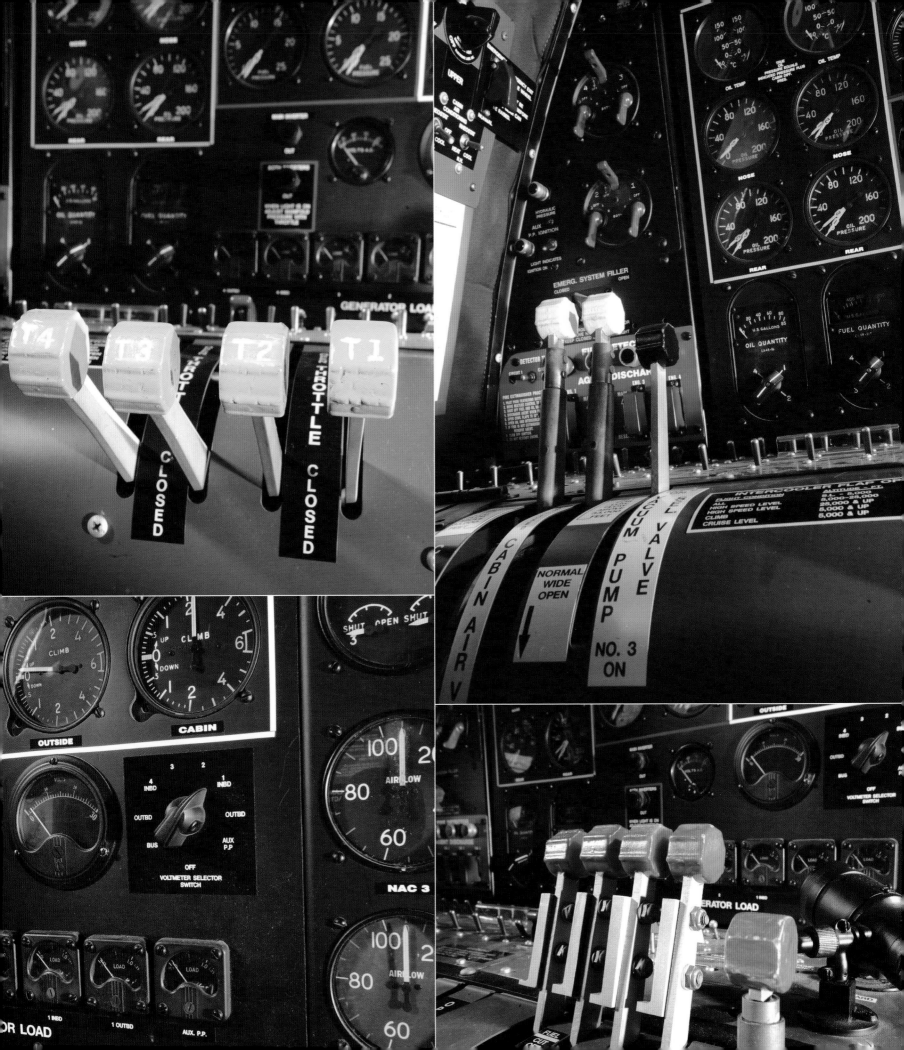

Unexpected outcomes

In the spring of 1944, early B-29 operations in China were dogged by a shortage of supplies, poor crew training, and lack of maintenance. The reasons were varied, but most of them were linked directly to the reliability of the Wright Cyclone R-3350 engine. Ralph M. Robert, flight engineer with the 468th Bomb Group, had to bail over the "Hump" (see pages 34 to 35) twice because of engine malfunction:

"When we went overseas we only had 30 hours in the B-29! We had one cross-country trip from Seattle to Denver and one gunnery trip; all of our training prior to that was in B-17s.

"We started across the Hump. We got up to altitude and we're up there for about an hour and a half, two hours, cruising along when all of a sudden the number two engine started to cough, snort and do whatever.

ENGINES FROM A SUPER-FACTORY...

POWER THE SUPERFORTRESS—The mammoth Dodge Chicago Plant, largest in the world and staffed from a nucleus of Dodge-trained personnel, is now in quantity production of 2,200 horsepower Wright Cyclone engines for the great new Boeing B-29 Superfortresses. Dodge Chicago represents the same high standards of workmanship that are being applied to Dodge engineered production of more than 300,000 Military Vehicles, thousands of Sperry Gyro-Compasses, Tank assemblies and Bofors Anti-Aircraft Gun parts — all backed by more than a quarter century of production leadership in fine motor cars and trucks.

DODGE DIVISION OF CHRYSLER CORPORATION

Remember to dial your CBS station Thursdays, 9 P.M., E.W.T. You'll enjoy Major Bowes and his Amateurs

Artist's sketch of the Dodge Chicago Plant

Above: *The Dodge Chicago Aircraft Engine Plant built most of the Wright Cyclone R-3350 engines; between January 1944 and July 1945, 16,000 had been produced.*

We feathered the propeller immediately and started back to our base. We didn't get very far when the number one engine caught fire and I remember the gunner saying, 'Hey, the flame is all the way back to the stabilizer.' We got ready to bail out. As we started letting down it was my job to open the hatch; at that altitude the open hatch looked bigger than the Grand Canyon.

"We all bailed out and landed in the jungle, but we did lose our radar operator; it was his first trip. We were separated by this river—we were on one side, and he was on the other. He tried swimming across but drowned; they found us a couple of days later.

"Thirty-seven days later, I was asked if I could fill in for a guy who was sick. I said 'sure,' another trip over the Hump! This time we made it all the way but our aircraft didn't. As we started to let down, the number two engine ran away. We lost complete control of the prop causing a huge amount of drag. We still had three engines but because of the 'windmilling' prop we were forced to bail out once again!"

As part of the bombing effort from China and India, flight engineer Jerry W. Noble and his fellow crewman tested the B-29 in combat for the first time. Breaking with regulations, Noble, of the 40th Bomb Group, kept a diary; below are two entries from 1944 describing some of the difficulties they encountered while trying to bomb targets in Japan and Manchuria:

Mission #1: Yawata, Japan

"Thursday, June 15 was the big day. Briefed at 09:00, when we found out that our target was in Japan, you could have knocked us over with a feather. Some parts of the briefing were rather funny; they said maybe you'll run into fighter planes and maybe you'll run into flak. Nothing definite, so we really didn't know what to expect. Ate dinner, rested a while, and then went back to the airplane for last-minute preparations and to sweat out takeoff.

"Took stations at 16:30, took off at 16:45, and set course for Japan at 10,000ft [3,048m]. We were the 12th ship to take off, but we passed about three ships before dark. Passed over some enemy territory before we reached the coast of China, but we were told the 14th Air Force had neutralized the airfields in that vicinity. As we neared the Initial Point, we all put on full battle dress—Mae West, parachute, flak vest, and flak helmet. Frankly, we were all pretty scared; we didn't know what to expect, and I think we were all expecting hell to break loose any minute. We turned into the target run, and as soon as we got to the mainland, searchlights started hunting for us. There was a little flak, but most of it was below and behind us. Bombs were away at 22:30, and we peeled off and got the hell out of there."

we ran into some weather. Since we were flying number three position, and on the outside, we turned to the left and started climbing; guess that's where we made a big mistake.

"Broke out of the weather at 24,000ft [7,315m], and not another airplane in sight; it was really beautiful. Nothing for us to do but go to the second rendezvous point and try to pick up at least two more ships, because we had instructions not to go in on the primary target with less than a three-ship formation. We circled that island for about three quarters of an hour and didn't pick up anything, so we headed for the secondary target, Dairen [China]. Looked as though we were going to have to drop on radar so we notified the radar operator to warm up the set. We were still about 22,000ft [6,706m], and the bombardier's window was all iced over; the radar set was frozen up also so we started descending.

"Got down to 18,000ft [5,486m] and everything was still frozen up so we had to level off. We could see the docks and

Above: *A posed picture of a flight engineer wearing a flight helmet, goggles, and B-15 flight jacket (rarely worn in the hot Pacific), probably taken Stateside. The flight engineer was reliant upon not only his instruments, but also the sound and vibration of the engines.*

Right: *B-29 Jo of the 58th Bomb Wing, 444th Bomb Group, 676th Bomb Squadron, suffered major damage when one of its Wright Cyclones was torn loose during an emergency landing on Tinian. The engine would never be used again (the damage would have been too extensive) and it was stripped for useable parts.*

Mission #3: Anshan, Manchuria, September 26, 1944

"Got off at daybreak this morning for our third mission. Got out to the rendezvous point to pick up our formation; it was a mess—about 50 to 60 B-29s milling around trying to pick up their formations. We finally found ours and took off for the target. Just about an hour out of the target,

warehouses at Dairen; Mac finally dropped our ten 500-pounders by guess—the gunners said they saw the bombs hit in the target area. Later we found out [that] Tokyo Rose claimed more damage was done at Dairen than Anshan. Our trip back was fairly uneventful except we were jumped by a couple of Tojos. They didn't fire a shot at us, though."

Unpredictable engines

Like the B-29, the Wright Cyclone engine was not ready for combat when it went to war; it was unreliable, and its faults were many and often deadly. But on November 21, 1944, flight engineer Elmo W. Gray of the 44th Squadron, while on a mission to Omura, Japan, had three engines knocked out. Elmo was forced to restart his damaged number one engine; this time, the Wright Cyclone came to the rescue. A portion of Elmo's combat report describes the action:

"The formation was tightened, the bomb bay doors opened, and we were on the bombing run when it happened. We were approximately 30 seconds before the bomb release point when it seemed as if the whole Jap Air Force concentrated on our plane.

"On the first pass, the number four engine propeller dome was pierced by a bullet and the engine had to be feathered. Before we had completed feathering number four, a second wave of attacking planes was on us. We could hear bullets ripping through the plane, and immediately the instruments on number one and number two engines indicated that they also had been shot out. The fuel pressure on number one dropped to below zero and the manifold pressure dropped to 15 inches [38cm]. The fuel supply was shut off to number one and number two engines. Number two was feathered, but number one was left windmilling because of the urgent need for electrical power to operate the turrets.

"Meanwhile, we reached the bomb release point and dropped our bombs. We could not stay in formation with only one engine running and we were losing altitude rapidly; we needed power badly and as a last resort the fuel shut-off valve on number one engine was turned on and the throttle advanced very slowly. The tachometer was operating normally, oil pressure was normal, fuel pressure was still out, and manifold pressure was fluctuating from 15 to 30 inches [38 to 76cm]. However, as the throttle was advanced still further, the manifold pressure settled down and it was evident by the instruments and the flying characteristics of the airplane that the number one engine was producing power.

"In the five minutes since the first wave of fighters had attacked us we had lost 6,000ft [1,829m] of altitude, but we had two engines running and were maintaining level flight even though the airspeed was very low. A 15-minute battle followed, during which our gunners destroyed three

2CU 6F 29-156-33

Left: City of Pittsburgh *undergoes maintenance. The in-commission rate of B-29s in the Marinas hovered at around 60 per cent during 1945.*

Jap fighters. Out over the Yellow Sea, free from fighters, our greatest problems at that time were: would the engines maintain level flight and was the gas supply sufficient to reach friendly territory?

"After landing at an emergency strip and inspecting the plane and engines, we discovered numerous bullet holes: the number one engine fuel pressure line had been shot up; the number four engine had been put out of commission by a bullet [shot] through the propeller dome; and the number two engine carburetor fuel metering valve had been shot away."

Flying over the "Hump" was hazardous; not only did crews have to negotiate some of the world's tallest mountains, but they also did it in the temperamental B-29. Paul Hunter, flight engineer with the 45th Bomb Squadron, recalls a flight in 1944, which ended with a tragic crash:

"We took off from Chakulia at 06:50, 19 June, 1944 on a gasoline ferry flight to Hsinching (A-1). After a few minutes into the flight, an oil leak was discovered in the number four engine and we returned; the oil leak was caused by an overfilled tank. After fixing the problem, we took off for a second time. After about two and a half hours into the flight, we leveled off at 23,000ft [7,010m]. That's when the number two engine began losing power and oil; the prop was feathered but it continued to windmill.

"We then began to lose altitude at the rate of 100ft [30.5m] per minute followed by an even higher rate of 200fpm [feet per minute], all this while flying over the highest part of the Hump. The bombardier salvoed the lower bomb bay tanks.

"The radio compass was inoperative; we called 'Sugar Queen' ground station for a heading, but this would have taken us into the overcast. Tom Brennan, our navigator, was able to see the ground and made a visual identification in regards to our position. We were over Hsichang which had an emergency landing field. Shortly after, our number three engine began losing oil and started smoking.

"We decided to return to Hsichang and land. We flew over the field and quickly realized an approach from the south would be the safest; high mountains to the east were very close to the field. Copilot Bill Clay instructed the crew to position themselves for the landing; the pilot,

A portion of Edwin L. Levenson's Flight Engineer's Log Book:

"FROM **APRIL 28** 1945"

FROM	TO	REMARKS OR INSTRUCTOR'S SIGNATURE AND CERTIFICATE NO.
DOBA	CHINA LULIANG	127,000 - 15,000' - USED 2635 - 18 PASS. - ON OUR WAY AGAIN. - 11,000' RUNWAY - ELEV. 6200' CALCUTTA - SNOW FRO - LASHIO
IANG	LULIANG	AIR ABORT - HIT #2 PROP WITH ROCK - 128,000 NOTE
IANG	LULIANG	AIR ABORT - HIT 8 TELEPHONE POLES OFF END OF RUNWAY - DAMAGED 3 BOMBAY DOORS - RADAR - FLAP & STAB. WHEW!
	MARIANAS	

Above: *A portion of Edwin L. Levenson's Flight Engineer's Log Book. Levenson flew B-29s with the 462nd Bomb Group, 769th Bomb Squadron, during 1944–45.*

Below: *After two engines were shot out over Tokyo on April 13, 1945, Ramblin' Roscoe limped back to Saipan, crash-landed, hit a truck and finally came to halt.*

copilot and I remained forward. The radar operator and navigator moved to the radar compartment. Right, left, and CFC gunners and the radio operator were in the gunner's compartment with the tail gunner in the tail. When we made contact with the ground, the field was so obviously short that I applied full brakes. The main wheels locked, and we skidded on the soft turf until we reached the end. Unfortunately, there were Chinese workers laboring at the end of the runway; they made no effort to get out of the way! Tragically, nine of them were killed instantly by our whirling propellers.

"When our nose-gear struck the slight ditch and the rough stones beyond the runway, it folded. The nose was 'ground off.' The engineer and pilot's compartments were completely wrecked. We were all uninjured except for scratches and bruises. The plane from the rear of the radio compartment to the tail looked to be intact. The props were ruined and there was some damage to the flaps from flying stones."

No easy missions

On December 14, 1944, a 12-plane formation from the 40th Bomb Group was ordered to bomb the Rama bridge in Bangkok. Unable to target the primary because of cloud, they moved on to the secondary: the railway yards at Rangoon. A "milk run" (an easy target) quickly turned into a disaster for flight engineer G. M. Etherington and his crew:

"The weather was clear as we approached Rangoon. Apparently we had taken the Japanese by surprise. Seconds after bombs away there was a tremendous explosion; we were hit and hit bad. The exact events of the next several minutes are not clear in my mind— I guess all four engines had been damaged: two engines were on fire, the number three and one other. My first concern was to get these fires out, which fortunately I was able to do. One of the other engines was running so rough we had to feather it. The gunners reported a big hole in the right wing and the control surfaces were badly damaged; Bob and Fletch [pilot and copilot] had a lot of trouble flying the plane but managed to control it. I had a scratch on my left arm and Julian Cochran had a small piece of metal in the sole of his shoe and a small piece in his leg.

"We were heading west, hoping to make the Burma coast. If we were able to ditch in the Bay of Bengal, we stood a good chance of being picked up by air-sea rescue. We were losing altitude so we re-started the engine that had been running rough. We began to throw out everything we could to lighten the plane. We had to feather number one again, leaving only number two running.

"We managed to fly 15 or 20 minutes after being hit and were somewhere over the delta of the Irrawaddy River at about 6,000ft [1,829m]. A higher mountain range lay ahead of us when number two engine started to burn. I don't remember who the first one out was, but I know I had to help Benny get out with his partially popped-open 'chute. I switched on the autopilot to give the pilots a better chance to get out and told Bob and Fletch to come right behind me; then I jumped and pulled the rip-cord. There was quite a jolt as the 'chute opened—but it sure looked good to me. Several 'chutes were open in the direction we had just come from; after what seemed like a long time, two more 'chutes opened. Soon the plane turned to the left and started toward me. The number two engine was now burning fiercely. It turned again to the

Left: The crew of Irish Lassie: the flight engineer, Lt. Robert E. Watson, can be seen second from the right on the front row.

Inset: Irish Lassie after her incredible crash-landing at Saipan, narrowly avoiding a cliff-edge drop.

left, lost altitude, flew away from me and finally crashed and burned."

The Japanese Army and Naval Air Forces were completely unprepared for the B-29: the numbers of fighters and well-trained pilots were very low. Add to this the poor high-altitude performance of their fighters, and the results were disastrous. In desperation, the Japanese adopted ramming tactics and formed specialized units.

For the crew of the *Irish Lassie* from the 497th Bomb Group, their bomb run over Tokyo on January 27, 1945, turned into a bitter battle for survival. Two fighters found their mark: the first was a Mitsubishi A6M5 Zeke that came in from directly above and slammed into the left wing behind the number one engine, ripping away 8ft (2.4m) of aileron and shredding a gas tank. The second was a Mitsubishi J2M3 Raiden 21 Jack that slammed into the tail compartment, tearing away the left side of the tail section and severing the left stabilizer. As the two rammers found their mark, flight engineer Lieutenant Robert Watson managed to keep his cool and help save the aircraft:

"There was surprisingly little jolt when the Jap hit us, and our navigator didn't even know we'd been rammed . . . thought we'd lost an engine for sure. However, I glanced at my instruments and found that it was still in good running order. To keep it in operation, I immediately transferred enough fuel from the damaged gas tank into another tank so that the level of the fuel

Right: "Blood chits"—identification or escape flags—provided identification to a downed airman and facilitated local assistance. These were used in the China-Burma theater of operations.

來華助戰

仰我

一體救護

國民政府

軍航空委員會

借用

字第　　號 W 69783

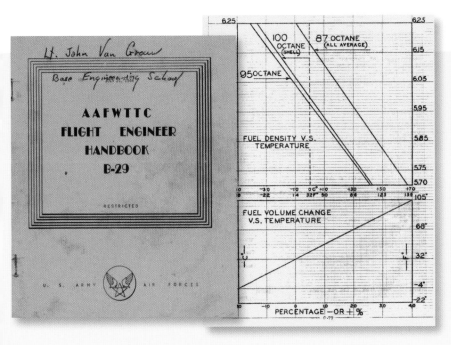

Left: *Flight engineers not only had to know the Wright Cyclone inside and out, but they also had to understand fluid dynamics. These graphs show the efficiency of different octane fuels and their performance under varying air temperatures.*

Below: *A B-29 of the 504th Bomb Group over Osaka. Early captions to this photo describe the number three engine losing oil, but in fact the dark area behind the engine was caused by the shadow of the B-29 from which this picture was made.*

in the cell was below the point of the leak; then I fed it back to keep the engine going."

[*Irish Lassie* made it back to Saipan, where she crash-landed. All crew members survived, although some were heavily injured. Nine were decorated for their part in this historic mission.]

Accurate weather forecasting in China was vital, and photo reconnaissance detachments were thus formed. But they suffered losses; *Brooklyn Bessie* **was the first. Jim Morrison (flight engineer) had to bail out and was captured by what he thought were Japanese soldiers:**

"We caught fire over North China when the order came over the intercom to bail out; I quickly left my station and dove out the forward hatch. I landed on the crest of a foothill about a 1,000ft [305m] high . . . [Morrison then caught sight of a group of men in what looked like Japanese uniforms.]

"With gestures I attempted to let them know I was willing to surrender; the largest of the group directed for some of the men to advance. They stationed themselves behind other rocks and aimed their guns at me; the leader advanced and started searching me. He asked to see my pistol; after examining it he then returned the gun. I took a chance and brought out my American-Chinese dictionary. After looking at it, the leader took my pencil and methodically wrote 'B-29' on the flyleaf."

[Writing "B-29" secured the crew's safety, as it would signify to other Chinese soldiers or authority figures that the men were genuine.]

The Wright Engine?

"When the brakes released on the old bird, it was like pulling your foot out of a gluepot. The running joke was, 'Everybody stand up; it'll make it lighter!' Down the runway we go with the airspeed indicator moving like the hour hand on a Mickey Mouse watch. When we got to the point where we had better think pretty seriously of flying, our copilot comes on the inter-phone with, 'The manifold pressure on number three is dropping! Abort! Abort!' Not another word was said. I had the throttles locked forward to the firewall with my feet. Well, we managed to get off, as I knew we would, because nobody was looking forward to a swim in the China Sea."—E. L. Davis, 307th Bomb Group, Korea.

The B-29 was in many ways terribly flawed; rapid development and too few hours' testing meant it suffered from endless "teething" problems. The most crippling of these lay with the notoriously unreliable Wright Cyclone R-3350 air-cooled engines. These huge 18-cylinder radials, produced 2,200hp each. (The famous B-17 had four Cyclone R-1280 engines of 1,200hp each.) The twin-bank configuration of the engine caused serious cooling problems; consequently, engine fires were common, along with runaway props, and units that simply disintegrated. The original design goal of the R-3350 had been to produce an engine that produced one horsepower for each pound (around 0.5kg) of weight; this aim proved to be overly ambitious. In order to reduce weight, the engineers replaced the conventional aluminum-alloy crankcase and other accessory housings with lighter magnesium-alloy parts, and in combat conditions the brittle magnesium tended to crack under severe vibration. Magnesium also burned at an extremely high temperature, making in-flight engine fires virtually impossible to put out. The B-29's onboard extinguishers proved inadequate, and were unable to deal with 87 per cent of reported fires.

General Curtis LeMay was one of the few high-ranking officers who knew a great deal about the B-29 and its engines. As a graduate engineer, he was ideally placed to understand that he had "the buggiest damn airplane that ever came down the pike" on his hands. For flight

Below: All B-29 maintenance was done outdoors. This group of ground crew has managed to construct a more permanent structure to make access to the B-29's engines easier.

Right: High above the Pacific Ocean, two 498th Bomb Group B-29s form up. This shot was taken through the small flight engineer's window, which offered him limited visibility.

Pair of nylons...Superfortress size

A BOEING SUPERFORTRESS lands on enough nylon to make 4,000 pairs of stockings. There are six tires—four like those above; and two others, slightly smaller, that hold up the nose. All have to be stronger than tires ever were before. For sometimes seventy tons of B-29 come down a little too fast, or hit a bump during a bomb-heavy take-off. Too bad if the tires couldn't take terrific loads.

So B. F. Goodrich builds B-29 tires reinforced with nylon.

Any woman can understand why. Nylon made stronger stockings than ever before, and it worked the same way with tires. Nylon plies *doubled* the strength of B. F. Goodrich airplane Silvertowns; resistance to bruising was also greatly increased. And all without adding weight.

B. F. Goodrich development work with special materials and with natural and synthetic rubbers has brought about many improvements in airplane tires . . . and many B. F. Goodrich

"firsts" important to car owners.

Typical was the lead B. F. Goodrich took in making and selling synthetic rubber tires. Long before Pearl Harbor, and *three full years* before any other company, B. F. Goodrich sold automobile tires containing synthetic rubber. They learned a lot from making and testing them.

Today, your B. F. Goodrich dealer sells the one synthetic tire that's three years ahead of all others! The extra experience behind it is showing up in

extra mileage, extra safety for car owners. *The B. F. Goodrich Company, Akron, Ohio.*

Skyway or Highway

B.F. Goodrich

FIRST IN RUBBER

Right: Goodrich Chemical pioneered the petrochemical-based synthetic rubber process during World War II. Airplane de-icers and B-29 tires were among more than 35,000 products made by the firm—founded in Akron, Ohio, in 1870—for American combat aircraft during the war.

engineers, the R-3350 was an unpredictable demon that could at any moment burst into flames. But that was just one scenario; a valve could burn off and chew up a cylinder, followed by the cylinder flying off and tearing up the whole engine. If there was a loss of hydraulic fluid and the flight engineer couldn't feather the prop, it would fly off; but

that would be preferable, because—in an even worse scenario—sometimes the whole engine simply seized and twisted right off the wing!

Takeoff was the most critical phase—full power was required from all engines. Nursing an overloaded B-29 down the runway required intense concentration by the flight engineer; if just one of the engines quit, caught fire, or even sputtered, the aircraft invariably crashed, killing its entire crew. Andy Doty, tail gunner with the 19th Bomb Group, recalls: "Among the saddest sights to be seen by departing crews as they took off was the flaming wreckage of a bomber below them at the end of the runway."

Tragically, in its short combat tour, the B-29 was responsible for the deaths of far more crewmen through mechanical failures and malfunctions, and causes unknown, than enemy fighters and flak.

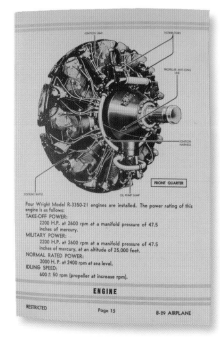

Four Wright Model R-3350-21 engines are installed. The power rating of this engine is as follows:
TAKE-OFF POWER:
2200 H.P. at 2600 rpm at a manifold pressure of 47.5 inches of mercury.
MILITARY POWER:
2200 H.P. at 2600 rpm at a manifold pressure of 47.5 inches of mercury, at an altitude of 25,000 feet.
NORMAL RATED POWER:
2000 H.P. at 2400 rpm at sea level.
IDLING SPEED:
600 ± 50 rpm (propeller at increase rpm).

ENGINE

RESTRICTED   Page 15   B-29 AIRPLANE

Above: For B-29 production alone, Wright and its subcontractor, Dodge, produced more than 5,500 R-3350 piston engines.

Left: The B-29 program was hindered by the R-3350's problems, which slowed its development during 1943 and into 1944. Here, Lady Mary Anna, *with 17 missions to her credit, is about to receive a new engine.*

Point of no return

The B-29s were often grossly overloaded. Crammed with fuel, bombs, and ammunition, they routinely exceeded the manufacturer's safe takeoff weight by thousands of pounds. Getting such a heavily weighted aircraft off the ground was never easy, and many crews considered it the most frightening part of the mission. Flight engineer Earl Rishell from the 45th Bomb Squadron recounts, in vivid detail, just one of many takeoffs from Tinian on May 25, 1945:

"What with critiques, briefings, and the constant readying and checking of aircraft between missions, flight engineers were the most sleep-deprived of all combat crewmembers; some of us had not fully recovered from a 15-hour mission only two days before.

"As daunting as the over-water flight to Japan was, the taxi out to the active runway on a maximum effort mission could be even more grueling. Getting 300 aircraft into the air at three-minute intervals meant a long, creeping promenade that stretched back over an extensive network of taxiways and parking revetments. Grossed out at 30 tons, the trip to the active runway was an endless series of high revving starts, lunging, wallowing turns and sudden full-braking stops. Loaded with fuel, bombs, .50 caliber ammo and crew, the engines, brakes and tires, [the B-29s] were brought close to— or exceeded—design limits. With engines idling and a rotisserie-like environment in the cabin, we sat drenched in sweat. The cylinder head temperatures . . . edged into the red. Memories of swallowed valves, engine failures and aborted takeoffs back in India came to mind. Now, only halfway to the active runway, the fuel gauge needles had begun their relentless, downward circle and would not stop until the night had come and gone.

Above: A Wright Field Flight Line Pass. Bomber Flight Test was located at Wright Field, Ohio, during World War II.

"When the active runway was reached, the Tinian takeoff was a five-minute exercise in white-knuckle concentration and silent prayer by everyone on board. When the pilot applied full throttle, the heavy plane seemed stuck in mire and unwilling to roll. But horsepower won out over weight and the plane began to move. The air speed indicator needle stopped bouncing and began to move slowly upward. At 30 knots or so, Mitchell began calling out the airspeed at 5-knot intervals. The rate of acceleration seemed so slow I was certain we'd roll off the runway and down the embankment long before we reached 60 knots, but the engines did their job; RPM and manifold pressure held. Cylinder head temperatures, that [were] in yellow or red for the best part of an hour, now crept back toward the green.

"The wings, accepting their responsibility, began to relieve the tires of their burden; the aircraft artfully rotated and we were safely in the air. As far as I was concerned the most harrowing part of the flight was now over."

Above: A B-29 from the "Red Raiders" 22nd Bombardment Group, 33rd Bombardment Squadron, sits on its hardstand at Kadena Air Base, Okinawa. The 22nd served during the Korean War from July to October 1950.

The appearance of a Soviet-built MiG-15 jet fighter over North Korea forced the B-29s to switch from daylight operations to night bombing. Many crews were relieved; as flight engineer Jesse Richey of the 345th Bomb Squadron, 98th Bomb Group, describes, on one night mission in December 1951 it wasn't just the MiGs one had to worry about:

"We were going to be flying a night mission this time, and we believed we would have little problem with MiGs or flak; we were half right.

"We had solid flak for 12 to 14 minutes going into the target. I had curtains over my window to prevent light from escaping, so I couldn't see the antiaircraft fire, but I could hear it—a kind of crinkling sound; as it intensified, it sounded like a hailstorm. Our aircraft was punctured by quite a few holes, although one was very large.

"As soon as we delivered the bombs, our pilot made a diving turn and got the hell out of there."

When the Korean War started, the call-up of experienced aircrew began. Many of them had seen service in World War II, and some of them didn't look forward to putting themselves into harm's way once more. Flight engineer Eugene L. Davies from the 370th Bomb Squadron, 307th Bomb Wing, Korea, recalls an event between an uninterested "retread pilot" (one that has served before, called up from the reserves) and a straight-up, no-bull major:

"B-29 combat crew training for the Korean War was rough on young teenage engineers, and on retread pilots who didn't want to be there in the first place. And it didn't help matters to know that after the training at Randolph (AFB, Texas), there was Korea waiting. Check rides, standboard exams, and flight checks were things to be despised, but we all knew the best thing to do was pass and get the hell out of Randolph anyway.

"On one particular day our crew was getting a check ride from a major who occupied the copilot's seat for the flight. He was a stickler for detail, and he demanded instant response and perfection from the flight crew. After minor skirmishes on pre-flight, takeoff and climb out, we settled down for the rest of the routine.

"Our aircraft commander was a retread captain who didn't give a damn for anybody or anything, and his nickname was Tex. We were sitting there, flying straight and level with everything working like a well-oiled watch, when the major yanked the number four throttle back to idle, slumped over the control column and yelled, 'You just lost number four and I'm dead! What are you going to do about it, Captain?'

"Old Tex punched the mike button, and in a cool, couldn't-care-less tone said, 'Engineer! Come up here and drag this dead bastard out and help me fly the son-of-a-bitchin' airplane!'"

The Radio Operator

"It was terrible. We had flown over many bombed cities including Tokyo. They were damaged, but nothing like what we saw below. I think we were the first persons to fly over [Hiroshima] and see what happened."

—S/Sgt. Lewis "Lew" Remy, radio operator on a B-29 named *Kaga Tsuchi: Scourge of the Fire God*, 315th BW (VH), Northwest Field, Guam

Seated aft of the flight engineer in the forward pressurized crew compartment, the B-29 radio operator was responsible for air-to-ground, air-to-air, and inter-phone communication, electronic aids to navigation, and the newly introduced Instrument Landing System (ILS). The position was standard in contemporary USAAF heavy bombers, and comprised much of the same equipment as in B-17s and B-24s. The USAAF preferred its radio school graduates to qualify as radio operator-mechanics (ROMs). Students unable to receive and decode the required 16 random, five-letter, Morse code groups per minute might graduate as mechanics, while students more adept at code, but less proficient in maintenance and electronics, could qualify as operators; both single-qualification ratings were generally assigned to non-flying positions. B-29 radiomen were expected to remain with their sets throughout most of the mission, and did not take the gunnery courses required for radio operators in other USAAF bombers.

The main radio set on the B-29 was the USAAF's standard four-channel, very high frequency (VHF) SCR-522 command set. The Twentieth Air Force generally assigned the set's four crystal-controlled channels as a wing (bomber-to-bomber) frequency, a bomber-to-fighter

Left: The radio operator faced the outer skin of the fuselage, with the back of the flight engineer's panel to his left and the bomb bay bulkhead to his right.

frequency, a Pacific Common (control tower) and air-sea rescue frequency, and a VHF homing frequency used by ground stations to vector in on an aircraft's position.

By the war's end, the Twentieth had begun installing the ARC-3 command set, essentially an eight-channel replacement for the SCR-522; both sets could generate homing signals for USAAF fighters, allowing the escorts to find a nearby B-29 for navigational assistance on the long missions across the Pacific. In addition to the command set, each B-29 carried an AM liaison set (comprising an ART-12 transmitter and BC-348 receiver) operating in the low-to-medium frequency range, and ARN-7 radio compass, a rudimentary navigational aid. A more precise radio navigation system used the Army Airways Communications System's ground-based high frequency direction finders: the radio operator could send the "QUJ" code letter combination to request a bearing to one of the ground stations. The response, generated almost immediately, gave a true course to that station; the navigator could then factor in the winds to guide the aircraft safely home. If his aircraft was in danger of ditching, the radio operator could request a "QTF" fix on his position; in three to six minutes, ground stations could triangulate on the aircraft and pass the B-29's latitude and longitude to the aircraft and to the air-sea rescue network.

The radio operator also operated the B-29's components of the SCS-51 Instrument Landing System (ILS), critical for bringing the aircraft down safely in the dark or in adverse weather conditions. To function at all, the system required the runway to be equipped with transmitters to indicate its center and the glide path, and with marker beacons to help indicate the aircraft's distance from the field. With a pair of dials, the radio operator could inform the pilot if they were above, below, left, or right of the glide path until the runway came into visual range.

The radio operator was also responsible for the SCR-578, a 34lb (15kg) portable emergency radio transmission set and hand-cranked generator. The unit was nicknamed the "Gibson Girl" in deference to its pinched waist (resembling the 1890s' fashion designs of Charles Dana Gibson); following an emergency landing or ditching, the operator held the set between his legs, deployed the antenna, and cranked the generator at around 72rpm. The set could broadcast an automatic SOS, or a manual code signal. The radio operator contacted the nearest ground station and gave the bearing (hopefully determined before the crash); the code word "Monster"

(indication that the downed aircraft is a B-29), the words "Goodyear" (survivors are in a life raft), "Yellow Jacket" (survivors in life jackets), or "Davey Jones" (survivors without floatation devices); the number of survivors; and, if the green dye marker was showing, "Evergreen." The information helped rescue forces locate the survivors and ensure that enough resources were deployed. The Gibson Girl also generated power for a signal lamp. (Cranking out all that electricity took a great deal of effort, and survivors were cautioned to relieve each other in that task frequently to avoid exhausting any single crew member.)

Page right, clockwise from top left: The back of the flight engineer's panel stored the radio operator's two handheld microphones; the headset hangs from its hook above the work table; the radio compass helped take bearings on ground stations, though the most accurate bearings were taken by the ground stations on a signal generated aboard the aircraft.

Liaison Radio

Between 1936 and 1950, the BC-348 (also known as the ARR-11) was the USAAF AM liaison radio receiver for heavy aircraft. Reliable and simple to use, more than 100,00 were produced, mainly by Belmont Radio and (below) Wells-Gardner. In B-29s, it was paired with the ART-12 transmitter and used to make emergency contact with ground stations, request and receive bearings, and send distress signals.

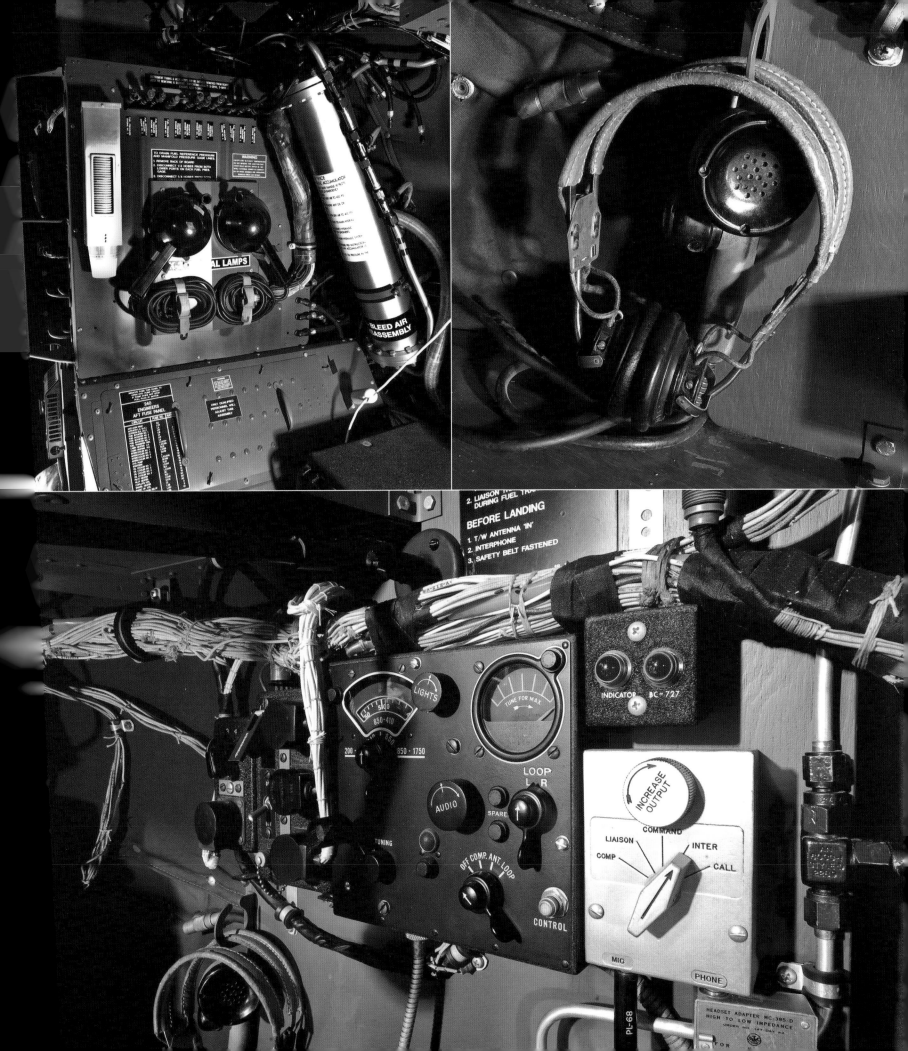

Lucky thirteen?

This was the 13th combat mission in which the 40th Bomb Group had participated. The primary target was the Omura Aircraft Plant. Of the 78 planes launched, 59 reached and bombed the target; one of those aircraft was *The Heavenly Body*, from the 45th Squadron. As part of the lead squadron *The Heavenly Body* was damaged by fighters, and Douyne McCullough, radio operator, was forced to bail out, along with the rest of his crew. Everyone made it out, but his flight engineer died shortly after. McCullough describes the action and his treatment after bailing out over friendly territory:

"Shortly after bombs away, there was a loud 'ping' sound. Someone said, 'We've been hit; put on your oxygen masks.' I looked over at Oblender [the navigator] and noticed that he had pieces of [what looked like] dried prunes all over his face; the small box he'd been carrying had been blown away. I asked if he was OK. He pointed to Miller—I leaned over and found him slumped forward with mucus running from his nose; I immediately put a small oxygen tank on him, and pulled him out of his seat [and] laid him over the wheel well hatch. I went back to my position. After flying for several hours, Ledford [the pilot] requested a

Above: *Advanced as it may have been, the B-29 was still a combat aircraft and as such was full of flammable liquids and gasses. These two diagrams illustrate the oxygen and fuel systems, both of which were vulnerable to flak and enemy fighters; a single cannon shell or small piece of shrapnel could be enough to disable a B-29.*

voice 'May Day' distress call be made in the hope of locating an emergency landing field; no luck. I remained in radio contact while bailout preparations were made.

"We bailed out at about 10,500ft [3,234m]; we landed in a narrow valley between two mountain ranges. While sitting there, I noticed a figure in the distance coming toward me. I was relieved to see he was a Chinese soldier. I got [out] my translation booklet and pointed to the phrase, 'take me to your garrison.' The soldier then pointed to the phrase, 'You stay here,' so that's what I did.

"Most of the communicating between us and the Chinese was

Left: *Pictured here was one of the first B-29s to arrive in the India-China theater of war. This example was one of the first aircraft to have rolled off the production line. Early production aircraft were painted olive drab on the upper surfaces and neutral gray underneath.*

handled by a Chinese civilian official and a Norwegian missionary woman. Their English was very limited, but they did tell us that Miller had died about ten minutes after landing. When we left the village each of us was carried on a stretcher-like pallet.

"After a while, I decided it would be much safer walking on the uneven surface than being carried. After walking along the mountain ridge, we came to a fortress-type structure; we spent the night there and were treated to a fine Chinese dinner with high-ranking officers. After breakfast the next day we were loaded into an old school bus with no seats; [finally] after a day's travel we arrived at an advanced fighter base. Shortly after, a C-47 landed to pick us up."

Right: *American aircrew fought in some of the world's most extreme climates. Most aircraft were well equipped with survival gear; what the crew lacked was training. This survival guide was produced to help redress the balance.*

Below: Old–Bitch-U-Airy Bess *served with both the 462nd Bomb Group, 769 Bomb Squadron and later with the 98th Bomb Group, 345 Bomb Squadron.*

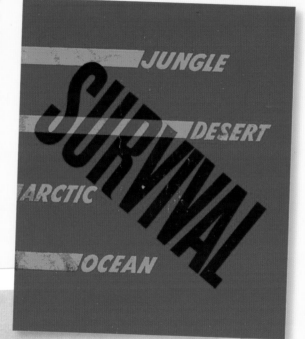

By August 1944, changes in the Pacific War and the destruction of Japanese shipping had diminished the importance of certain targets, one of them being the Pladjoe refinery at Palemburg, Sumatra. Washington was adamant that the target be hit, though. On August 10, 54 B-29s took off along with radio operator Clay Sandhofer of 462nd Bomb Group. It was to be a 19-hour mission that would use every last drop of fuel:

"The transfer of fuel was arranged between him [the flight engineer] and Major Thompson [the pilot], so that the best balance was obtained and the aircraft was 'on the step.' This gave the best fuel economy. Unfortunately, after 15 hours into the mission we could not transfer the fuel from one of the bomb bay tanks; this was serious and a great concern as we had no way of removing the fuel from the rear tank—something had gone wrong. Furthermore, we could not salvo the tank for some reason . . . as a result, additional weight was added with a loss of usable fuel . . . we became badly unbalanced because [of] the added gas weight in the back of the aircraft.

"One hour from Ceylon we had passed our original flight plan of 17 hours; we were convinced we'd have to ditch and started planning. To keep the aircraft from losing control, Major Thompson had the crew in the rear move forward. All 11 members crowded into the nose compartment. Although dangerous for ditching, it did put the aircraft back 'on the step.' We pulled the engines to minimum rpm and managed the fuel as best we could. We discussed cutting one engine so we could run the other three at a slightly more efficient speed, but no change was made [in the end].

"We made a straight-in approach and landed [on Ceylon] at high speed; we were afraid of losing the engines and with full flaps and gear down we couldn't depend on them. Our trip had lasted exactly 19 hours—as we taxied off the runway the engines cut due to lack of fuel."

Survivors

The B-29 was an extremely tough aircraft, a quality shared by most American combat aircraft built during World War II. Howard T. Anderson, a radio operator with the 44th Squadron based in China and on Tinian, owed his life to the B-29's solid constitution. In two separate events in 1945, Anderson's aircraft was severely damaged, and in both cases the mighty Boeing held together and brought his crew home:

"It seemed a routine mission. We maintained radio silence while I kept listening on the Wing's high frequency for any weather reports and/or changes in plans. It was to be a 14-hour mission to Omura and back. As we neared the target the formation joined at 22,000ft [6,706m], our bombing altitude; our aircraft was stacked high on the left side of the formation.

"When we departed the IP, I climbed up in the tunnel and looked through the astrodome to watch for enemy fighters. As I recall, it was the radio

OFFICIAL PHOTOGRAPH
NOT TO BE RELEASED
FOR PUBLICATION
NAVY YARD MARE ISLAND, CALIF.

RESTRICTED
DECLASSIFIED

2836-44
45° OFF CENTERLINE.   (SS411)
MARE ISLAND, CAL.   11 MAY 1944.

Right: *Fourteen subs—including USS* Spadefish, *seen here off Mare Island, California—were assigned to air-sea-rescue duties around Japan.*

Below: *Ditching a heavy bomber like the B-29 into the sea was a hazardous prospect at best. Even in the calmest of seas the aircraft could be heavily damaged. This unidentified B-29, its tail broken, begins to sink.*

operator's duty to observe (through the window of the bomb bay hatch) the release of the bombs; as I slipped down to my radio position, 'all hell broke loose.' It seemed that the entire Japanese air force had hit our B-29 and the aircraft seemed to shudder and shake. I heard Elmo Gray tell the Major that he had lost number four engine and to feather it. Then another wave of fighters pounded us and I knew that we had lost cabin pressure.

"We were also losing altitude fast. After several minutes of repeated attacks the fighters left; we were now alone. Major Roberts told Ford [the navigator] to point us toward the Yellow Sea and the air-sea rescue submarine USS *Spadefish*. I attempted radio contact with the sub on the emergency frequency, but with some difficulty. The gunners had shot away the fixed wire antenna and the trailing wire antenna would not reel out. I set the emergency frequency on the high frequency 274N command radio, which utilized a different antenna. I then contacted 'Funny People' [the call sign of the submarine].

"We talked briefly about heading north to Vladivostok, Russia, but decided to make it back into friendly China; attempts to notify the submarine failed. All non-essential equipment was thrown overboard in order to lighten the aircraft. Studying the maps, our navigator suggested to Major Roberts that the emergency strip at Laohokow would be a suitable place to set down [and] we landed on the short grassy strip. Early the next morning, with the aid of many Chinese, we refueled the aircraft with 5 gallon [19 liter] cans and took off.

"We were happy to be back at our forward base. The mission was a tribute to those Wright 3350s! Major Roberts was awarded the Silver Star for gallantry in action. The remainder of the crew was presented with the Distinguished Flying Cross and/or the Air Medal."

Now based on Tinian, Howard Anderson and his crew once again found themselves at the mercy of their damaged bomber. On May 19, 1945, after they bombed the target, problems arose with the number two engine; the aircraft got them home, but landing was impossible—it was a question of ditch or bail out:

"We were bound for our target, an aircraft factory at Hamamatsu. As we climbed to our bombing altitude, Irv Smith reported what seemed to be an oil leak in number two engine.

"The target was under 10/10 cloud cover as we approached so the bomb run was made by radar. The oil leak, meanwhile, had become worse; Joe Phalon's [flight engineer] assessment was the number two had blown a cylinder. He decided to feather the prop, but it wouldn't go all the way . . . Soon after bombs away, it began windmilling and further attempts at feathering were unsuccessful.

"Major Roberts asked me to notify Tinian about our troubles via the ART-13 liaison radio. I also contacted the super-dumbo B-29 rescue plane which normally carried a range of droppable equipment, including rafts, rations, survival kit, and radios. The propeller windmilling gradually increased, sending vibrations throughout the plane; we considered the possibility of ditching. Radio contact was made with a rescue submarine. They advised us that the seas were very rough and ditching would be extremely difficult. The alternative was to try to make it to Iwo.

"The propeller began to really wind up as we headed south toward Iwo. Major Roberts told Vince Ford and me to leave our positions; it was evident the prop would come off and possibly strike the plane. By this time, three P-61s from Iwo and a super-dumbo were flying formation. The noise from the engine was unbearable.

"Approximately 45 minutes north of Iwo, the prop sheared off. On its upward swing it tore a large jagged hole in the fuselage immediately aft of the navigator's station. It ruptured the small hydraulic tank and cut some control cables and electrical wiring. Luckily, the number one engine seemed untouched. Major Roberts and Colonel Schaaf decided it would be futile to attempt a landing at Iwo with such a damaged plane.

"Since we had no intercom or radio communications, Major Roberts asked me to crawl through the tunnel with bail instructions for the aft

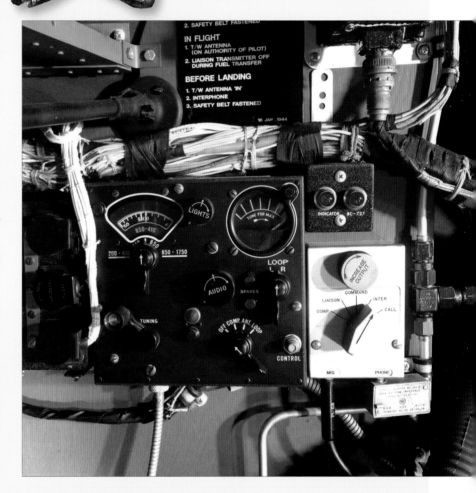

Left: The Silver Star was established for the army in 1932; it is awarded to persons cited for gallantry in action that does not warrant the award of the Medal of Honor or the Distinguished Service Cross.

Below: Communication between crewmen was vital. The intercom control box let crewmen direct their messages to the appropriate position. Most of the radio operator's communication was with the pilot and navigator.

crewmembers. We would make two passes over the Island in an effort to drop as many crewmembers as possible.

"From approximately 2,500ft [762m], Iwo Jima didn't look very large. It was extremely quiet after bailing out, like being in a vacuum; after my 'chute opened it seemed like just seconds before I was on the ground. A few of us landed by the water's edge where some Seabees helped gather our 'chutes. As they took us to the dispensary tent, we watched as #271 crashed into the ocean. That's when my knees began knocking!"

Super-dumbos

The radio message would look like this: "Nelly's Belly three, this is Armpit five; number two is out but have advised Room Service of our arrival with an ETA of 09:30 hours." The wit is self-evident but it had a purpose: to confuse the Japanese. These codes referred to rescue submarine number three on station and to aircraft number five of a specific squadron, which had been shot up over the target and was signaling its estimated time of arrival to the tower at Isely Field. Almost every crewmember in a battle-damaged B-29 felt that if their aircraft could get beyond the coast of Japan, then they would be home free; however, chances of rescue were just about even.

Early in the B-29 campaign, rescue at sea was a problem for the USAAF. Most of the flying was over water and the distances were vast. Responsibility for air-to-sea rescue was originally assigned to the theater commander and a rather loose system was established. While there were boats and aircraft that patrolled near the Marianas, and longer-range aircraft along with destroyers and submarines covered most of the B-29s' routes, success was limited: up until January 14, 1945, only 23

Left: This patch was worn on the left sleeve of the B-29 radio operator's dress uniform.
Below left and below: Early air-sea rescue efforts were haphazard. Before March 1945, fewer than one in three aircrew were retrieved. By the end of May, eight out of ten were saved. By mid-August, nine super-dumbos were on duty, with 21 PBY Catalina flying boats.

per cent of the crewmembers from 32 presumed-ditched aircraft were actually rescued.

The capture of Iwo Jima greatly improved the chances of rescue success; this forward base was 600 miles (966km) closer to Japan and could serve as a base for a variety of aircraft. The B-29 was modified in haste and quickly pressed into the rescue effort. Soon nicknamed "super-dumbos," these modified aircraft were equipped with additional radios and operators, homing transmitters, and extra survival equipment. Based on Iwo, the super-dumbos would circle 50 to 100 miles [81 to 161km] off Japan until called in.

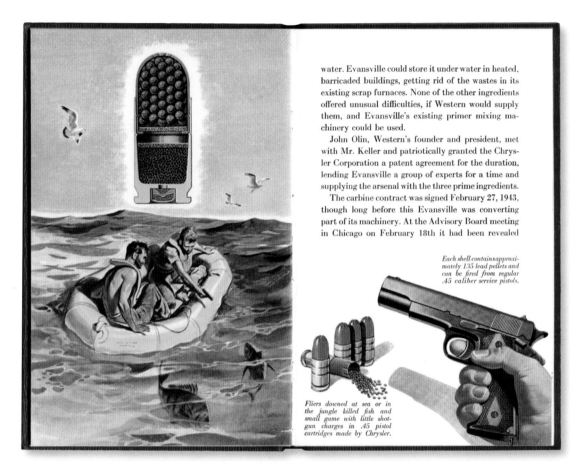

water. Evansville could store it under water in heated, barricaded buildings, getting rid of the wastes in its existing scrap furnaces. None of the other ingredients offered unusual difficulties, if Western would supply them, and Evansville's existing primer mixing machinery could be used.

John Olin, Western's founder and president, met with Mr. Keller and patriotically granted the Chrysler Corporation a patent agreement for the duration, lending Evansville a group of experts for a time and supplying the arsenal with the three prime ingredients.

The carbine contract was signed February 27, 1943, though long before this Evansville was converting part of its machinery. At the Advisory Board meeting in Chicago on February 18th it had been revealed

Each shell contains approximately 135 lead pellets and can be fired from regular .45 caliber service pistols.

Fliers downed at sea or in the jungle killed fish and small game with little shotgun charges in .45 pistol cartridges made by Chrysler.

Above: *Downed B-29 aircrew had well-equipped life rafts. All were stocked with food, water, flares, medicines, and so forth, and a small amount of specialized equipment, such as the .45 caliber pistol and rounds of shells containing 135 lead pellets, designed to kill fish or small game.*

Right: *All Allied aircrew rescued by submarine owed their rescuers a big debt of gratitude. For submariners it was a satisfying mission and on some occasions it was celebrated with humor and ceremony. Jean Vandruff, a downed B-24 pilot, was offered this parting certificate as a gift from the captain of the USS* Cobia.

In many ways B-29 crews were not well equipped for ditching (this was true of almost all heavy bomber crews during World War II)—ditching a damaged four-engine bomber was an extremely dangerous operation. Weather, waves, and darkness made the situation even worse. None of the pilots had any practice of ditching, and it

was a matter of "getting it right" the first time; not getting it right often meant the difference between life and death. If the aircraft survived intact, it would float long enough for the crew to launch life rafts and survival gear (the B-29's large fuel tanks would be more than half full with air, giving the aircraft some buoyancy).

The B-29 carried two E-2A six-man life rafts. These rafts contained a signal kit, emergency drinking water (seven cans), sea marker (three cans), life-raft rations (seven cans), and twenty-three other accessories, including aluminum oars, bailing buckets, and sun protection ointment. Individual crewmen, meanwhile, were equipped with the B-5 Pneumatic Life Preserve vests and the AN-R-2A one-man life raft. However, the aircraft's fuselage had a tendency to break near the trailing edge of the wing, which caused many tail gunners to perish.

By August 1945, the rescue forces were much better equipped, with 14 submarines, 21 flying boats, 9 super-dumbo aircraft, and 5 ships deployed for air-sea rescue. Downed crewmen could be rescued by seaplane, submarine, or destroyer; destroyers were stationed at 100 mile (161km) intervals between Iwo Jima and Japan, while submarines and amphibious aircraft, along with modified B-29 super-dumbos, patrolled enemy coastal waters. A staggering 2,400 men were assigned to the effort.

US attitudes toward air-sea rescue stood in stark contrast to those of the Japanese. Whereas the Americans valued their fighting personnel, the Japanese military showed apparent callousness toward their men when the latter were in danger; air-sea rescue in the Japanese Air Forces was nonexistent. Overall, 654 of the 1,310 US army fliers known to be downed were saved at sea; of that number, half had been aboard bombers that were ditched.

Log of a radio operator

Aircrews were not permitted to keep diaries. However, Richard A. Wachs of the 61st Bomb Squadron, 39th Bomb Group, ignored the rules. Wachs's account is short and to the point, and a casual glance through it might give the reader the impression that combat flying was a routine event. But closer scrutiny reveals the "routine" to be a series of long, boring periods punctuated by short bursts of adrenaline and fear:

Mission 1—May 4, 1945
Target: SAEKI Naval Air Base. Combat Flying Hours: 15:10.
Remarks: 20 general-purpose 500lb [227kg] bombs, little flack [sic], three fighter attacks, flew with crew number 37.

Mission 2—May 11, 1945
Target: Kobe, Kawanshi Aircraft Plant. Combat Flying Hours: 18:00.
Remarks: Heavy flack [sic], 15 fighter attacks, number two engine controls and hydraulic brake system shot out, landed at Iwo Jima with aid of parachute (Received Distinguished Flying Cross for mission).

Aborted Mission—May 15, 1945
Mission 3—May 17, 1945
Target: Nagoya. Combat Flying Hours: 15:45.
Remarks: Night mission, radar run, 24 incendiary bombs, no flack [sic], no fighters.

Mission 4—May 19, 1945
Target: Hamamatsu. Combat Flying Hours: 17:05.
Remarks: 20 GP [general purpose] bombs, cloud coverage, radar run, bombing altitude: 26,000ft [7,925m], little flack [sic], no fighters, landed at Iwo Jima, low on gas, seen crew bail out over water.

Mission 5—May 26, 1945
Target: Tokyo. Combat Flying Hours: 16:50.
Remarks: Night mission, 16 incendiaries, intense flak and search lights, jettisoned 12 bombs off coast, front bomb bays inoperable, landed on Saipan.

May 28, 1945
Our CFC gunner, Edgar Tuttle, shot himself in the foot while cleaning his gun.

Mission 6—May 29, 1945
Target: Yokohama. Combat Flying Hours: 19:00.
Remarks: 116 100lb [45kg] gasoline jell bombs, visual run, altitude:

19,000ft [5,791m], intense flak, one fighter attack plane, number P-1, hit over target, buddied with them, four men bailed out. Contacted sub and dumbo to give position; one man picked up by sub. Landed at Iwo Jima to refuel. On June 6, three men picked up; to date, Reck (radio operator) missing . . .

Aborted Mission—June 1, 1945
Mission 7—June 5, 1945
Target: Kobe. Combat Flying Hours: 16:30.
Remarks: 116 100lb [45kg] gasoline jell bombs, visual run, altitude 15,000ft [4,572m], meager flak, five fighters, one hole in horizontal tail. Made it back to base, low on gas.

Mission 8—June 7, 1945
Target: Osaka. Combat Flying Hours: 17:05.
Remarks: Altitude 21,000ft [6,401m], incendiary bombs, radar run, little flak, landed at Tinian to refuel.

Mission 9—June 10, 1945
Target: Chiba. Combat Flying Hours: 14:45.
Remarks: Aircraft Assembly Plant, altitude 15,000ft [4,572m], GP bombs, no flack [sic] or fighters, landed at base.

Right: A post-strike photo of Nagoya City. Nagoya was attacked several times in May 1945, resulting in seven square miles (18 sq km) of the city being completely torched.

Mission 10—June 18, 1945

Target: Kagoshima.

Combat Flying Hours: 17:05.

Remarks: Night mission, altitude 8,500ft [2,591m], 116 gasoline jell bombs, moderate flak, no fighters, landed at Iwo Jima to refuel.

Mission 11—June 20, 1945

Target: Shizuoka. Combat Flying Hours: 15:00

Remarks: Altitude 8,000ft [2,438m]. Industrial Center, incendiary bombs, little flak, no fighters, returned to base.

Mission 12—June 22, 1945

Target: Tamashima. Combat Flying Hours: 15:10.

Remarks: New aircraft assembly plant, altitude 15,500ft [4,572m], GP bombs, meager flak, three fighters, no attacks, returned to base.

Mission 13—July 4, 1945

Navigation Escort. Combat Flying Hours: 16:40.

Remarks: Escorted P-51 fighter planes to Tokyo area. Fighters strafed the area and rendezvoused with us to return to base. Mission flown from Iwo Jima.

Mission 14—July 17, 1945

Target: Hiratsuka. Combat Flying Hours: 14:00.

Remarks: Naval installations, night mission, radar run, 40 incendiaries, no flack or fighters, returned to Guam.

Mission 15—July 20, 1945

Target: Okasaki. Combat Flying Hours: 14:10.

Remarks: 184 gas jell bombs, night mission, visual bombing, no flak or fighters, returned to base.

Mission 16—July 27, 1945

Target: Omuta. Combat Flying Hours: 15:40.

Remarks: Night mission, incendiaries, visual bombing, no flak or fighters, returned to base.

Mission 17—July 29, 1945

Target: Ogaki.

Combat Flying Hours: 14:50.

Remarks: Night mission, radar run, incendiaries, no flak or fighters, bombing run broadcasted to States from "K" ship, returned to base.

Mission 18—August 2, 1945

Target: Mito. Combat Flying Hours: 15:45.

Remarks: Night mission, incendiaries, flak, no fighters, number one engine caught on fire on bomb run, feathered it and returned to base.

Mission 19—August 6, 1945

Target: Mikage (Nishinomiya). Combat Flying Hours: 15:05.

Remarks: Night mission, incendiaries, number two engine lost oil, feathered it and bombed Shingu, a city on the coast of Honshu, returned to base.

Mission 20—August 10, 1945

Target: Tokyo. Combat Flying Hours: 14:30.

Remarks: Day mission, four 2,000lb [907kg] and five 500lb [227kg] bombs, intense flak, eight holes in plane, returned to base. (Announced Japan's acceptance of Potsdam peace terms.)

Mission 21—August 15, 1945

Target: Isesaki. Combat Flying Hours: 14:40.

Remarks: Night mission, incendiaries, no flak or fighters, returned to base. (Last Combat Mission.)

Mission 22—August 31, 1945

Target: Tokyo. Flying hours: 16:40.

Remarks: Flew over Tokyo in formation as a display of power.

Tokyo Rose: The Voice of Treason?

"She played a lot of melodies that were popular back home. She talked a lot about how we were losing the war and how many planes had been shot down. It was a lot of crap."—Pilot Nolan Strange, 91st Reconnaissance Squadron.

Japan's World War II propaganda machine faced many challenges. The peoples of invaded nations had to learn that Japanese intervention in their lands was for their own protection from Western imperialism. The people at home in Japan were told of their country's unending string of victories against weak and unworthy foes; those foes, while still doomed to defeat, would soon be redefined as cruel and barbarous when the B-29s brought the war to the home islands. The Japanese fighting man was reminded of the racial superiority of all things Japanese, of the pure motives of Japan's leaders, and of the Samurai code of glorious death for the emperor. For the Dutch, British, Australians, New Zealanders, and Americans, the Japanese propaganda message warned of inglorious death and defeat; a familiar theme portrayed Western leaders leaving their

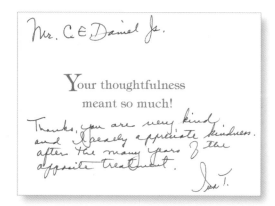

Mr. C.E. Daniel Jr.

Your thoughtfulness
meant so much!

Thanks, you are very kind and I really appreciate kindness, after the many years of the opposite treatment.

Iva T.

Left: A note from Iva Toguri to former B-29 crewman C.E. Daniels reflected Toguri's years of suffering as much as her eventual acceptance by the country of her birth.

soldiers to die at the hands of a relentless enemy while "4Fs" (the US draft board's code for anyone physically exempted from military service) romanced their wives and sweethearts back at home.

Japanese strategists hoped that their English-language broadcasts on Radio Tokyo would be an effective means of getting the message directly to the Allied troops. Playing popular American music to draw more listeners, the stations then switched to "news" broadcasts that emphasized Western casualties while downplaying any Japanese losses. Even clear-cut Allied victories were presented as temporary gains, while Japanese reinforcements prepared to destroy all enemies. At the Superfortress bases, the occasional grain of truth—such as when the deaths of individual B-29 crewmen were reported—could bring closure, sadness, or anger, but few placed much faith in the accuracy of anything reported by the Japanese.

The most famous of Japanese broadcasters was known to the troops as "Tokyo Rose," though no Japanese announcer was ever introduced by that name. Hoping to ingratiate themselves with the thousands of young Americans far from home, Radio Tokyo employed roughly a dozen English-speaking female broadcasters whose task it was to read scripts as part of *The Zero Hour* program; the Japanese expected that the female voice would have the most power, and that its seductive and alluring tones would resonate deeply with the troops, becoming the voice of every serviceman's anxieties. Collectively, all these women were remembered as "Tokyo Rose," though, after the war, one woman would be tried and convicted under that sobriquet.

The Foreign Broadcast Intelligence Service (FBIS), the American government agency responsible for monitoring enemy broadcasts, singled out Iva Toguri (whose on-air identity was "Orphan Ann") as the woman most servicemen identified as Tokyo Rose. The FBIS characterized the stories collected about Toguri as "apocryphal"—in fact, some of the broadcasts attributed to her dated to a time before she had joined the radio station.

Iva Toguri was *Nisei*, a first-generation American citizen born of Japanese parents. She had traveled to Japan in 1941 to care for an ill relative, planning to return on December 2

Below: A group of B-29 crewmen on Saipan relax with their radio and with the aid of some unusual-looking pipes. Crews enjoyed the broadcasts of Radio Tokyo as much as those of their own locally managed US military stations.

of that year. But a foul-up with paperwork stranded Toguri in Japan where, following the declaration of war, she was classified as an enemy alien and denied rations. In order to feed herself, she worked at any available job before becoming an English-language typist for Radio Tokyo in 1943. This work led to her participation in live broadcasts of music and comedy sketches on *The Zero Hour*, where she and her scriptwriters (both coerced POWs) reportedly conspired to covertly undermine the Japanese by crafting their content to avoid anti-US propaganda.

In September 1945, Toguri was arrested by US military authorities for her part in the broadcasts, and she languished in prison for more than a year. No charges were ever filed, and the Army Intelligence investigators found no evidence that she had ever broadcast greetings

Above: (Left) Iva was arrested in Japan in 1948 and returned to the US. Here, an MP takes her from a military prison to a plane bound for the US. (Right) US Deputy Marshall Herbert Cole escorts Iva to the Federal Court in San Francisco.

to units by name, predicted military movements, or violated any military laws. Nonetheless, she was tried in the US for violations of the Espionage Act of 1917, was convicted, and sentenced to ten years in prison. Released in 1956, the government attempted to revoke her citizenship and threatened her with deportation. However, she would be pardoned by President Ford in 1977, following revelations that the primary witnesses against her had committed perjury.

Toguri died in 2006. Despite her pardon and all evidence to the contrary, she is remembered by many veterans as the real Tokyo Rose, a mythical voice responsible for a long string of unsettling broadcasts.

Radio Waves

Gerard Rau, navigator, 497th Bomb Group records: "Tokyo Rose was a propaganda person that spoke English. She played modern music and tried to lower the morale of American soldiers, not just flyers, but American solders anywhere. She would suggest our wives were having affairs back home. Anything to start lowering our morale, or make us worry.

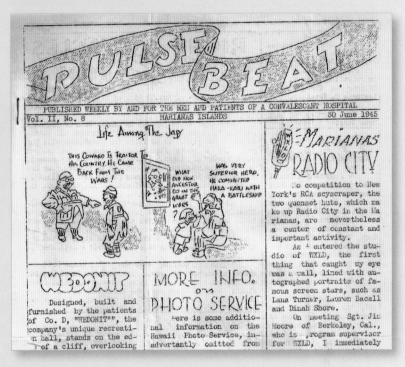

Above: This June 30, 1945 issue of Pulse Beat *included an article on WXLD, the military's entertainment and information radio station based in the Marianas.*

"Her radio station, Radio Tokyo, broadcast from Tokyo. We had our own station for our own use down in Saipan, called Radio Saipan. It did play music and we'd get the news and what baseball team was winning the World Series and stuff like that. In fact, I even used the Radio Tokyo signal to see where Tokyo was. When the radio operator tuned into a certain station he had a dial that would tell you where [that] station was in relation to the airplane. Those radios signals did help with our navigation."

[Twentieth Air Force was aware that its navigators would take bearings on Radio Tokyo, and discouraged the practice. The Japanese, who had used Honolulu's radio broadcasts to navigate to Pearl Harbor, occasionally switched transmission stations to confuse the Americans. Still, the practice continued aboard B-29s, and there are no reported incidences of bombers being led off course by Japanese radio signals.]

One of the first

August 6, 1945, was the day the first atomic bomb was dropped on Japan. Because of the importance of the attack and the destructive power of the new weapon, it is often assumed that there was only one B-29 flying over Japan on that day; in fact, there were hundreds of Allied aircraft bombing and strafing targets in Japan that same day (six B-29s were involved in the Hiroshima attack). In one of those aircraft was radioman Lew Remy from the 315th Bomb Wing meteorological flight:

"Most B-29s were equipped to fly for 18 hours tops, but with extra fuel tanks we could fly for 24 hours; I think we even flew for 30 hours on one flight. We could see Japanese planes, but they never attacked us; they were looking for big flights of bombers and we always flew alone. Sometimes we would fly very low, almost at treetop level. Sometimes we might be as high as 30,000ft [9,144m]. We were pressurized and didn't need oxygen masks. Of course, we knew nothing

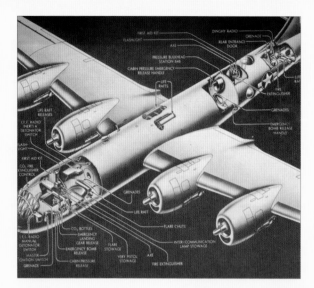

Left: B-29s were well equipped with first aid and emergency equipment. From axes to morphine, fire extinguishers to life rafts, B-29 crews had the tools to hand to deal with most emergencies.

about atomic bombs. We were listening to a Stateside shortwave radio and heard about a huge bomb being dropped on Hiroshima. We were so close; our pilot told us we would drift over the city to see what happened. It was terrible. We had flown over many bombed cities, including Tokyo; they were damaged, but nothing like what we saw below. I think we were the first people to fly over and see what happened."

Martin L. Zapf was a radio operator with the Fifth Bomb Squadron, Ninth Bomb Group based on Tinian. Martin had considered the job of radio operator to be "boring," but on one of the last missions of the war (August 15, 1945) he would experience the sheer terror of bailing out of a burning bomber, being lost at sea, an attack by Japanese villagers, and becoming a prisoner of war. Last, but not least, he would witness the horrible effects of radiation sickness on his fellow countrymen:

"Being a radio operator was a terrible job: I just sat there and wrote down what came over the radio. I sat next to the front bomb bay and there was a little, round door with a small window. Over a target, with the bomb bay doors open, I could see the bombs dropping—that's the only time I saw anything.

"On the day that we were shot down we lost power and had difficulty staying in formation. As we dropped out, we got hit by antiaircraft fire, causing the number three engine to catch fire. We quickly realized it wasn't an engine fire but the gas tank that was burning; it was a bad fire. The order came, 'prepare for ditching.' But there was a problem: [the] bombs were hung up, so now we had to jump.

"It was a beautiful, calm day when we splashed into the sea; we wound up with eight life rafts for ten people. Two aircraft flew over us, radioing our position, and we thought, 'we'll be picked up soon.' We waited for two or three days but nothing happened. We had no food, just a few pints of water; we had to do something, so we started paddling towards Japan. It took us three-plus days before we saw land and were picked up by Japanese fishermen—

Above: B-29 crewmen wore three different kinds of parachutes. This photo clearly illustrates the AN-6510 seat type parachute (left) made by the Irving Air Chute Company, and the B-8 back type parachute (right); a chest type was the third 'chute. The type worn depended on the position a crewman occupied within the aircraft.

Above: *A lead crew B-29 (identified by the black, yellow, black stripe on the rear fuselage and vertical stabilizer) from the 9th Bomb Group, 1st Bomb Squadron, climbs for altitude. Crews that displayed excellence in navigation or bombing were often chosen to lead entire squadrons to and from Japan.*

they didn't treat us very well. They hit us with things, and the kids threw stones and spat on us, until the military came.

"We left the village and they took us to Hiroshima for execution. A Japanese officer came to our rescue; he debated with his commanding officer and fortunately won the argument. One night, an English-speaking officer said he was going to take us away the next day. He took us through the city, and that's when we saw Hiroshima, ten days after the bomb. He put us in a civilian jail for a couple of days [where] we met two Americans who had been POWs in Hiroshima when the bomb was dropped. One was a B-24 gunner and the other was a Navy flyer.

"They both died while we were with them. It's difficult to describe what they looked like; they had puss [sic] running out of their mouth, ears and nose—they were in agony. They wanted to die. Later [the Japanese] took us to a POW camp and told us the war was over; you can't believe the feeling we had at that time. It was just amazing."

Lucky Break

T/Sgt. Stanley Tecoma told his daughter of one mission while serving as a B-29 radio operator: "One day we were on an overseas mission which required radio silence, and ran into extremely bad weather. We lost aircraft formation. The situation was becoming critical as we were approaching enemy aircraft. I decided to break radio silence and was able to get a fix on our position. We were able to navigate to a safe landing, but I really thought I was in for a serious reprimand. Several days later, the military police hunted me down while I was relaxing at the Club and I was sure I was in deep trouble. Instead they handed me travel orders for a long R&R trip, commending me for my actions. While I was away, I missed some very dangerous missions."

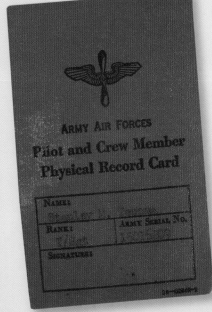

Above: *T/Sgt. Stanley Tecoma's Physical Record Card. Before going overseas, crewmembers had to be inoculated against a variety of diseases.*

CFC Top, Left, and Right Gunners

"CFC gunners of the B-29 named Command Decision of the 19th Bomb Group (Medium), 28th Bomb Squadron (Medium), shot down five MiG-15s in the Korean War; three during a single mission, to become the one and only Superfortress known as The Jet Bomber Ace." —Airman First Class James G. "Jim" Ewen, Okinawa

Since its introduction in World War I, defensive gunnery had been an integral part of America's strategic bombing doctrine. In the B-17 and B-24, some gunners sat in power-operated turrets, flanked by their heavy machine guns as they turned toward enemy fighters. Others held on to pintle-mounted guns, swinging their bodies from side to side. They wore bulky, electrically heated flying suits, and inhaled dehumidified oxygen in heavy masks. As the lowest-ranking members on the Flying Fortress or Liberator, most gunners noted that crew discomfort increased the farther one got from the "officer country" at the front of the aircraft. This was not the case in the B-29, where the three principal Central Fire Control (CFC) gunners sat in a pressurized, shirt-sleeve environment in the Central Station Fire Control (CSFC) compartment—better known as the Central Fire Control compartment. There, the cabin air was heated, breathable, and relatively humid (reducing the parched throat and fatigue associated with hours of breathing "dried" oxygen in other aircraft). Their guns were situated in remote turrets, isolating the gunners from the vibration,

Left: *The right-hand gunner's station, with the gunsight mounted in its blister and the gunner's seat swiveled to face aft. The yellow handles around the Plexiglas blister allow it to be jettisoned for use as an emergency exit.*

recoil, and fumes experienced by gunners in earlier bombers. B-29 gunners also enjoyed one other advantage: rank. Based on their experience, their training in the CFC system, and their duties in other aviation specialties, nearly all B-29 gunners were rated as sergeants.

The fully armed B-29 carried five remotely operated gun turrets: a forward dorsal (top) turret (with either two or four .50-caliber machine guns), a forward ventral turret, aft ventral, and aft dorsal (each with two fifties), and a tail turret (with either two fifties, three fifties, or two fifties with a 20mm cannon). The CFC allowed the sighting and firing of those turrets to be switched between the gunners. The bombardier (considered the officer in charge of the gunnery team) had primary responsibility for the two forward turrets, while the tail gunner was primarily responsible for the tail turret. The two lateral CFC gunners sat at clear Plexiglas sighting blisters on either side of the aft fuselage; they shared primary control of the aft ventral turret, with secondary control of the forward ventral turret and, when necessary, the tail turret. The senior CFC gunner sat beneath his sighting blister atop of the fuselage, with sole control of the after dorsal turret and secondary control of the forward dorsal turret.

While defensive gunnery training for earlier bombers had stressed the ability to track and hit a moving target, the B-29 required gunners to know also how to manage the sharing of their weapons. As such, CFC training schools instructed gunners in five-man teams.

But the CFC system was neither perfect nor automatic; it required a gunner to enter the wingspan of an attacking aircraft. The gunsight's reticle (sometimes written as "reticule") then helped compute the target's range, which was also entered into the computer. The gunner smoothly tracked the fighter, keeping the reticle center dot on the center of the target; the computer corrected for ballistics, parallax (variance caused by the distance between the gunner and the guns), and lead (the target's position once the bullets arrived at their destination).

Nearly all B-29 gunners entered CFC training with experience in B-17s or B-24s, which meant that many old habits had to be "un-learned." While earlier gunners learned to adjust their sighting to ensure a hit, CFC gunners needed to keep their sights centered on the target. And the old fallback of sighting with tracers became totally ineffective, confusing the CFC to the advantage of any attacking enemy aircraft.

However, all this proved to be superfluous once Curtis LeMay switched to low-altitude night missions, eliminating all defensive weapons except the tail guns. On those aircraft, the three CFC gunners were replaced by a pair of observers.

Page right, clockwise from top left: The right-hand gunner's position; the upper CFC gunner sat beneath his sighting blister on a seat known as the barber's chair; the pedestal gunsight was only part of the central fire control system. An outlet for a (rarely used) electrically heated flying suit and a breathing oxygen regulator and control; brackets held a thermos bottle and cup dispenser, pry bar and ax, and a first aid kit.

The Central Fire Control Computer

The heart of the Central Fire Control system was a series of four, 50lb (23kg) electromechanical computers, one linked to each remote gunnery station. Designed by General Electric (though often manufactured by other companies such as Singer), the computer received data from each of the pedestal gunsights, adjusted one or two turrets to follow the target, and fired the guns as the triggers were squeezed. Produced years before the invention of the transistor, the computer relied on vacuum tubes, gears, servos, motors, and amplifiers for computations and to control the turrets electrically. Despite being protected by armor plate, the computer could be knocked out of action by enemy fire or a simple system failure. In such an event, the gunner could switch to manual mode. While there are no known records of aerial victories in the manual mode, any action that fired back at the enemy was more encouraging than watching helplessly as a fighter bore in to attack!

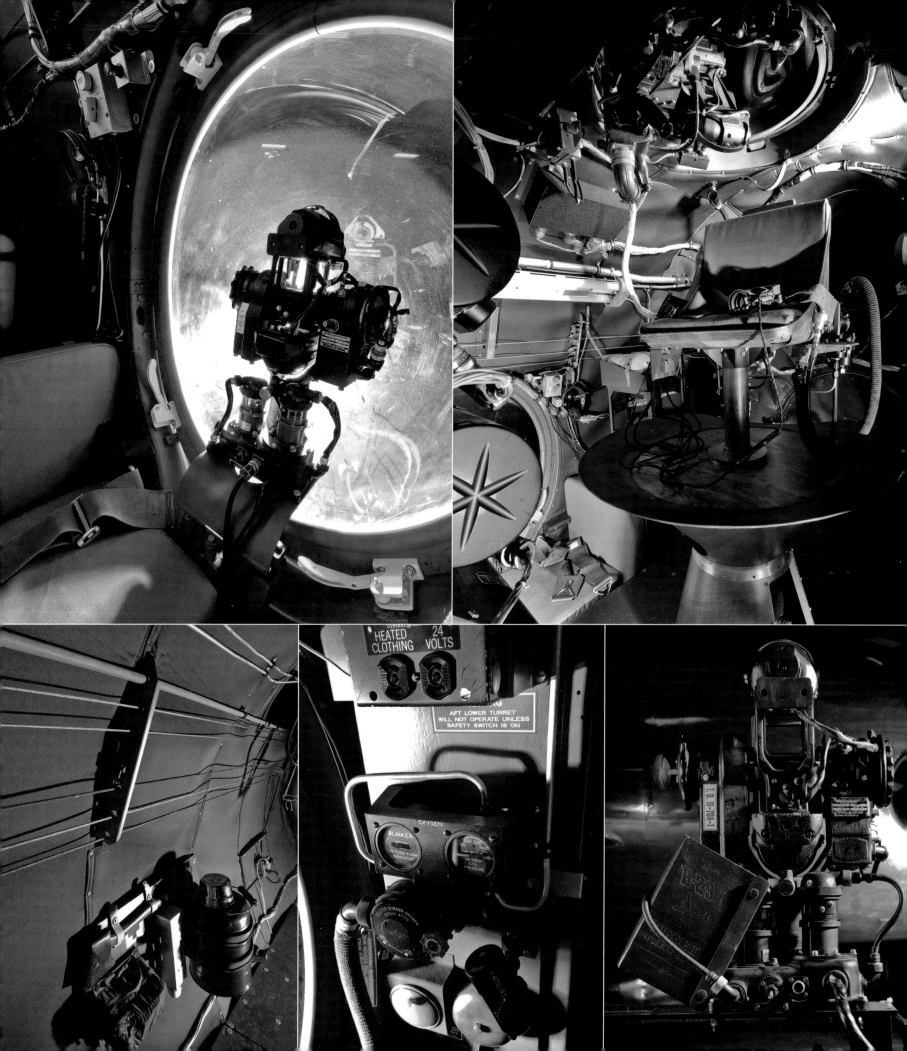

Wide awake

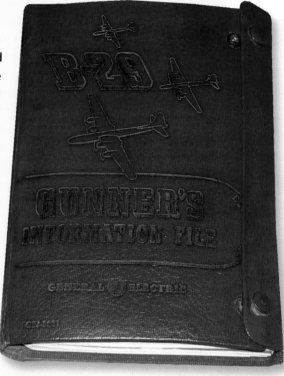

Left: *The* Gunner's Information File *was the gunner's bible; a manual designed to give the gunner the best possible chance of success.*

The first strategic bombing mission to Japan occurred on the night of June 15, 1944. Not since the Doolittle Raid in 1942 had US bombers flown over Japan. For CFC gunner Robert L. Hall of the 58th Bomb Wing, 40th Bomb Group, 44th Bomb Squadron, it was a mission that made him question why he had volunteered to fly in the B-29 in the first place:

"Inside the briefing room there was a big sheet of brown paper covering the maps at the front of the room. Someone told us to look at the persons on our left and right; if we did not know them, raise a hand; security precautions. After everyone was identified, they uncovered the map. There was an audible gasp; a piece of yarn marked the course, eastward across China, across the Yellow Sea, to Japan. This was what we had been training for. The time had come. I felt worried. I wasn't concerned about enemy action; I was more worried about the aircraft and whether it could make it there and back.

"As the briefing proceeded, my concern about enemy reaction increased. We'd be within the range of all kinds of ground fire, but there wouldn't be enough fuel to climb to a higher altitude. As I recall, things went smoothly: pre-flight checks, startup, taxi and takeoff. I don't remember all the flight details on the way out, except to say I was very careful to remember my training; reminding the gunners early in the mission to turn on auxiliary power, then AC power, and finally, as we neared the target, the turret power.

"It was dark over Japan. I strained my eyes staring into the darkness, searching for other planes. As we neared the target, searchlights and tracers from automatic weapons flashed through the sky. There was a strangeness to everything, an uncertainty about what to expect. It played on your nerves. Thoughts raced through my mind. I was scared, but no worse than the time we nearly ditched our

plane in the stormy Atlantic, and the time we made a very heavy takeoff and kicked up a lot of dust at the end of the runway. I thought combat couldn't be any worse. What had ever possessed me to volunteer for B-29 flying? I must've been crazy.

"After bombs away, and with a great sense of relief, we turned toward home base. It could have been much worse. Of course, I did not know it then, but later missions would be far more challenging. The trip home was a test of endurance; I'd had little or no sleep before the mission, and we had been flying all night. Exhausted, I struggled to keep alert and watch for other planes. On later missions the flight surgeon issued packets of Benzedrine sulfate tables to help us stay awake, but on this one I had nothing."

Not all Superfortress missions were to deliver bombs on target. Other duties included air-sea rescue, fighter escort, and reconnaissance. During one such reconnaissance mission, on October 26, 1944, CFC Gunner John K. Jensen and his crew were flying a solo post-strike photo mission when the Japanese decided they would take on the lone intruder, despite the fact that B-29s flying on their own over Japan were often left alone. The gunfight that followed was known as "the mission that saved the CFC system" because it had been proven in battle. There would be no going back to the old manual system now:

"Just as we turned north, [Cliff] Bell reported nine fighters coming up through the clouds behind us followed by seven more. As we approached the new target the first group was now in attack position. Donahue and I coordinated the use of the upper forward turret to maximum effect. The first group came at us in ones

Right: *The forward lower turret with its twin .50 caliber machine guns. With its four .50 caliber guns of the forward upper turret, the B-29 was well-equipped to deal with frontal attacks.*

and twos. The first fighter came in at 12 o'clock level. Donahue took both forward turrets. This fighter made the mistake of climbing after his attack, allowing Donahue to put both turrets on him. He was smoking as he passed over our right wing—so close, in fact, Eigenmann [the aircraft commander] said he could almost read his dog tags.

"On the next pass, two came in, one high and one low. Donahue took the lower turret and I used the uppers [both upper turrets]. Just as the high fighter rolled over and started into us I fired both . . . He never made it all

Above: *Following the October 25, 1944 recce mission the crew is seen being interrogated by a group intelligence officer. John K. Jensen is second from the left; Clifford Bell is on the right.*

Left: *Pages from the gunner's essential manual, the* Gunner's Information File. *The B-29's fire control was unique in that one gunner could control multiple turrets. This diagram illustrates clearly the primary and secondary controls built into the system.*

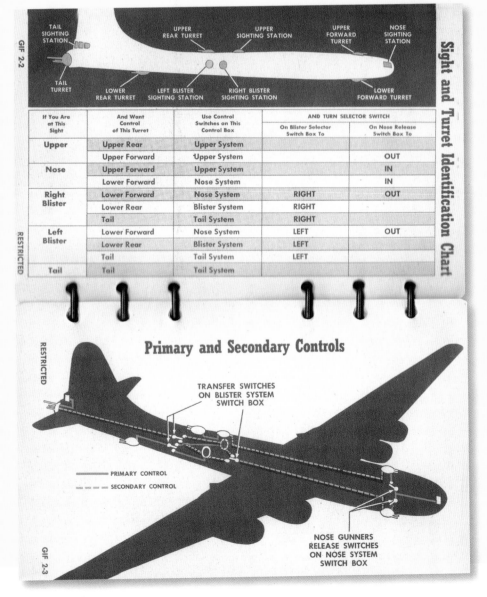

Sight and Turret Identification Chart

If You Are at This Sight	And Want Control of This Turret	Use Control Switches on This Control Box	AND TURN SELECTOR SWITCH	
			On Blister Selector Switch Box To	On Nose Release Switch Box To
Upper	Upper Rear	Upper System		
	Upper Forward	Upper System		OUT
Nose	Upper Forward	Upper System		IN
	Lower Forward	Nose System		IN
Right Blister	Lower Forward	Nose System	RIGHT	OUT
	Lower Rear	Blister System	RIGHT	
	Tail	Tail System	RIGHT	
Left Blister	Lower Forward	Nose System	LEFT	OUT
	Lower Rear	Blister System	LEFT	
	Tail	Tail System	LEFT	
Tail	Tail	Tail System		

Primary and Secondary Controls

TRANSFER SWITCHES ON BLISTER SYSTEM SWITCH BOX

——— PRIMARY CONTROL
- - - - SECONDARY CONTROL

NOSE GUNNERS RELEASE SWITCHES ON NOSE SYSTEM SWITCH BOX

the way around. His nose dipped and he went into a dive, straight down. While this was happening, one fighter from the second group attempted a tail attack, but Cliff Bell shot him down.

"Another one came in at 12 o'clock high. As he rolled over and started his attack, I fired at him with both uppers—his plane just seemed to stop. A second later his nose dropped and he went down.

"Shortly after, three more came in at one o'clock level and here's where Eigenmann's ability came to the fore. His evasive maneuvers either threw off the attacking fighters or brought the upper turret's fire power into full play. Donahue fired all three turrets and hit every one of them hard. Smoke was streaming from all of them. Another fighter came at us from ten o'clock high, and I shot him down. He passed so close he snapped off our radio antenna. If my memory is correct this was the first of 16 attacks with the remaining being far less aggressive.

"All in all, we were attacked by 30 or 40 fighters in a three- or four-hour running gun battle. We were credited with nine shot down and two damaged. We all believed, however, that we shot down eleven with four or five more damaged."

[The photographs that were made during this mission showed that the attack had been a success.]

Put on the spot

Karnig Thomasian was a left waist gunner/electrical specialist, 40th Bomb Group, 45th Bomb Squadron, who was shot down over Burma in 1944. Thomasian's training could not prepare him for the cultural shock, heartache, and pain he would experience as a young man flying to India and as a prisoner of war; yet he remained resolute, never giving up information in the face of repeated beatings and the threat of death:

"We were based in Chakulia, India and [were] the first group of B-29s to be put into combat. We were there primarily to test the B-29s, [and] send a message to Japan. These missions were not tremendously successful in the destructive manner, but they were very successful in the psychological aspect.

"It took us almost two months to go overseas for various reasons. First we went down to Florida, then to Puerto Rico, and then [to] Belem, Brazil. From Belem we flew to Accra on the African coast. From Accra we went to Khartoum, Sudan; at this point we had to wait because of the monsoons in India. So all we did was sit around—watch movies, play cards. We had little bearers; they'd take care of our room, clean up things. We were playing cards once when we saw this one little kid and we said, 'come here play with us, play with our money.' Shortly after his father came in and grabbed the kid by the ear. This is part of what we should have been indoctrinated about, the cultures we were going to face. He came back and told us, 'No gamble.' This is against their religion. This is not a small thing. I felt it then and I feel it now. I felt very bad. This was a sweet kid. So two days later we're going to go off when he comes up like Tom Sawyer with a little bag on the end of a stick and he wanted to come with us. I'm telling you, it broke my heart. I said, 'Look, we're going to war. We can't take you.' I don't know how to explain it, it was very touching. I wonder what happened to him.

"I flew three missions before I was shot down. On December 14, 1944, we got orders to bomb a bridge in Bangkok. Up until that moment I thought we were invincible and I couldn't believe that my plane

Above: *Gunner Paul Griber of the 29th Bomb Group sits shirtless, demonstrating the relative comfort of the B-29.*

Left: *This game was developed to help improve everyone's aircraft recognition abilities.*

was damaged and going down. I had to get out, so I jumped. As I landed, the Burmese surrounded me with pitchforks and knifes. The Japanese soon followed and I finally saw my enemy face to face.

"Shortly after, they got us into interrogation; during the interrogations I quickly discovered the cultural differences between us and the Japanese. It was totally different. They made it very clear, if there's a Japanese soldier coming by your cell you had to stand at attention, otherwise you'd be beaten.

"[During the interrogation] they asked me why I was fighting. I answered quickly that my country was attacked and I volunteered to fight and do my part, and I told them that we were fighting for the rights and freedoms of people and that his people were trying to destroy those rights and freedoms. The guards and interrogator snickered and got pretty mad at hearing all this. They reminded me that I would be shot, but they realized that I had made my decision."

Gunners had to react quickly and often improvise to repair damage and look after injured crewmates. Robert L. "Bob" Hall, a CFC top gunner with the 40th Bomb Group, 44th Bomb Squadron, recounts his experiences in February 1945:

"At the briefing on February 25, 1945, we learned that our target would be Singapore. I had been on three previous missions to Singapore and regarded it as an especially tough target; the Japanese had accurate flak and good naval fighter pilots.

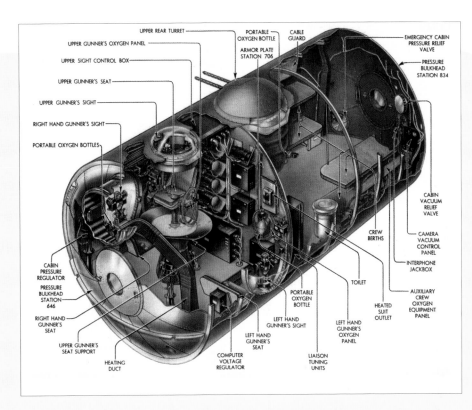

Above: *This cutaway of the CFC gunner's compartment and radar operator's area shows the positions occupied by the top, right, and left gunners, and the radar operator.*

Left: *The B-29's remote turret system allowed for more streamlined turrets compared with the B-17 and B-24.*

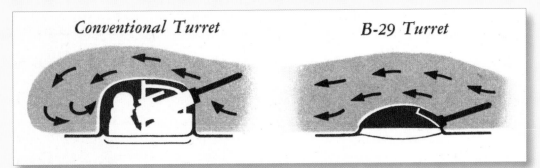

"The mission involved a daylight bomb run at an altitude above 20,000ft [6,096m]. We saw no fighters before bombs away, but antiaircraft fire started bursting around us. I was sitting in my 'swivel chair' [known as the barber's chair] in the upper blister, scanning the sky for fighters. As the bombs fell away and as we turned, there was a sickening 'plunk' of flak striking us and a strange sensation as the cabin suddenly depressurized. At the time I was facing to the left of the plane. I spun around to see where we were hit. I saw a gaping hole, perhaps 5 or 6ft [1.5 or 1.8m] in diameter along the trailing edge of the right wing behind the number three engine nacelle. My first impulse was to push the intercom button to report the damage, but [the] intercom was dead; for me, that was the most frightening part.

"At this point, Everett Nygard, the right gunner, reached up from his position in the right blister and tapped my leg; he was trying to tell me something. After the decompression you couldn't hear a thing; we were all using oxygen and I couldn't understand him. I kept scanning for enemy fighters. I had the panicky feeling that they were bailing out up front.

"Sometime later, with all the engines running and the condition of the plane stable, someone (probably Leonard Morris, the flight engineer) decided that we should repair the holes in the fuselage and repressurize the cabin. Fortunately there was a large supply of chewing gum in the flight lunches; we used it, together with torn pieces of cabin insulation. We discovered dozens of holes in the gunnery compartment and in the tunnel. Restoring cabin pressure would minimize our need to use pure oxygen [to breathe].

"In preparation for landing, A/C [aircraft commander] Brown consulted with various crewmembers, and made detailed plans. It was going to be a flaps-up landing at high speed. Normal and emergency hydraulic brake pressure read zero. We quickly rigged a parachute in the rear escape hatch. If the brakes failed, he would give the order for the tail gunner to spill the 'chute to slow us down.

"It was the smoothest landing I have ever experienced. The gear held and the brakes worked. The next day I never felt so tired. Maybe it was a hangover from the hypoxia and extreme tension. My jaw also ached for a couple of days. Must have been the chewing gum."

Running the gauntlet

A CFC gunner with the 883rd Bomb Squadron, 500th Bomb Group flying from Saipan, Al Agee was one of the few gunners to be credited with two victories during the war. The date was April 7, 1945, and the target was Yokohama:

"April 7th was the wildest fighter attack; I got credit for two kills on that trip. The first one I saw coming—as he came in, I figured out that I could open up on him quite a lot further out than my gunsight indicated. Somebody up front was screaming, 'get that fighter in front.' I opened up on him at about 1,200 yards [1,097m]. The crew said he started losing pieces as soon as I opened up on him; by the time he got to us, he bailed out. The other Japanese fighter was a little high and slightly behind us. That was more a reflex action—I had seen several fighters come in and appear to stop momentarily. This fighter looked like he was trying to make a hard turn and come around to make an attack or follow us. Our central fire control system required smooth tracking and framing of the target to be accurate. By anticipating where he would stop, my guns were with my sight. I had my guns set and waited, because I knew he was going to stop momentarily. When he did, I let him have it. At the time, I thought somebody else was shooting at him, but my two turrets were converging on him."

During this mission, the inter-phone communications between all the crewmembers were recorded on a Dictaphone, and a portion of that transcript appears below. Although it's not always clear who was talking to whom, it documents the intense focus, and frantic fear, as the crew made their bomb run through a gauntlet of Japanese fighters:

Mission No. 39 A/C No. Z Dictaphone

[Bombardier from Navigator]

Can you make out the IP?

Roger, it should be about eight o'clock.

[Pilot from Navigator]

Are we on our own? Don't want to miss the radar aiming point.

OK Navigator, we'll do the best we can.

Good radar picture.

P-51 on the side of me on the left.

Good deal.

Ships, capital ships in Yokosuka harbor.

Will make a note.

Left: Ground crew were the unsung heroes of World War II. They worked day and night and in all kinds of weather conditions, and for hours on end.

Below: B-29 incendiary attacks were incredibly destructive. This photo shows Tokyo as a burned-out shell after one of several attacks that devastated the city during the spring and summer of 1945.

Notice the white lines.

Those are phosphorous bombs—two of them—there's a third.

How about that vapor trail you were talking about?

Should be turning soon.

There's Yokohama.

There are a few ships in Yokohama harbor.

Roger.

IP is at nine o'clock.

Two planes ahead—three coming in—a Jap. Get him!

One coming in at ten o'clock, low, eight o'clock, nine o'clock level.

Eleven o'clock low.

Can you make out the target area?

Will have to turn in.

Fighter coming in low at ten o'clock.

We're streaming oil. Am feathering No.1.
Twin engine outside right.
Are you taking over?
One coming in at nine o'clock.
Ten o'clock high.
Four o'clock low.
What the hell are we doing here?

Right: A map showing the very large number of POW camps located on the Japanese mainland. At the end of the war, there were no fewer than 154 known POW camps spread across Japan, China, and Korea.

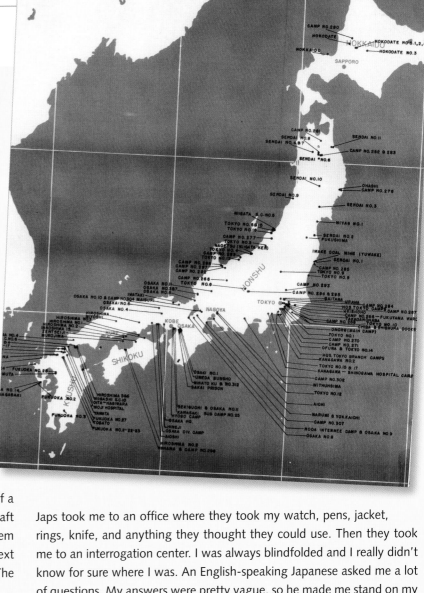

For the two nights of May 24 and 26, 1945, Tokyo was attacked by 500 B-29s. Between 3,500 and 4,000 tons of incendiaries were dropped—but at a high cost, with 43 B-29s lost and 169 damaged. One of those damaged aircraft was crewed by Dale Johnson, a right gunner with the 44th Squadron:

"Everything was going well until we made our turn toward the target. Our altitude was pretty low. The searchlights started to pick us up and it was so bright I could have read a newspaper in the gunners' compartment. Before we dropped our bombs we were hit; I thought it was antiaircraft fire. There was no communication from any of the crew after we were damaged. There was a big hole near my position, and I felt as if the aircraft was falling, so I rolled out through the hole, waited a few seconds, and pulled the ripcord on my 'chute. That was the last I saw of my crew. I landed on the edge of a bay or lake [and] needless to say, I was scared to death. An antiaircraft Gun Camp was about a half-mile from where I landed. I watched them shoot down two planes. I hid out for the rest of the night. The next morning, I walked to the Gun Camp MP booth and gave myself up. The Japs took me to an office where they took my watch, pens, jacket, rings, knife, and anything they thought they could use. Then they took me to an interrogation center. I was always blindfolded and I really didn't know for sure where I was. An English-speaking Japanese asked me a lot of questions. My answers were pretty vague, so he made me stand on my head with my feet on the wall, and then he beat me on my back and rear. After I collapsed on the floor, they finally quit asking questions . . . Most of the other men in my cell were from previous island invasions. We were not allowed to talk. With so many of us crowded into one room and a shortage of food, it was hard for many of the men to get along. Some would get greedy and demand more than their fair share. After the US dropped the A-Bomb, a truce was declared and we were moved to a regular POW camp [where] conditions were much better. We even got to wash and take baths—the first time since I bailed out. After a few days, American planes began dropping clothes and food—what a beautiful sight!"

Left: The B-29 was pressurized, and so the gunners had to be housed in the aircraft, making remote control an absolute necessity.

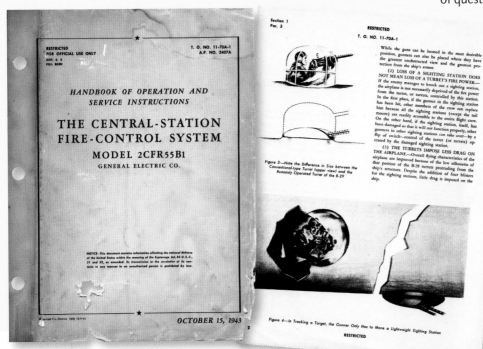

The B-29 Hunters

"Every day our fighters went up to slash at the B-29s, and every day we achieved spectacularly little success."—Saburo Sakai, legendary Japanese fighter pilot.

The Japanese could do very little to stop the B-29; by the time the Americans had begun their aerial bombardment of Japan in 1944, both the Japanese Army Air Force (JAAF) and the Japanese Navy Air Force (JNAF) were spent forces. The aerial battles in the southwest Pacific from 1942 until 1944 and the invasion of the Philippines in 1944 had virtually destroyed both air forces as a fighting force. Even more surprising was the fact that no more that 26 per cent of the total Japanese fighter force was ever assigned to the defense of the homeland. At the beginning of September 1944, between 30 and 40 per cent of the Japanese army's fighters were deployed in the Philippines, with the rest in the China and Burma theater of operations.

Right: *Saburo Sakai—Japan's most famous Zero ace (more than 60 aircraft destroyed or damaged)—later befriended the Americans he once doggedly fought.*

Below: *Fortunately for B-29 crews, the potent Kawanishi N1K2-J Model 21 Shiden-Kai were few in number and their engines were unreliable and prone to failure.*

Below: *Saburo Sakai's signature and motto: "Never give up." Saburo was blinded in combat, but survived until his 84th year.*

Right: *Two captured Mitsubishi J2M3 Raidens, code-named "Jack," in RAF colors.*

Below: *Mitsubishi A6M5c Type 52 Zeros warm up for a mission. Poor high-altitude performance and relatively weak armament made this plane an ineffective bomber interceptor.*

Even if the Japanese had poured what remaining fighters they had into the defense of Japan, the outcome would have been the same. Pilot training by this point was nonexistent, due in large part to the chronic lack of fuel, and the new pilots who did join the fight had fewer than 200 hours of flight time. It would be up to the surviving veterans to carry the battle, but they were few in number. There was also another glaring problem: the inadequate performance

of Japanese aircraft at high altitude. Almost all the single-engine fighters employed by the Japanese (Mitsubishi A6M7 Zero, Nakajima Ki 44 Tojo, Kawasaki Ki 61, Mitsubishi J2M3 Raiden, Nakajima Ki 84 Frank, and Nakajima Ki 43 Oscar) did not have the high-altitude efficacy needed to cope with the high-flying B-29s. It took all a pilot's skill just to keep his fighter under control at those heights. And, while the Japanese did have radar to warn them of attacks, they could only detect a B-29 raid at a maximum range of less than 190 miles (306km). This left very little time for them to scramble their fighters and get to height; as a result, most intercepts took place after the B-29s had hit their targets.

In every respect, Japanese pilots were fighting a desperate battle. Taking a page from their Kamikaze brethren, the idea of ramming attacks—*"Taiatari"* (body crashing)—was put forth as a means of destroying the B-29. Special attack units were hastily formed, most equipped with the Ki 61 Tony. To gain better altitude performance, selected fighters were stripped of all armor and armament, but even when a Japanese fighter did make it to the required height and found itself in a good position for a ramming attack, the task demanded considerable skill, something most of the inexperienced pilots did not have.

However, for the crews of the B-29s the Japanese ramming tactics were terrifying; the notion that a pilot would deliberately crash his aircraft into another was incomprehensible. Ivan Potts, a pilot with the 40th Bomb Group's 25th Squadron, recalls: "We were flying number one in our formation. Number three plane, which was the plane on the right, was deliberately rammed in the back by one of the Kamikaze Jap fighters. This was a horrible experience for our crew to see, especially the gunners, right off our wing. I don't think our gunners completely recovered from that for the balance of our missions."

Culture shock

Staff Sergeant Clyde G. Durham was a left gunner for the 28th Bomb Squadron (M), 19th Bomb Group, based at Kadena, Okinawa, during the Korean War. For many gunners, the Korean War offered few opportunities to actually fire their weapons and, like the World War II experience for many B-29 crewmen, it was a case of long periods of boredom punctuated by moments of sheer terror:

"We flew a total of 26 combat missions over North Korea. Our first combat mission was on a Friday the 13th in June 1952 and our last was on Thanksgiving night on November 26, 1952.

"Many of our missions were memorable in some ways, but the one I will detail here stood out the most. Our primary airplane was a B-29 named *Top of the Mark* after the famous restaurant/cocktail lounge on the top floor of the Mark Hopkins Hotel in San Francisco. When we flew in her we felt rather charmed because she was never hit by flak or fired upon during fighter attacks.

"Then came combat mission number 18! Our target for the night of October 30th was the Namsan-Ni Chemical Plant. They told us to expect rather strong resistance, mostly antiaircraft fire. We were also scheduled to bomb from 26,000ft [7,925m], the highest combat mission of my tour.

"Everything went as briefed on the first part of the bomb run and then all hell broke out. We were suddenly bracketed by multiple searchlights. Shrapnel from flak shells was rattling off the skin of our B-29. They had us locked in and we felt naked. After what seemed like hours, but was actually just minutes, we took a huge hit in our left wing. There were no flames but a large amount of smoke.

"After a few seconds the aircraft commander was able to right the B-29 and ordered the bombardier and us gunners into the waist to hit the salvo switches. But nothing happened! Finally one of the salvo switches worked and all 40 500-pounders fell at once.

"A quick crew check found everyone okay but our '29 was marginal. Getting out of the flak gave us a few minutes to collect ourselves and plan our next move. The aircraft commander told the navigator to plot a course for Itasuki AFB on the southernmost Japanese main island.

"It was still dark when we landed, but looking at the damage sent a sharp chill down our spines. There was a 2 by 3.5ft [61 by 107cm] hole in the wing; the shell had exploded inside the fuel cell.

"It was even scarier looking at it in the daylight. We did not know it at that time, but the flak fragments found in our aircraft had come from

Above: A CFC gunner sits in the barber's chair. From this position he had a clear 360-degree view and could take control of all four fuselage-mounted turrets if needed.

Below: Before future B-29 pilots earned their wings they had to endure flying school, beginning with Primary Training aircraft such as the Stearman PT-17 Kaydet. This image shows notes taken by one such cadet.

a German 88mm antiaircraft gun! We knew the Russians were manning most of the antiaircraft artillery batteries, but we never realized they were using captured German weapons from World War II!"

Each and every crewmember was affected by turbulence and bad weather. There was no escape. If not strapped in, any individual would be thrown around like a rag doll. On August 19, 1945, left gunner Calvin Brown and his crew were flying a return trip from India to China when they ran into violent weather. Brown soon found himself defying gravity, if only for a few seconds:

"When we left India to fly the Hump, we forgot to take along our portable toilet. It

Right: A B-29 from the 98th Bomb Group, 344th Bomb Squadron, unleashes high explosives on a target in North Korea. The 98th was based at Yokota near Tokyo.

was no big deal until the return trip when our right gunner, Bill Rogers, had to answer nature's call. Bill borrowed Theodore Urban's [left gunner] cigarette lighter, melted the wax on the end of a 'C' ration box and removed the contents. He answered nature's call and very carefully resealed that box and laid it aside for the rest of the trip.

"I was riding the barber's chair and watching the top of the airplane and maybe dozing off now and then. I could see a huge cloud ahead of us which didn't look any different from the many we had flown through before. As we flew in, lightning started jumping all over the airplane, from the tail to wingtips, including the nose and every other part of the ship. That woke me up. Suddenly, I was pushed down into the barber's chair so hard I couldn't move. The next thing I knew I was out of my chair. I tried to get my 'chute on but I was floating in mid-air

along with everything else in the gunner's compartment. Then I hit the floor and couldn't move. This was repeated a number of times. Floating, hitting the top of the airplane and my gun sight, and then back to the floor again. I now know what it feels like to be weightless.

"The other two gunners were strapped in so they stayed in place. After that, things seemed to settle down. I looked out a side blister and saw we were pretty close to the ground and [that] it was raining.

"Someone from up front told us our compasses were all out of whack. The turbulence had caused us to go up, then down, up again and finally over and upside down. This was followed by a nosedive straight down. If I remember right, Bill Johnson, our copilot, said we went into that cloud at 11,000ft [3,353m] and came out at 3,000ft [914m]. This was thanks to the powered trim tabs because both he and Captain Turner couldn't budge the yoke during the dive.

"It seems to me, because the compasses were all out of whack, we got back to Chakulia by radio contact. When we landed we were

Above: Two views of the upper rear turret and sighting blister. Because the gunner was not subjected to noise and vibration when firing the guns, his sighting accuracy was greatly improved. From the upper blister position the CFC officer had a 360-degree view, giving him the ability to assign turrets to the other gunners when needed.

met by the operations officer; when Captain Turner told him what had happened, he said, 'You guys need a drink.' He brought out a jug of whiskey—after one drink apiece that jug was gone. Later, we looked the plane over from stem to stern and we never did find that 'C' ration box."

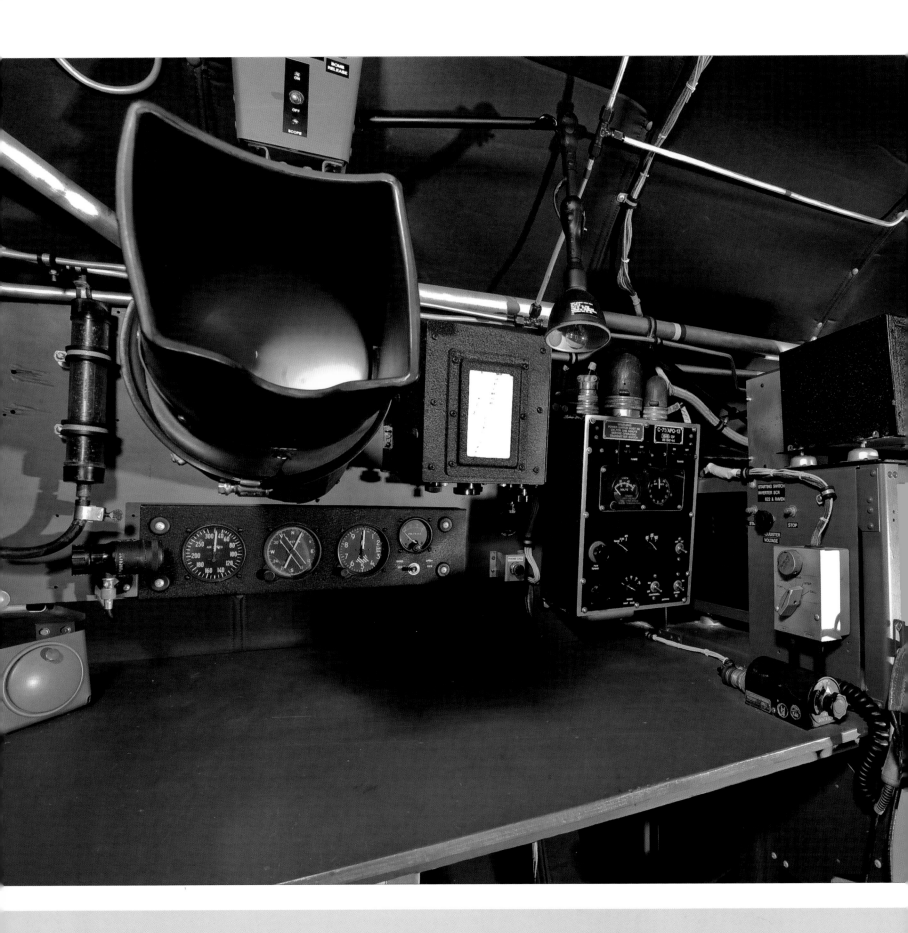

The Radar Operator

"This was our first strike, our inauguration into the clan of combat flyers we had looked upon as out of our sphere of experience. We 'rhubarbs' could not join in the tales and yarns of the missions to Japan. We were looked down upon and we were told what it would be like, what the 'score' was, but now we were off on our own to bomb the [Japanese] mainland. At last we, too, would have a tale to tell, we would 'belong'."

—1/Lt. William C. Atkinson, Radar Navigator, 73rd BW (VH), 498th BG (VH), 874th BS (VH), Isley Field, Saipan

The first operational radar carried by the B-29 was the APQ-13 Mickey, a development of the APS-15 Mickey BTO (Bomb Through Overcast) radar carried by Pathfinder B-17s and B-24s over Europe. (The APS-15, also known as H2X, was a development of the British H2S.) These early bombing radar sets were far less sophisticated than the systems used today: only features such as large, flat, factory roofs, waterways, or rail lines were distinguishable. If the target happened to be at a fork in a river, the radar operator could be sure of an aiming point and talk the bombardier to the target. But in other cases, there was less certainty; the radar operator combined a fix on an identifiable terrain feature with photographic or cartographic intelligence sources to determine where the target should be on the scope.

Seated in the aft fuselage, the radar operator was physically separated from the bombardier and navigator; any cooperation between the three men was accomplished over the inter-phone. (In USAAF inter-phone procedure, the radar operator was addressed as "Mickey" rather than "Radar," to avoid confusion with "Radio," the radio

operator.) The radar operator was expected to calculate the aircraft's approach to the drop point, then communicate the data to the bombardier. Since visual bombing was far more accurate, the bombardier remained at his bomb sight, making course corrections and hoping that he could take over visually. If the target remained obscured, the radar operator would continue to relay the distance to the target in five-degree increments.

Mickey was also helpful for search-and-rescue missions over the Pacific; at the beginning of 1945, the US military began equipping life rafts with small radar reflectors, giving a rubber raft the same radar visibility as a small ship and thereby increasing the chances of its discovery.

In the spring of 1945, the first B-29s equipped with Eagle radar (APQ-7 or APQ-10) arrived in the Marianas. The power and clarity of the Eagle gave the radar operator (still called Mickey) a greatly improved view of the earth below. The 20th Air Force continued to favor visual bombing, but radar bombing with the Eagle produced dramatic improvements over the older APQ-13.

The radar operator's job was as much about maintenance as bomb aiming. Most B-29 radar operators had prior training as bombardiers or navigators, with a subsequent ten-week course (usually held at Boca Raton

Left: The original B-29 design had a four-bunk rest area at the rear of the aft pressurized compartment; when radar was added, two bunks on the port side were replaced by the radar operator's station.

Army Air Field, Florida) introducing the radar equipment and its use, though practical flight training was limited by the shortage of radar-equipped aircraft. But the limitations of time and equipment meant that most training would come in the field.

By 1944, combat experience had proven the need for radar jamming; the defensive radar net over Japan never equaled that built by Germany, but it was enough to require a response. The new position of RCM Observer was created, seated on the crew's chemical toilet. With the addition of shelving, radio equipment, and a pair of headphones, several B-29s were prepared for electronic warfare. The observer scanned the standard frequencies for Japanese radar signals, then jammed them with his own signals. Eventually, special B-29 jammers code-named "Angels" (often called "porcupines" by the crews, in reference to their extra antenna) would be sent to each target expressly to counter Japanese radar.

The Korean War saw B-29 radar bombing reach both its apex and its nadir within the space of a few short months. Of the first three Superfortress groups to enter combat in 1950, one (the 22nd BG) had been assigned to the Far

East Air Forces (FEAF) and had no radar. The other two groups (the 22nd and the 92nd BGs) had been assigned to the Strategic Air Command (SAC) and deployed with upgraded APQ-13 Mickey sets. On July 30, 1950, the 22nd and 92nd struck the Chosen Nitrogen Explosives Factory at Hungnam, North Korea. The accurate, radar-guided initial attack created fires hot enough to burn away some of the cloud cover, allowing trailing squadrons to bomb visually. SAC's peacetime radar bombing training had paid off: 30 per cent of the factory was destroyed, with another 40 per cent heavily damaged. Subsequent operations produced similar results, and North Korea's few strategic industrial targets were soon destroyed.

Page right, clockwise from top left: Part of the control system for the APQ-13 search radar; a rack to the right of the radar operator's desk held most of his electronics (the galvanized bucket just visible here on the right was part of the crew's chemical toilet); the APQ-13's radar dish—seen here on separate display—was normally mounted the other way up and set in a ventral radome between the two bomb bays.

Eagle-eyed Radar

While wartime radars were revolutionary, their usefulness for identifying individual targets was limited. This image, taken from an Eagle radar scope, was considered a major improvement over earlier Mickey images, but it still did not have the resolution to pick out individual buildings and structures. The coastal targets were the naval facilities at Tokuyama and the petroleum refineries at Kudamatsu. Twentieth Air Force B-29s hit each target twice between May and July 1945.

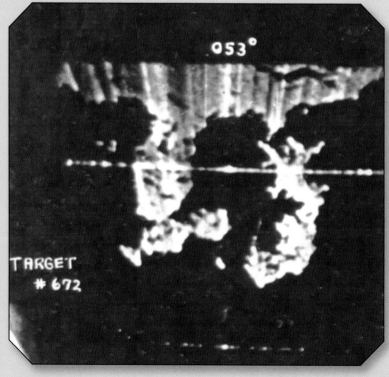

Countermeasures

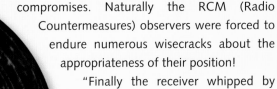

On the first B-29 raid to Japan (June 15, 1944), radar operator Tom Friedman of the 468th Bomb Group was flying in the newly created position of "radar countermeasures observer." With his gear tucked into the windowless and crowded radar compartment, Friedman found little comfort in his new position:

"I was preparing to monitor one frequency range to see if the Japanese were using any German-designed equipment.

"A small electric motor swept the receiver back and forth across the band while I listened with earphones for the first sign of enemy activity and tried to assume a comfortable position on my 'seat'—the chemical toilet. Radar countermeasures equipment had been installed at the last minute, after the B-29 had been completely designed, so it had been necessary to make certain compromises. Naturally the RCM (Radio Countermeasures) observers were forced to endure numerous wisecracks about the appropriateness of their position!

"Finally the receiver whipped by a whining signal and I flipped off the motor and tuned the station manually; a half-minute's work with the analyzer revealed that the situation was one of the early warning types. We had been detected well back of the China coast and several hours from the target. As we neared the coast other signals came and increased in strength . . . a glance in the radarscope showed the mainland of China receding . . . at the initial [point] the radar activity of the Japanese reached a high level and signals were starting to crescendo until my earphones were whining as if a thousand devils were screaming in unison at us. It was an eerie feeling to know that far below our every move was being carefully watched on scopes and plotting boards."

The first strike by B-29s targeted the steel works at Yawata. The mission was conducted at night, but only 15 B-29s bombed visually while the rest used radar (only one bomb hit the target). Radar operator Ferris A. Albers flew in that historic mission (his first) and describes the problems associated with night bombing using radar:

"The final turn had been made on autopilot. When we came out on course, Hunter [the pilot] told Mac [the bombardier] it was all his; Mac took over but it was so dark he couldn't see a thing. We were hoping the B-29s ahead of us had started some fires, but there was nothing. Mac called me and said it was going to have to be a radar show, and asked if I had spotted the target. At that time, I had located the general area of the steel mill some 40 or 50 miles [64 or 80km] away.

"As we neared the island of Kyushu, the southern and westernmost island of Japan, bursts of bright orange flak appeared. I was back in the 'dark room' and didn't see a thing. From the inter-phone I got a clear picture of what was going [on] outside the aircraft. For Mac, our bombardier, sitting out in the unprotected glass nose, the scene must have been really impressive. In order to throw the Japanese gunners off he

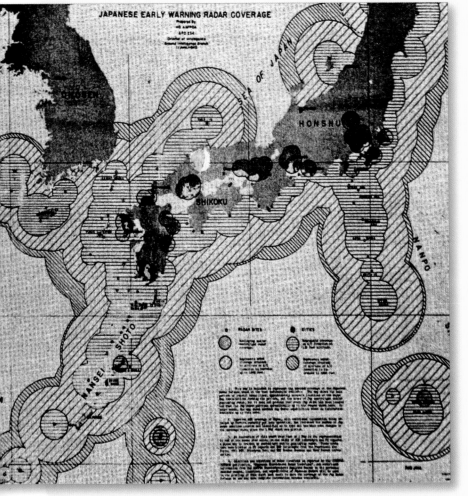

Above: A typical radar image of the Japanese coastline.

Left: Japanese land-based radars could detect inbound B-29 formations but could not determine their altitude or composition. This intelligence drawing illustrates the ranges of Japanese radar coverage. Kyushu is the darker central area.

began taking evasive action; he put the ship into a series of twisting turns. Of course, during each turn my radar scope was useless. When he called back to ask where the target was, I told him he'd have to level out before I could see it; he did level out, but for just a moment. I was confused by these unexpected gyrations and I should have been more forceful in my commands. Mac and I had not spent a lot of time working together; we didn't understand each other's jobs! He had no idea his evasive tactics were fouling up my radar, and now because of our great speed we had little time left for an accurate bomb run.

"Our training and abilities were being pushed to the limit, but I wasn't afraid. There was only the swift rush of time in this strange and unnatural situation. I knew how long the run to the target should have taken and when we finally did level out it was almost gone; we were off course by a wide margin. Something resembling the target area passed beneath us; I hit my bomb release switch and I cried 'Bombs away.' Hunter immediately took over manual control of the ship—we turned sharply to the left to get out of the flak area."

Above: *The early electronics devices developed by the Allies were only as good as the men who used and maintained them. Operations in China highlighted the devices' lack of reliability. Here, technicians service LORAN (long range navigation) sets.*

Left: *The silver eagle clutching arrows is the insignia worn by a colonel.*

Apart from the bombardier and the gunners, the crew could usually only look on as the Japanese made their attacks. But when radar operator Alex Rearwick got his chance, the results were not what he expected:

"The radar sets didn't work very well. They were having problems with them all the time. At first they didn't work, but eventually they got some mechanics to work on the problem. After about 12 missions they finally got the radar sets fixed, and they worked fine.

"When you start flying missions you're scared to death, but then you get used to it. I did what they called a 'super-dumbo' mission. If one of our planes got shot down over the target and ditched, we'd circle round then call for a submarine to pick them up. The submarine was a couple of hours away, so it took a while to get there. That's when this Japanese floatplane came snooping around. We ended up chasing it, trying to shoot him down. It should have been the other way around. Our pilot was the very impressive type. All he wanted to do was shoot down more Japanese planes and cause more damage than anyone else in the squadron.

"My most memorable trip was the raid on Kawasaki. They sent us in at low level to drop some sea mines and that's when we almost got shot down. We came in around 6,000 to 7,00 [1,829 to 2,134m] and almost immediately the searchlights caught us; it seemed as if every gun in the city turned on us. Our navigator had made a mistake and sent us over a Japanese military installation when they just unloaded on us. I looked out the blister at one point to see tracers hitting the plane. It sounded like somebody was throwing bricks at us. Our pilot did some maneuvering to throw the gunners off.

"The thing I hated about being the radar operator was I never got to do any shooting; you just sit there . . . The only time I ever got to man the guns was when the tail gunner got wounded during the Kawasaki raid. They sent one of the side gunners up to the tail position; I was told to go up and take over one of the side blisters. No sooner did I sit down and belt in when this big Japanese twin-engine night fighter came in. It filled my whole gunsight. I pressed the triggers, but there was no ammo left! Fortunately he never shot at us. It was a pretty scary mission and we were damn lucky to get back. When the chief mechanic came out and looked at the plane he said, 'You know these things are expensive, you need to take better care of it.' Yah, we got a big kick out of that one."

Turbulent heights

October 25, 1944. Target: Omura Aircraft Plant. For radar operator Gilbert Rodencal of the 45th Bomb Squadron, this mission represented a change in tactics. Large formations would now be used, but there was confusion at the assembly points. High tail winds and different radio frequencies caused some aircraft to miss their rendezvous points, making it difficult to join the formations, and Japanese fighters took advantage of the situation. After "bombs away," Gilbert's aircraft came under heavy fighter attack and was hit. Gilbert's aircraft commander, Jack Ledford, was wounded, causing paralysis in his legs. The flight engineer suffered a bad head wound and was unconscious. As "first aid" man, Gilbert had to attend to the wounded before bailing out of his stricken aircraft:

"The fact that Ledford had his backpack 'chute on had helped to prevent more damage, but it was serious enough. The whole bottom corner of his 'chute was blown to shreds. Miller [the flight engineer] was unconscious. McCullough and Oblender laid him on top of the wheel well hatch. The only visible wounds were three very deep scalp wounds over the right ear where shrapnel had penetrated his skull.

Above: A B-29 suffers a direct hit by Japanese antiaircraft guns and goes down in flames. Flak (antiaircraft fire) was not primarily designed to bring down individual aircraft; its purpose rather was to cause enemy bombers to fly higher, and so to disrupt their aim.

Left: Lt. Harold T. Oblender. Inset: From left to right: S/Sgt. Charles D. Bacon, right gunner S/Sgt. D.V. McCullough, radio operator Sgt. Gilbert H. Rodencal, radar operator, 2nd Lt. Harold T. Oblender.

"When the time came to jump, Halpern was the first to go. Gardner, Elwell, Paslay, Clark, and I followed. My first attempt wasn't very good; I stuck my head out, lost my glasses, and got slammed against the door frame. The second time, I made it. I was now alone, flat on my back at 10,000ft [3,048m]. My 'chute opened with a jolt and then it was very quiet—just the swish of air from the 'chute.

"I came down near the top of some mountains. Some Chinese appeared and motioned me to follow [them]; I was worried because I did not know if they were friend or foe. After a while we came to a house which seemed to have several generations living in it. I tried to use my pointy-talky, but none of them could read. After a while, a boy came in who could read, and I got the message across that I wanted to get to the village I saw just after I landed. He and an adult took me down the mountain to the village where the rest of the crew had already arrived.

"Later that evening, a runner went to the next village and came back with some police/soldiers to guide us out. The next day, we arrived at the village, where we met a Mr. B. T. Chang who spoke English. After one day on a riverboat and several days on foot, we ended up at grass landing strip; we stayed there with some missionaries who fed and took care of us. There was also a small unit of GIs (maybe four or five) who took care of the strip. We ended up staying for several long days. Every time a C-47 came in to rescue us, the Japs sent fighters to strafe the place. One day I got so damn mad I opened fire with my .45!"

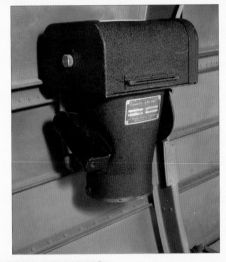

another aircraft from our squadron was hit and went down. On the 18th we were hit by enemy fighters and flak over the target. We limped back to Saipan, but crash-landed with only one engine.

"In December we were bombed three times by the Japanese for no real damage. On the 22nd, I flew with another crew. Flak damage over the target forced us to land at Tinian. In January 1945, I was transferred to the Third Photo Recon Squadron on Guam. Their job was to take post-strike photos. We carried no armor or guns and had no escorts—my job was to sit in the open bomb bay and take pictures; it was no picnic and sometimes I could see the flak coming up at us.

"On my seventh and last mission we took a hit, forcing us to ditch about 100 miles [161km] from Guam. No one suffered any injuries and a destroyer came by to pick us up. I flew 40 combat missions, including the group's first and last over Japan."

Above: B-29s had two fixed aerial cameras, which produced photos for assessment. If these failed, the Garaflex K-20 handheld camera (shown here) would be used.

Below: Chinese laborers employed in the construction of B-29 bases. A massive amount of human labor was used in the construction of bases in India and China.

UNIT No. 115A

COMPRESSED

TRIANGULAR BANDAGE

(1 ONLY)

STERILIZED

ckaged by **MEDICAL SUPPLY COMPANY** Chicago, Illinois

Above: Accidents could, and did, occur; on-board first aid kits carried a supply of bandages for different injuries.

Many B-29 crewmen were trained to perform three jobs: gunner, radio operator, and radar operator. It made good combat sense. As a radar operator, radioman, and gunner, Sergeant Murray Juvelier flew with the 498th Bomb Group from Saipan. In late 1944, he also managed to add one more job to his B-29 resume, that of aerial photographer:

"December 1944 was a month I will never forget. We bombed Nagoya three times. It was also the time when I experienced the full horror of war. On December 13th I flew as a gunner. Our ship was damaged after a runaway prop burned off and crashed into the side of the aircraft. We were lucky;

Sea dog and eagle

On February 25, 1945—while on a photo mission to Singapore—radar operator John Topolski and his crew of the 40th Bomb Group were attacked by Japanese fighters and were forced to bail out. Fortunately, John and most of his crew were rescued by a British submarine. In this extremely rare case, the HMS *Seadog* brought to safety nine out of twelve crewmembers:

"Someone spotted a single Jap plane off in the distance; he came in head on. When he was in range we opened up, but nothing happened;

Above: The view that a Japanese pilot would have had during a head-on attack. The B-29 bombardier and the Japanese pilot would have just 3.5 seconds to react.

Right: PBY Catalinas played a large part in the successful rescues of ditched B-29 crewmen. This February 1943 Popular Mechanics *feature tells their story.*

we were dumbfounded. The enemy fighter managed to hit our nose section and came in for a second attack. I could hear everything that was said with my headphones. There was a fire in the forward compartment when the number two engine started losing power. We got orders to jettison everything in the plane [and] I went into the back bomb bay to try and kick the auxiliary tank out.

"When we bailed out I saw all 11 'chutes in the air in addition to my own. The instant my 'chute opened, I saw the aircraft's left wing break off and hit the water; it was incredible. I know I was in shock afterwards.

"Before hitting the water you were supposed to release the 'chute and drop into the water; when I

landed, the 'chute dropped on top of me. Somehow I freed myself and it was a great relief to see another aircraft circling. They dropped all of their ditching equipment, including a small dinghy. Calling out to each other, the rest of the crew managed to find each other—except for me.

"A Mae West does not keep you afloat; you have to keep fighting. I got bumped by sharks several times—you bob like a cork on a fishing line. You have to keep the back of your head into the waves and you have to do this constantly.

"One of the PBY search planes flew around the area. At times it seemed as if the aircraft was within 50ft [15m] of me. I waved and tried to signal to them, but they didn't see me. I can't describe the desperateness [sic] you feel being alone in the water; the worst part was seeing the B-29 making its last circle. I said to myself, 'I'll never last another night.' I was in the water for almost three days. I know that you should never give up, but I was ready. Just then this giant submarine surfaced directly in front of me; the crew threw me a line and I resolved to never let go.

"A surfaced sub in enemy waters was always in great danger; after they [had] picked up the first three crewmembers, they were anxious to leave. My rescued buddies pressed the sub commander to keep searching, and that's why they found me."

Not all those who trained for war made it to the frontlines. In 1945, the aircrew training system was producing thousands of well-trained men, many of them eager to serve. However, circumstances would prevent many from seeing any action. Technical Sergeant Bill Patterson was training to operate the new "Eagle radar" when the Japanese surrendered:

"I had mixed feelings when Japan finally surrendered—we all enlisted with the idea of 'just send me.' It was that kind of attitude; you were volunteering for your country.

"On the day I went to enlist at Patterson field, April 1944, I remember seeing a B-29 take off and fly over old route four. It was the first time I ever saw a B-29 and I recognized it immediately.

"My time in the service was almost all spent in school. Radio, radar, and ultimately high-altitude bombing radar. I had basic training and then went to Wisconsin to study basic radio. That's when they began to hint at other things, new weapons and so on. At Chanute Field in Illinois I began my radar training. Then it was off to Boca Raton, Florida, and that's where I was introduced to the Eagle radar. There were two kinds of radar at the time—one had a sweep of 360 degrees and the other, the Eagle, had a 90-degree sweep toward the front. It was very precise and reliable. You could actually count the cars of a train with the Eagle radar; I thought the technology was pretty special. Back in Illinois, they even had television-guided bombs; that was all new to me and [it] was secret at the time.

Above: *When the B-29 arrived in India and China, it was the world's most advanced bomber; but its runways were built using simple human labor.*

Left: *US airmen mostly used the B-3 and B-4 "Mae West." This is a B-3, which was different from the B-4 in that it had a leather square in the front.*
Inset: *A B-29 crewman adjusts his B-3 prior to takeoff.*

"I did most of my flying and training aboard the B-17. We would fly low-level practice radar missions by bombing Tampa Bay. The thing I remember seeing on the scope was the causeway. Sadly, I only made two trips in the B-29 and, shortly after, the war came to an end."

BTO—Bombing Through Overcast

"This outfit has been getting a lot of publicity without having really accomplished a hell of a lot in bombing results."—Curtis LeMay.

The numbers from Operational Analysis made for grim reading: it would take no fewer than 400 B-29s to destroy an industrial target via high altitude on a day with good visibility—and over Japan, such days occurred only around five times a month. Radar held some promise—but would it be enough?

Thus, the great hope of the B-29 as a daylight precision bomber had been cruelly dashed: of nine priority targets—including the Mitsubishi Aircraft Plant, Kagamigahara, the Nakajima Aircraft Plant, Tokyo, and the Kawanishi Aircraft Plant, Mimejiand—not one had been destroyed after months of bombing. And the crucial factor had been the weather—adverse frontal conditions drained fuel, broke up formations, and complicated navigation. Weather conditions over Japan were unpredictable, too, and with the newly discovered jet stream causing its own unique set of unsolvable problems, accurate forecasting was nigh-on impossible. At one point, the USAAF

Left: *2,000lb (907kg) general-purpose bombs sit ready for loading. The crewman standing by one of the bombs illustrates the massive size of these weapons.*

even tried to decipher coded Soviet weather reports (the Russians seldom shared information with their allies).

But there was an answer, in the shape of radar—radar could "see" through the clouds. The AN/APQ-13 radar fitted to the B-29 was an improved version of the British H_2S radar—the first ground-mapping system in the world to be used in combat. It was good at identifying open and built-up areas such as large cities, as well as coastlines, rivers, lakes, and other bodies of water; most of the Japanese cities were located on the coast. General LeMay's switch to low-level night incendiary attacks brought the APQ-13 radar and its operators to the fore. Precision was now replaced with the area-bombing method: find a city, dump as many incendiaries as possible, and burn it down.

Unfortunately, radar had come late to the B-29 program and, not surprisingly, many operators had received insufficient training; many, in fact, were extraneous gunners. Convinced that radar could play a vital role, LeMay established a radar school for both current and new operators. Shortly afterward, the number of cities successfully bombed went up, and so did the tonnage of bombs dropped. But there was more advanced radar waiting in the wings.

In May 1945, the last wing—the 315th—joined LeMay's command. This new unit was equipped with brand-new B-29Bs, which carried the AN/APQ-7 Eagle radar—the most advanced in the world at the time. The antenna was housed in an 18ft (5.5m) wide airfoil-shaped section under the fuselage. Optimized for precision targeting rather than navigation, as the APQ-13 was, it would give the new crews exceptional accuracy.

Left: *Four newly arrived B-29s—their tail markings have not yet been applied—sit on their hardstands at North West Field on Guam.*

makes propellers. Since it was socked in, the run was by radar. We made IP at Motosu-ko, the southernmost of a string of lakes northwest of Fuji, and rolled in over the cloud blanket to bombs away. Of course we dropped on the lead ship [the aircraft that bombed first—all the other aircraft would wait for this aircraft; once they saw the bombs they would drop theirs]. Altitude 20,000ft [6,096m]; neither flak nor fighters were observed."

In just six weeks, the 315th and its Eagle-equipped B-29s were credited with shutting down what was left of Japan's oil industry. In characteristic laconic style, LeMay indicated how impressed he was: "This performance is the most successful radar bombing of this command to date."

Left: A flight of 9th Bomb Group, 1st Bomb Squadron B-29s climb out of Tinian in the spring of 1945. The circled "X" on the tail, white flash atop the vertical stabilizer, and white engine cowl stripes distinguished all 9th Bomb Group aircraft; the group's three squadrons were identified by ranges of aircraft numbers painted on the aft fuselage.

On June 26, 1945, the 315th launched 38 bombers bound for the Utsube River Oil Refinery in central Honshu, the largest island of Japan; it was an ideal precision target and one of Japan's largest petroleum plants. Of the original 38 bombers, 30 found the target—for no losses, this small number of bombers was able to destroy and damage 30 per cent of the facility. In July, two groups attacked the Maruzen oil refinery and left it smoldering and forgotten with 95 per cent of it destroyed. William Atkinson, 874th Bomb Squadron, 498th Bomb Group, recalls a bombing run that was carried out with the aid of radar:

"The secondary target was urban Hamamatsu on the coast west of Omae-zaki; the banjo factory there now

Above: These two images of Japanese cities reveal the AN/APQ-13 radar's limited detail. Originally designed as an aid to navigation, it was pressed into service as a blind bombing device, which worked well when the target was the size of a city.

Left: Victory Mail was based on the British Airgraph, in which mail was censored, photographed, and reduced to a thumbnail size. Reels of film would be shipped to the US, developed, and delivered.

Proving ground

Nothing in their training could have prepared William C. Atkinson—a radar/navigator assigned to the 874th Squadron, 498th Bomb Group—and his crew for the harsh reality of combat. Each new crew had to prove itself; every crewmember had to steel himself against the unknown and hope that he would perform to the best of his ability. Twenty-year-old Atkinson and his crew wouldn't have to wait long. Below is a further excerpt from Atkinson's navigator's log dated April 2, 1945, which he kept while serving on Saipan:

"At Isley Field it was common on takeoff for the pilot of a fully loaded B-29 to hold the wheels to the runway until the final few hundred feet, hauling back at the last possible instant to lurch over the road along the cliff edge; then diving full throttle for the sea far below, gaining airspeed while retracting the wheels; and finally beginning the long takeoff climb as the belly of the plane virtually skimmed the water.

"Unlike the later missions, no one slept on the 7½ hour trip to the target. Things had to work out; we dared not miss a trick. John [Shaw, the navigator] did celestial all the way and there wasn't an island or a ship that I missed on the radar for a wind determination or a fix. Iwo appeared

Right: Crews kept hydrated with water from the thermal jugs located in the front and rear of the aircraft.

as a yellow ghostly friend on the scope to the right of us. John made a correction to course and we droned on between the stars and the vast chasm of the sea.

"Three hours later, Capt. James R. Norris informed us that we were within 50 to 100 miles [80 to 161km] of the Empire. For the first time since before takeoff, the tension again became evident; our stomachs tightened; I needed a drink of water. Everything was checked.

"I was to make a radar approach to the target while Max bombed visually by moonlight. The radar was the Western Electric Eagle AN/APQ-7 or APQ-13 developed for navigation and for bombing at night with cloud cover. It was electronically linked to the Norden bomb sight and the autopilot. By twisting a knob, I could direct the plane.

"We came in over Oshima, the first enemy island of any size, on course. The control point showed in radar and I strained my eyes for the coast. Gradually it made itself evident and the IP at Eno-Shima appeared. We altered course. First flak! Capt. Norris and Max could see the orange flashes ahead of us. Although we weren't in the searchlights they could see icy fingers of light probing the sky in search of the 'enemy;' we were alone. Max saw the Tama River gleaming in the moonlight and the radar confirmed the position. He said he thought he could see the target and he set the telescope sight on it. He started the rate motor and began to synchronize.

"Then it all happened. 'Lights converging on the boys ahead! Flak!' The intercom clicked and crackled. A light flashed momentarily on the wing from below and immediately snapped back. In an instant, every searchlight in the area was on us. The ship must have shone like a Christmas tree. We could hear the flak now. Thumping and rattling outside the ship. Max called up, 'I can't see; the goddam lights! I've lost the target!' Then there was a rock, a loud thump, and number four engine roared into a mass of flame. The whole wing seemed afire and the radar

Above: 500lb (227kg) general-purpose bombs lined up ready for loading. According to the Bombardier's Information File Manual, the 500lb (227kg) bomb was designed to be used against "steel railroad bridges, subways, concrete docks, light cruisers."

Left: T52 (42-63524) Passion Wagon, of the 875th BS (VH), is shown at rest between missions within its designated parking spot at Isley Field on Saipan.

Above: In April 1945, the four bomb groups of the 73rd Bomb Wing enlarged their tail markings to improve air-to-air identification. The "T-Square-45" is in the process of being repainted with a giant "T."

Left: Cigarettes and tobacco products were widely available for American servicemen throughout World War II. Chesterfield was one of the more popular brands.

compartment was alive with the angry orange light. Harris [right gunner], terrified, screamed over the intercom. We were panic-stricken. Max took a chance and said, 'Bombs away!' Bill slithered out of his position and fumbled with his 'chute, his hand on the bomb bay door, all set to jump. I was almost paralyzed with fear. We waited for the order to jump. It never came. Harris broke in to say that the fire seemed to be lessening. The bombs had not gone away—the intervalometer was stuck. In the next instant Max salvoed the bombs. Everyone was confused and scared stiff. Capt. Virgil Olds took over (he was from Operations as backup copilot for support).

"All this took less than a minute; a second later the Japanese lights went out! They must have gone after the ship behind us. We turned off the bomb run with the fire almost out. We never understood why, but Gins' [the flight engineer] quick thinking with the fuel system control probably saved us. In nine cases out of ten a tank fire is fatal.

"We learned later that we had almost lost Rocky, the tail gunner, as he had prepared to bail out when he saw the fire, and had received no communication from the crew. He had jerked his head left to see the sudden plume of flame pass the tail and then waited, patiently, like the rest of us, for the order to bail out; everything had seemed to him to go silent as the ship droned on.

"The crew settled down and headed for Iwo Jima. We had lost nearly 500 gallons [1,892 liters] of gas. The three-engine landing on the dirt and muddy runway was successful; it was discovered later that a Japanese shell had pierced the right wheel-well door resulting in one flat tire."

The Tail Gunner

"'Tail to crew,' I called out. 'A fighter just came out of the clouds at seven o'clock low.' . . . I narrowed the circle of dots down to his wing tips, and began squeezing off bursts. I hit his engine, he broke off his attack and banked down into the clouds, a long, black plume trailing behind."—Sgt. Andy Doty,

314BW (VH), 19BG (VH), 93BS (VH)—B-29A-15-BN, *City of College Park* (42-93996)

The B-29's tail gunner sat in his own compartment at the rear of the aircraft, physically cut off from the rest of his crew whenever the aircraft was flying at altitude and pressurized. At the beginning of each mission, his duties included starting the "putt-putt" auxiliary power unit as the aircraft taxied and watching for any collision danger from other aircraft. As each unit fell into formation, he could move forward to join the other gunners, but as the aircraft approached 10,000ft (3,048m) he hurried back through the unpressurized rear fuselage to his capsule beneath the rudder. There, the difference in pressure between his gunner's station and the rest of the aircraft meant he would be physically unable to open his hatch to move forward until the aircraft was depressurized. As with the Superfortress's other gunners, the tail gunner never handled his weapons in flight. His lead-computing gunsight tracked the enemy, and deflected the guns ahead of where the target was going. The guns were originally specified as two Browning model M2 .50-caliber machine guns and a single M2 20mm cannon, but the "twenty" (which fired on a different trajectory than the "fifties" and was subject to jamming) was soon eliminated. On some aircraft,

Left: A heavy, quilt-covered armor plate and armored glass protected the tail gunner from enemy fire. The gunsight would compute firing solutions, then rotate the electrically powered gun turret to fire at defending fighters.

armorers installed a third fifty, though most flew with only two. The tail guns could traverse 30 degrees above or below the horizon or to either side, but the sight could be turned 105 degrees left or right, straight down, or 60 degrees up; tracking an enemy aircraft over this large expanse of sky allowed the tail gunner more time to adjust his sight and a better chance of scoring a kill as the enemy moved into the arc of his guns.

The sight was accurate enough that the gunner could open fire at a distance of 1,000 yards (914m), a 400 yard (366m) improvement on the range for the B-17 or B-24 tail guns. To conserve ammunition and keep his weapons from overheating, the tail gunner fired in short bursts, with no more than 30 rounds fired in a minute. If the enemy closed within 300 yards (274m), the rate of fire could safely be increased to 10 rounds every 15 seconds.

If an attacking aircraft was out of the tail gunner's field of vision or if the gunner was injured, he could release the action switch on his sight and control of his guns could pass to either side gunnery station. (This was particularly useful if one of the side gunners was tracking an aft-moving fighter; the fighter risked being sprayed by the two ventral turrets and, as it slid to the stern, the tail gun, all while being tracked by a single gunsight.)

Despite their unique position in the aircraft, tail gunners were fully trained members of the gunnery team and could be reassigned to other stations. For example, 39th Bomb

Group tail gunner Karolis "Charles" Buchinski was transferred from his regular bomber to the squadron's weather reconnaissance aircraft, a B-29 with no bombs or bombardier. Now flying in the aircraft's nose, Buchinski managed the two forward turrets and was redesignated the "nose gunner." (Following the war, Buchinski changed his last name to Bronson, moved to Hollywood, and began a 50-year acting career in movies and television.)

On some aircraft, the tail turret was "enhanced" by the addition of APG-15 gun-laying radar (see box below), but the system—which was cantankerous and ineffective—was soon removed from most aircraft.

When General Curtis LeMay ordered most defensive weapons to be removed from his B-29s to save weight, he retained the tail guns and gunner. Tail gunners continued to fly on all World War II Superfortress missions. Tail gunner Technical Sergeant George Robert "Bob" Caron was carrying a hand-held camera over Hiroshima on August 6, 1945 as his aircraft, the *Enola Gay*, raced away from its target. Moments later, Caron became the only member of the crew to witness the first combat detonation of a nuclear weapon. Remarkably, through a series of serendipitous flukes, Caron's photos became the only surviving still images of the explosion and mushroom cloud.

The Korean War saw the return of the B-29 to combat, and, again, B-29 tail gunners flew every mission. On daylight missions, B-29s began to encounter the new Russian MiG-15 jets, whose speed of over 650mph (1,050km/h) made them difficult to track with the Superfortress's 1940s-era gunnery system. Although several of the MiGs were destroyed, the B-29 was unable to defend itself against this new threat, and all of the aircraft's subsequent bombing missions took place at night to take advantage of the communists' lack of a night-fighter force.

Page right, clockwise from top left: The "putt-putt" auxiliary power unit (APU) was located just forward of the tail gunner's pressurized compartment; the tail turret guns could be deflected 30 degrees to the left or right, up or down; spent rounds dropped through a slot beneath the guns and spilled into the slipstream; when the aircraft was pressurized, the tail gunner's only contact with other crewmembers was over the inter-phone. The small reserve "walk-around" oxygen bottle (yellow, beneath the inter-phone) delivered about 20 minutes' breathing air.

Tail Gun Enhancements

There were three primary production versions of the Superfortress manufactured during World War II: the B-29 (Boeing-, Bell- and Martin-built), the B-29A (Boeing-built), and the B-29B, which benefited from a new system for the tail gunner:

The Bell Aircraft Corporation of Buffalo, New York, manufactured 311 B-29B airplanes at its Atlanta, Georgia, plant between January and September 1945. These were built to appease Lieutenant General Curtis E. LeMay's desire to field lighter and faster B-29s.

To achieve this, Bell built these B-29s without the four upper and lower fuselage-mounted gun turrets. Moreover, no 20mm cannon was installed in the tail turret. Instead, for self defense, the two .50 caliber machine guns were retained in the tail turret. And to better defend itself, the B-29B was given a tail-mounted AN/APG-15B S-Band Tail Gun Radar system (the spherical object seen below the guns), which was used to lock on to attacking fighters for "can't miss" kills. This system was retrofitted to some earlier models, too.

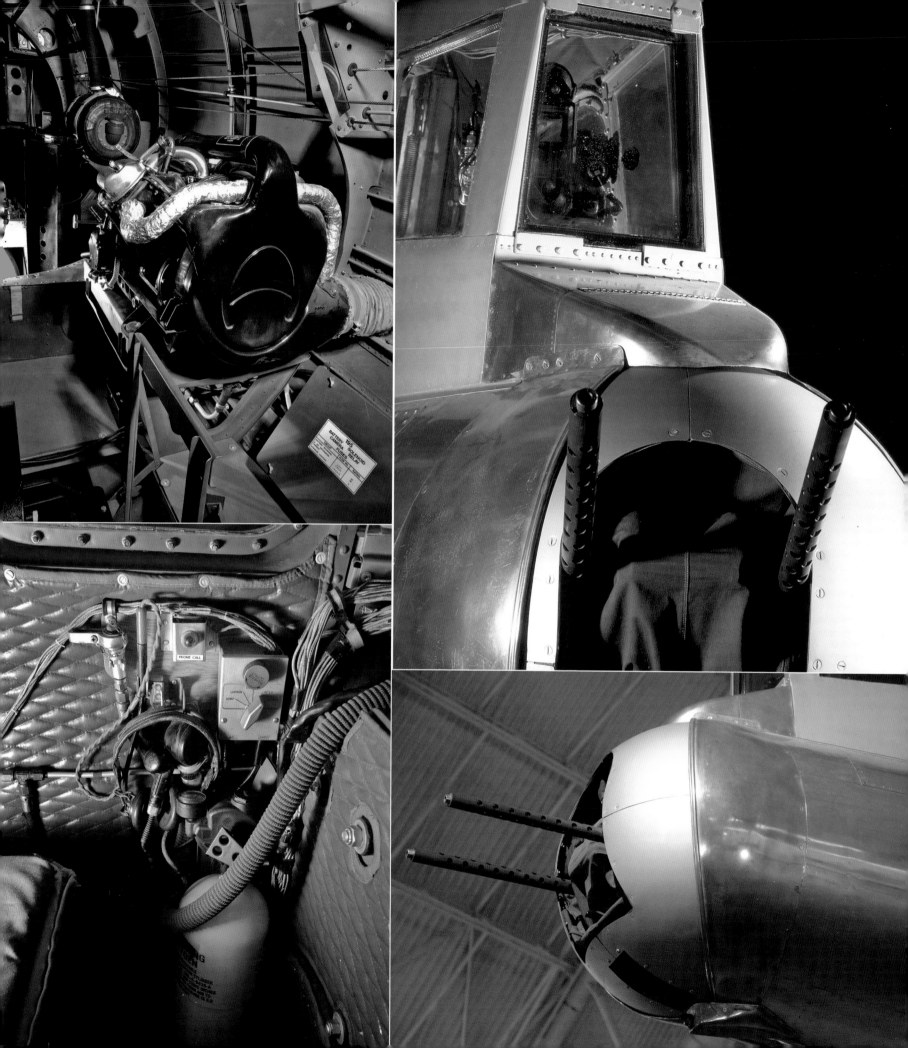

No more nightmares?

For many young men, the scars left by war would remain with them for many years. William H. Carter was an 18-year-old tail gunner with the 60th Bomb Squadron, 39th Bomb Group, on Guam in the spring and summer of 1945. For years after the war, William was plagued by vivid nightmares in which he relived the deaths of friends and crewmates. "A good friend told me I needed to talk all this out and I have done so almost to the point of overdoing it. [But] thanks to him and my wife, I am now able to talk about the war, and I am able to sleep peacefully."

"During daylight raids, all aircraft had to stay in formation. Our formations consisted of four planes in a diamond formation, and each set of four planes formed a larger a diamond. This type of formation gave all the planes greater protection. One particular and very skillful daredevil Japanese pilot had a habit of flying in and through our formation. He particularly liked to torment me and would get as close as he possibly could. He would then wave to me and grin. He did this to me a number of times, and I would pound my gunsight in frustration; I was unable to shoot him because I didn't want to hit one of the other planes in the formation. I am 76 years old now, and in my mind's eye I can still see his face, his grin, and his wave.

"On one particular daylight mission, one of our planes was heavily damaged; our plane also received serious damage, and we both had to pull out of the formation. We were not damaged as badly as the other plane, and we used all our guns and ammunition to give this plane coverage since the Zeros [Mitsubishi A6Ms] were coming in for the kill. I was able to dismantle several of the Zeros, and I believe I shot down five, but was credited with only three. By the time both planes were able to make it to the ocean, some of the gunners were out of ammunition while others, myself included, were very low.

"Our radio operator called in a [rescue] submarine and gave the sub the grid coordinates as to where the more damaged plane would ditch. We stayed with this plane and flew cover until the submarine was able to pick up the entire crew. I received the Distinguished Flying Cross for that mission.

"A few short months after we arrived on Guam, we went out on a daylight raid. While flying formation I saw the next squadron's lead plane hit and shudder. I saw my friend, George, standing on the tail section, and I watched as he jumped. When his parachute opened he made a circle with his arms, which indicated 'I'm okay.' Minutes later a Zero zoomed in and strafed George; I exploded with frustration—I couldn't shoot that Zero for fear of hitting our planes in that diamond formation. Just before we turned south I saw George hanging in his parachute, his limp body covered in blood."

Above: *The B-29's original tail gun position had an impressive sting: two .50 caliber machine guns and a single 20mm cannon. The cannon was soon removed in the field and on the production line.*

Right: *Getting the range to the target required turning the reticle (circle of dots) down so that it spanned the wingtips of the oncoming enemy fighter. The computer took care of the rest.*

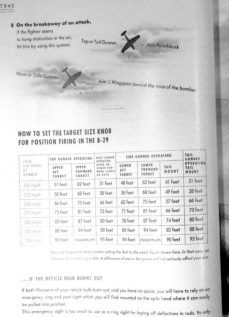

Below: *The 55 Sentai, armed exclusively with the Ki-61 Tony, was formed in March 1944. Its main duty was home defense, but the unit achieved no real success against the high-flying B-29s.*

Above: *Sixteen B-29s were converted to SB-29 super-dumbo rescue aircraft during World War II. All were equipped with an A-3 life boat that could be dropped, as seen above, by parachute to downed crewmen.*

Left: *The Champion Spark Plug Company provided spark plugs for both the Wright Cyclone engines and the Auxiliary Power Unit (APU) located in the rear of the aircraft. This period print ad extols the virtues of their product and the part they played to help win the war.*

Jack Halpern of the 45th Bomb Squadron was trained both as a flight engineer and as a tail gunner. On October 25, 1944, while aboard his aircraft *The Heavenly Body*, Jack's formation was attacked by numerous Japanese fighters, including Tojos (Nakajima Ki-44s), Tonys (Kawasaki Ki-61s), and Oscars (Nakajima Ki-43s). The aircraft was heavily damaged and his flight engineer severely wounded. Jack had to abandon his position and take over as flight engineer:

"I noticed fighters in the area. They were doing 'rollover' maneuvers, but they were out of range. Shortly after bombs away, I saw those same fighters; this time I noticed small flashes of light coming from the underside of their wings. At that moment, the inside cabin pressure, set for 8,000ft [2,438m] immediately dropped to the bombing-altitude pressure of 20,000 to 22,000ft [6,100 to 6,700m]. My tail gunner's compartment fogged up. My ears popped and it felt like they were going to burst [due to the very sudden decompression].

"DeCoster called me to come up and man the flight engineer's position. At that moment I couldn't leave; enemy fighters were now coming in. I fired my guns in a scatter fashion to ward off any accurate attacks. Firing my guns in this manner was not an effective way of shooting down enemy aircraft, but it did [at least] have the effect of dispersing the Jap fighters.

"When I took over the flight engineer's position, I remember clearly seeing Ledford's [the pilot] parachute torn to shreds. When he moved out of his seat, I could see the bones of his hip socket . . . The fuel mixture control levers were in 'full lean' and I remembered what a Boeing Tech. Rep. had said before we took off: 'Move the mixture controls out of the full lean detent and move them aft toward the closed or fuel cut-off position about one quarter to three-eighths of an inch. Do not move them beyond that point or you may cut off the fuel entirely, due to cable rigging. A leaner fuel mixture is a means of conserving fuel.'

"We were approaching the China mainland at this time and I was hoping this setup would give us some extra range. Our fuel situation was not good and after I transferred all the fuel from the bomb bay tanks, I let Gardner know it was okay to salvo the two tanks—due to battle damage they wouldn't budge; Gardner told me to go into the bay and salvo them manually. Without a parachute I crawled out into the forward bay. With the bomb doors open I struggled across the narrow metal structure and pulled the emergency release lever; both tanks dropped. The resulting vacuum almost sucked me out—I hung on with all the muscle I could muster. I then crawled back into the cockpit and resumed my seat at the engineer's panel. I remember seeing 40 gallons [151 liters] of fuel total remaining in the wing tanks. I knew bailing out was inevitable."

Pictures of war

Staff Sergeant William R. "Dick" Keefer was a tail gunner on an F-13 with the 3rd Photographic Reconnaissance Squadron (PRS); he was based at Harmon Field on Guam from early April to late December of 1945. Normally immune to fighter attacks, the high flying F-13s would sometimes find themselves flying over some very sensitive areas, causing the Japanese to react; the following account is from June that year:

"We of the 3rd PRS were known informally as 'The Official Photographers of Japan.' We flew photo missions to assess bomb damage following raids on Japanese cities. The F-13 version of the B-29 had the usual crewmembers, except there was a photo navigator instead of a bombardier. It was his job to guide the flight during photo runs while over the Japanese mainland. We also had an aerial photographer who operated the six big cameras that were housed in the waist compartment over Plexiglas ports cut in the fuselage floor.

"A normal mission schedule was a briefing the afternoon before the flight and then takeoff at 2am the following morning. After a relatively low-level flight and about an hour before entering Japanese airspace, we would start climbing to our operating altitude. Shortly after, we'd start the 'photo runs' as briefed, many of which included flights over several cities, and then we'd start the long flight home. These planes carried some 8,000 gallons [30,280 liters] of gas on takeoff (there were extra fuel tanks in the bomb bays), but we still had to refuel on Iwo Jima following missions that lasted 15 hours or more.

"We also flew pure reconnaissance missions such as the one we flew over Hokkaido. The primary purpose was to obtain aerial coverage of steel factories in the city of Muroran near the south coast. In fact, we were only the second US aircraft to fly over that northern island during the war. Photo missions were normally flown at high altitude, typically 25,000 to 30,000ft [7,620 to 9,144m]. Being a single-plane mission, we always flew without fighter escort. But for this particular target we were met with intense antiaircraft fire, and were attacked by five fighters, which was surprising since we were at an altitude of 25,000ft [7,620m] plus. We shot one down and claimed another as a 'probable.'"

Sergeant Andrew M. "Andy" Doty was a 21-mission tail gunner with the 93rd Bomb Squadron, 19th Bomb Group, 314th Bomb Wing, based on Guam on April 26, 1945. He describes the perils of flying, the steps needed to prepare for battle, and the act of shooting at an enemy fighter:

"The stress of the takeoffs cannot be overemphasized. The pilot needed full power as long as he could have it to haul his overloaded bomber into the air. The B-29 was designed to carry a gross weight of 120,000lb [60 tons] and a maximum of 135,000lb [67.5 tons], but they often weighed in at more than 140,000lb [70 tons]. The rule of thumb was that a bomber needed to gain a mile an hour [1.6km/h] of takeoff speed for every thousand pounds [454kg] of weight.

"If an engine failed after the 'point of no return' was reached, tragedy could result. Among the saddest sights to be seen by departing crews as they took off was the flaming wreckage of a bomber below them at the end of the runway.

"Once we were on our way to Japan, we spent our time watching the engines, talking about the war and when it might end, napping on the radar room floor, or listening to radio broadcasts from San Francisco.

"Hundreds of miles from Japan, we returned to our positions; I crawled back into the tail to set up shop in my small domain. I put on my light helmet with its small intercom receivers in the ears and inserted the line into the jack box . . .

Left and above: The Garflex K-20 handheld camera was built for day reconnaissance at medium altitude; it was loaded with 100 9 x 9in (23 x 23cm) frames. The photo of Kominato City on the east coast of Japan is an example of one of thousands of photos taken from the air during the war.

Left: *A newly arrived B-29 in China sits minus its unit tail markings. This B-29 still has the 20mm cannon fitted in the tail turret.*

Below: *B-29s in tight formation from the 314th Bomb Wing, 39th Bomb Group, drop their loads of incendiaries on the city of Hiratsuka, July 16, 1945.*

I put on my hard rubber oxygen mask, fastened it to my helmet and plugged the long hose into the ship's system.

"A multi-pocketed survival vest fitted over my flight suit, and my parachute harness went over that. I fastened my harness leg and chest straps, and clicked the chest 'chute in place . . . I switched on my gunsight and turret.

"The second time I encountered a fighter was the time we were jumped coming out of Osaka. It was a twin-engine fighter, and I know darn well he was trying to take us by surprise. To this day, I shudder to think what might have happened had he been able to catch us napping. We were unwinding because once you got a hundred miles [161km] off the coast you began to relax. There was a cloud base down below

Above: *The A-11 was an intermediate helmet made of sheepskin and lined with deerskin. Because of the hot conditions in the Pacific the A-11 was rarely worn by B-29 flight crews. The plug connected directly to the intercom for inter-crew communication.*

us, and for some reason I was still watching when I saw this guy pop up and drop back down. The first thing I knew, he overhauled us down through the clouds and then popped up behind us. I alerted everyone. I was able to open fire when he swung across the back of me; he was firing, I was firing, and I can still see my bullets smashing into his engine and wing, with parts . . . flying off. I could see my bullets were hitting his right engine, but I couldn't force myself to swing my guns over to the pilot's compartment. We were told to trust the sight and not the tracers; so I did, of course. If I had shot at the pilot's compartment, I might have killed some poor guy and I'm glad now I didn't."

Faith and salvage

On May 25–26, 1945, tail gunner John Blackard of the 45th Bomb Squadron and his crew headed toward Tokyo aboard *Harry Miller*. The target was the financial, commercial, and government districts of the city, including factories and homes—together with earlier missions, 86 per cent of the target area was destroyed. It was a low-level night mission (10,000ft [3,048m]), but just as they reached the IP, enemy searchlights found their mark and the flak came up with a vengeance. His aircraft received ten direct hits and lost an engine. Fire in the bomb bay only added to the confusion. After the harrowing action, Blackard and four of his crewmates were awarded the DFC (Distinguished Flying Cross). Blackard was the only one to receive a Purple Heart. He describes the action in the following passage:

"We were put on alert a couple of hours before we got to Japan. Once we got over land, the searchlights started to pick us up; it was so bright, all I could see was a blanket of flak—but no Jap fighters. The turbulence in the tail gunner's position was very strong.

"We were hit several times in the bomb bay section. Sgt. William Treanor could see a fire in the bomb bay; he reported [it] to Captain Wriston, but the Captain and Jim O'Keefe had the plane on automatic pilot and the bombs were dropped on target. With the bombs gone, the fire in the bomb bay went out. And just as we were leaving the Empire, one of our engines was hit and had to be feathered.

"After we left the target we stayed on alert for a couple of hours; we felt helpless—at this point we [were] just passengers. We didn't talk about what we had just gone through; we knew the plane was flying with three engines and was hit in several other places, but we'd been told that the B-29 could fly with three engines—two if for just a short time. We had to put our faith in Captain Wriston's flying skills. He did a magnificent job along with the navigator who kept us on course. I don't remember any

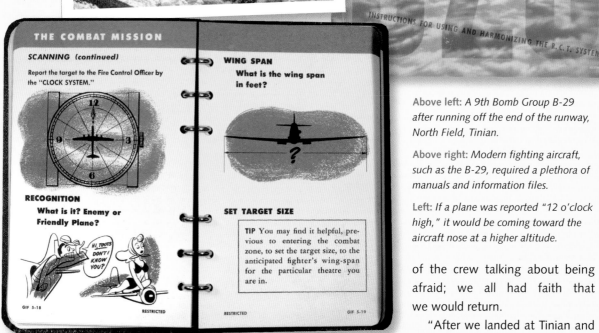

GUNNERY IN THE B·29

Above left: *A 9th Bomb Group B-29 after running off the end of the runway, North Field, Tinian.*

Above right: *Modern fighting aircraft, such as the B-29, required a plethora of manuals and information files.*

Left: *If a plane was reported "12 o'clock high," it would be coming toward the aircraft nose at a higher altitude.*

of the crew talking about being afraid; we all had faith that we would return.

"After we landed at Tinian and got out of the plane, we were able to see the massive destruction that had been inflicted on our aircraft. We were so close to being wiped out, and yet no one was hurt. The damage was so complete the aircraft was declared [only fit for] salvage."

Staff Sergeant Joseph J. "Joe" Majeski Jr. was a 35-mission tail gunner and a recipient of a Distinguished Flying Cross. He was a member of the 40th Bomb Squadron, 6th Bomb Group, and flew aboard the B-29 named *Lady Annabelle*. Majeski describes what it was like to be shot at, and, though he was trained to shoot down enemy fighters, in 1945 he found himself shooting at targets of a more maritime nature:

"On 29 May 1945, our 16th mission, we were assigned to bomb Yokahoma, Japan. Over the target the flak was thick and accurate; one piece hit and cracked my left window and came straight through, tearing my jacket over my left shoulder—it missed my skin by a quarter of an inch.

Flak also hit our number one engine; with three engines we headed for Iwo Jima and an emergency landing.

"We stayed on Iwo Jima for four days while our plane's engine was repaired. The next morning, at about 3am, air raid sirens began to wail. Joe Ryan, our radar operator, and I jumped into a ditch, landing on our stomachs; Japanese bombers were overhead. The bombs didn't land close but they were enough for us to feel the concussive waves. For a moment I felt compassion for the Japanese people we were bombing—it was a feeling of helplessness.

"That same morning we were asked to fly a photo reconnaissance B-29 to the coast of Japan and search for survivors from a shot-down B-29. We flew a rectangular pattern at an altitude of 100 to 150ft [30 to 46m] over the ocean; this enabled us to better locate survivors floating on the surface. We sighted two rafts and circled over them until we contacted the rescue submarine. The sub soon appeared and picked them up.

"We volunteered the next day as well and flew another search mission. We spotted a Japanese junk which had what appeared

Above: *A newly arrived B-29 at West Field, Tinian (1945) is painted with the two parallel stripes for the 468th Bomb Group, 793rd Bomb Squadron.*

Left: *North Field, Guam. North Field became operational in January 1945 and was home to the 314th Bomb Wing.*

Below left: *A P-51 Mustang crashes into a B-29 while landing at Iwo Jima. Sadly, accidents were not uncommon.*

[to be] a 20mm flak cannon on deck. We had been informed that the Japanese were using these boats as 'picket ships' in order to warn the mainland about approaching B-29s. Our aircraft commander, Capt. Percy Tucker, called back and asked: 'How about we sink it?'

"We were about 40 miles [64km] from the Japanese coast when we began our dive. Our bombardier, Joe Krogman, using the front top turret, got first shot with four .50s. Rob Ryan, one of the CFC side gunners, strafed him as well, and last of all I blasted away as we passed over and away. Our first pass set him on fire; we came in for a second run leaving him half sunk and burning. We didn't locate any survivors on that mission. Our plane was still not repaired when we returned to Iwo, so we flew back to Tinian in a 58th Bomb Wing B-29. We often thought of painting a Japanese junk next to the mission bombs painted on the side our B-29's fuselage, but we never did."

MiG Alley

It was October 1951, and US Air Force chief of staff, Hoyt S. Vandenberg, brushed aside the reports; "I want to talk to a tail gunner," he insisted. He wanted to speak to the men involved. B-29 losses to the Soviet Union's new MiG-15 during the Korean War had reached unacceptable levels; the new jets were simply too swift and the B-29's armament too weak. While several gunners were officially credited with MiG kills, none seriously believed they had actually done so.

In 1950, the B-29 had one more war to fight. On the morning of Sunday, June 25, North Korean armed forces smashed across the 38th Parallel and headed for the capital of South Korea. Almost immediately, the small force of B-29s from the Far East Air Force, based on Guam, reacted to the threat with

attack by North Korean piston-engine World War II fighters of Soviet vintage. Losses were light, but in the autumn of 1950, swept-wing fighters began to appear on airfields along the Yalu River. The new fighter was the Soviet MiG-15 jet fighter. In November, the first RB-29 was shot up by a gaggle of MiG-15s; it survived the attack but crash-landed on the return to base. The tail gunner, Corporal Harry J. La Vene, was credited with having shot down the first MiG by a B-29 gunner. Just 24 hours later, MiG-15s shot down a B-29 from the 307th Bomb Group near the Yalu River. Over the next two weeks, more B-29s would feel the sting of the MiG-15. Intelligence reports at the time stated that it was Chinese pilots in the MiGs and that China had no intention of joining the war; for B-29 crews both assertions were false—the early MiGs were flown by Soviet pilots, and the Chinese joined the conflict on November 28 with a force of 200,000 men.

Left: A 1950s Zippo lighter with the Strategic Air Command's (SAC) coat of arms. The SAC was in charge of US land-based strategic nuclear bomber aircraft. Four SAC bomb groups equipped with the B-29 saw service during the Korean War.

Above: Command Decision was the most famous B-29 of Korea. On one mission, it was said, the crew shot at two MiGs, claimed three, got credit for four and then painted five kills on their B-29.

Right: A few B-29 Bomb Groups were kept on strength with the newly created USAF and called into action during the Korean War.

a bombing mission on June 28. Early B-29 operations focused mainly on tank concentrations, supply dumps, troops, and trucks. The results were not very effective; the B-29 was a strategic bomber (more suited to large-impact targets) and these targets were tactical in nature. Early threats to the B-29s consisted of flak and the odd

Left: A pilot and a ground crewman inspect some minor damage caused by a MiG-15 to the inboard nacelle tail fairing. The MiG-15's armament of two 23mm and one 37mm cannon was specifically designed to down enemy bombers. A well-aimed two-second burst was often enough to bring down a B-29.

The MiG-15 posed a serious threat to the B-29. Equipped with two NR 23mm cannons and one 37mm cannon, it was the most heavily armed interceptor in the world. The MiG represented the next generation of combat aircraft, while the B-29 was a relic from World War II; it was simply outgunned, and on "Black Tuesday" its weakness was tragically revealed. For many B-29 crews it was their darkest day of the war.

On October 23, 1951, eight B-29s from the 307th Bomb Group were tasked with the bombing of Namsi airfield along the Yalu River. A fighter escort of straight-winged F-84 jet fighters proved ineffective; more than 50 MiGs tore in to the B-29s. As the MiGs began their runs, the B-29 gunners fought a desperate battle—out-gunned and out-ranged, they didn't stand a chance. Three were shot down, three were heavily damaged, and two badly damaged (heavily damaged is worse). Later, USAF chief

Above, left and right: The arrival of the MiG-15 forced the B-29s over to night operations. This one was flown to Kimpo Air Base by defecting North Korean Peoples Air Force pilot Ro Kim Suk on September 21, 1953, just weeks after the war came to an end. Both Chuck Yeager and Apollo astronaut Tom Collins test-flew this aircraft.

of staff, Hoyt S. Vandenberg, ordered a halt to daylight bomber operations over North Korea; B-29s would operate only at night.

While outclassed, the B-29s gave as good as they got: B-29 gunners were credited with 27 enemy fighters destroyed (16 MiG-15s) and 17 probably destroyed (all MiGs). B-29 losses totaled 34: 16 lost to fighters, 4 lost to flak, and 14 to other unspecified causes.

A dangerous position

The tail gunner was much like the radar operator—all alone within his combat station—and both of them occupied the tail end of the aircraft. But they did not occupy their respective stations all of the time. Generally speaking, while inbound or outbound to and from targets, while flying over the ocean, the tail gunner and CFC gunners would occupy the radar operator's area where the putt-putt, bunks, and toilet were located. But when the aircraft neared the danger zone, the tail gunner, CFC gunners, and radar operator returned to their respective stations. Frank "Bud" Farrell talks of his experiences in the Korean War:

"I was not a tail gunner but had flown the position a few times in training. The tail position in a '29 was not nearly as 'cramped' as was the case in the B-17 and B-24 . . . a good-sized six-footer could access and fit in the '29 tail very comfortably, [comfortable] apart from the cold back there. Re toilet facilities: of course there were none back there nor in any other position other than the relief tube and 'honey bucket' ["porta-potty"] in the radar compartment behind the gunner's compartment. Prudence or

discretion generally required last-minute relief in the boondocks near the hardstand just before boarding the aircraft . . . and very little drinking of coffee or water during a long flight!

"The tail gunner usually did not access the tail position until just prior to crossing the 38th Parallel or frontlines headed into enemy territory, and left his position at about the same landmark position on return, thus he was not in any more difficult relief situation than any other crewmember, i.e. that was the last thing on anyone's mind on a combat mission.

"The B-29 tail position was generally not regarded as any more dangerous in Korean operations than that of other positions in the aircraft . . . and in fact may have had more bullet-proof glass/plastic protection and surrounding armor than others . . . again, none of which might have been too protective against cannon fire of a MiG or heavy antiaircraft artillery/flak! The mass of metal in the three .50 caliber guns in our tail mounts, and the rather heavy metal of the gunsight afforded modest protection from shrapnel, but hardly against direct enemy cannon fire."

Left: Millions of leaflets were dropped during the Korean War. This one warns civilians to stay away from unexploded bombs and to stear clear of military targets, such as roads, railways, and military factories.

Below: During the Korean War, B-29s were often called upon to bomb tactical targets. This photo shows a strike by B-29s on the bridges across the Chongchon River in October 1952.

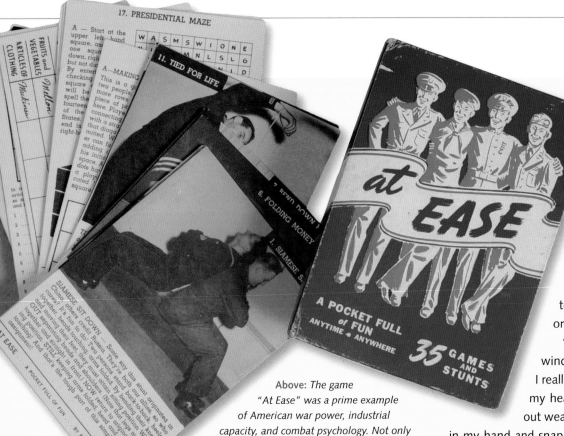

Above: The game
"At Ease" was a prime example
of American war power, industrial
capacity, and combat psychology. Not only
were crews equipped to fight, they were also
given games and other distractions to improve morale
between missions during both World War II and Korea.

Right: Two 93rd Bomb Squadron, 19th Bomb Group B-29s head
out for another mission over Korea in 1950. By the end of the Korean War, B-29s had
flown no fewer than 21,000 sorties and dropped 167,000 tons of bombs.

fur-lined flight suit and huge fur-lined flight boots over my regular shoes. Our bombing altitude varied, but it was generally around 25,000ft [7,620m]. Outside temperatures at that altitude [are] often 40 to 50 degrees below freezing; I generally encountered one to 2 inches [around 5cm] of frost accumulation on the interior of the tail compartment. After 'bombs away' we lost altitude as quickly as possible; in the warmer temperature, the frost would melt; the result was one cold and damp tail gunner.

"The tail compartment had a removable side window, which was the emergency exit. However, I really doubt if I could have squeezed through it with all my heavy clothing, and I know I could not have gotten out wearing a chest pack parachute unless I tried to hold it in my hand and snap it in place during free fall. My plan, if I had time to execute it, was to exit the tail the same way I got in and grab the 'chute at the rear door, buckle it on, and jump. However, the egress procedure

Tom Stevens joined the Air Force in 1951 because he "didn't know what to do with his life." Trained as a tail gunner, he would soon find himself flying night bombing missions over North Korea with the 307th Bomb Wing. Stevens never shot his guns in anger and spent most of his time watching the war raging below him; this gave him a lot of time to think, and he soon realized that if he had to bail out he would never make it:

"As a tail gunner I had the best view of the target area; my aircraft commander was always eager to hear my report of target destruction. Seldom did I see secondary explosions, but I had a good view of our bombs exploding. We were always given a primary, secondary, and tertiary target; the tertiary target was often frontline support. I found this fascinating because I could see the flashes of small arms fire and mortar rounds.

"Being a tail gunner had some unique and often uncomfortable aspects; there is a long, unpressurized area from the rear bulkhead door to the tail compartment, which also had its own bulkhead door. This area gets progressively smaller as one crawls toward the tail gunner's compartment, [and] is not large enough for a person to get through while wearing the heavy clothing needed for high-altitude combat; I wore a

would require that I stand, rotate 180 degrees, raise the tail gunner's seat, go down on my knees to open the tail compartment bulkhead door, and crawl forward about 25ft [7.6m] to the rear exit door. If the aircraft was going down in a steep dive and/or spin, this would have been impossible. I sometimes reflect on this and realize that for all practical purposes I was virtually trapped and would no doubt have [gone] down with the aircraft if we were shot down."

A Devastating Conclusion

"**And then one day we were getting ready to take off when they started loading the *Enola Gay*. There was a ring—all the way from wing tip to wing tip—of Marines with submachine guns standing in a circle around that airplane. A high-ranking officer was watching to make sure they were facing out.**"—Captain Davis Bunn, 482nd Bomb Squadron, 505th Bomb Group.

By the beginning of World War II, the capabilities of bombers had grown exponentially, yet air forces—whether practicing precision bombing or area bombing—were incapable of destroying either an enemy's will or ability to make war. US B-29s had started against Japan with a precision bombing campaign, which, thwarted by a variety of difficulties, had moved to an area bombing campaign, fire-bombing entire cities to decimate Japanese industry. During 1944 and 1945, the XX and XXI Bomber Commands would burn out 40 per cent of the built-up urban areas of 66 cities, destroying nearly one-third of all Japanese houses, and 106 square miles (274sq km) of Japan's six leading industrial cities. For many in Japan, the arrival of the B-29s would be the first sign that they could lose the war. For those controlling the Japanese government, the only hope was to bring the Allies to the negotiating table

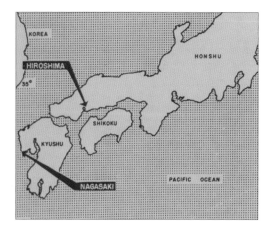

Left: A map showing Hiroshima and Nagasaki released from the Office of US Strategic Bombing Survey on July 19, 1946, stamped "No Obj. to Pub."

by making any victories overwhelmingly costly in terms of men and *matériel*.

World scientists had examined the possibility of a bomb powered by nuclear fission before the war began; both Germany and, to a lesser degree, Japan had explored the development of just such a weapon, although their programs bore no fruit. The US program can be traced back to an August 1939 letter from Albert Einstein to the president, Franklin Roosevelt. Einstein explained that a bomb detonating uranium could result in unimagined destruction. Nevertheless, the creation of such a weapon was not deemed to be a high priority until the US entry into World War II on December 7, 1941. Within just a few weeks, Roosevelt had appointed a committee to examine the feasibility of a nuclear bomb. By summer 1942, the committee reported that an accelerated program with the right funding could produce an atomic weapon by July 1944. That September, the US Army Corps of Engineers began the highly classified "Manhattan Project," and the US took its first steps toward a nuclear weapon.

Above: Silverplate B-29s participated in 51 practice bombing sorties using "Fat Man"-shaped "pumpkin" bombs.

Left: Two days after the Nagasaki mission, the crew of Bockscar stands in front of the plane. Charles Sweeney is fifth from the right.

Above: Enola Gay, *the most famous B-29 of them all, on her return from bombing Hiroshima. This Martin-built B-29-35-MO 44-86292 carried the standard circle "R" on its tail, representing the 6th Bomb Group during its historic mission.*

Also that September, the XB-29 made its first test flight—an event critical to the atomic bomb project, since no other aircraft under development had the projected capability of delivering the weapon. Although the Superfortress's range would eventually be a factor in the war against Japan, the aircraft's payload was its original advantage: the B-29 was expected to use the atomic bomb against Germany.

In December 1943, the 55th production B-29 flew to Wright Field in Dayton, Ohio, to undergo modification as the world's first atomic bomber prototype. Project Silverplate (a name taken from a directive describing the modification program as the "Silver Plated Project") was soon to become the USAAF's highest priority project, and also included any action needed to equip, organize, and train the crews that would deliver the world's first atomic weapons.

In October 1944, the men who would fly the Silverplate B-29s assembled as the 393rd Bomb Squadron. Two months later, the 393rd would be assigned to the 509th Composite Group, the highest numbered combat group formed by the USAAF during the war. (Although the group's second squadron was the C-54-equipped 320th Troop Carrier Squadron, the "Composite" designation may have been made to disguise the 509th's purpose.) The group's commander was 29-year-old Colonel Paul W. Tibbets, a former pilot with the 97th Bomb Group in Africa before he was assigned to General Doolittle's Twelfth Air Force headquarters as a "bombardment expert." Tibbets had been preparing the B-29 and his unit since late 1943. Now based at the isolated facilities of Wendover Field, Utah, he began training over the deserts of the American Southwest.

With Germany's surrender in May 1945, the 509th now had Japan in its sights. In June, the 509th began arriving at Tinian in the Marianas. Training missions soon began, with the crews dropping five-ton, orange-painted "pumpkin bombs" on Japanese targets. After 38 pumpkin sorties,

Little Boy; Fat Man

The US detonated three nuclear devices during World War II: the first was a test blast that took place on July 16, 1945; the other two devices were dropped on Japan.

The first to be dropped was "Little Boy," a uranium device that was 10.5ft (3.2m) long with a 29 inch (73.7cm) diameter. Its explosive yield was the equivalent of 12,500 tons of TNT. The power of Little Boy was derived from the rare isotope uranium 235, which had to be separated from the more plentiful uranium 238; this took a vast amount of energy and technical ingenuity, the result being that when the bomb was dropped on Hiroshima, it used all of the U-235 in existence.

Little Boy was a simple gun-type fission weapon: a specific mass of U-235 was "shot" into another mass of U-235, creating the required critical mass for an explosion.

The device dropped on Nagasaki was a plutonium bomb. "Fat Man" was 10ft 8in (3.25m) long and 5ft (1.5m) in diameter, with an explosive yield that was the equivalent of 22,000 tons of TNT. Fat man used a spherical explosive wave that compressed a sphere—hence the shape—of plutonium at the center of the wave to achieve critical mass, and thus a nuclear explosion.

Above: *The spherical "Fat Man" loaded into the forward bay of Bockscar.*

Right: *"Little Boy" in Enola Gay's forward bomb bay. Once dropped, the bomb moved on a forward trajectory and exploded several miles ahead of its release point. This gave time for the B-29 to bank to the right and away from the detonation.*

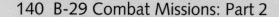

I going to fly an airplane around that tight turn? So I immediately pulled mine off and flew the airplane around this way. There was . . . a brilliance in the airplane. Everybody else was wearing goggles except me. There were also three shock waves from the Hiroshima weapon. The first one was a good jolt. The second one was quite noticeable. The third one was only visible to the tail gunner. He could see it coming."

While the final death toll is unknown, an estimated 70,000 people were killed outright. The message flashed to Tinian: "Clear cut. Successful in all respects." Tibbets and his crew landed safely 12 hours after takeoff. He was awarded the Distinguished Flying Cross by General Spaatz himself—it was a short and wordless ceremony; Spaatz simply pinned the medal on and walked away.

Despite expectations of Japan's surrender, later that evening, Tibbets informed 25-year-old Charles Sweeney, squadron commander of the 509th, to prepare for a second atomic bombing mission. And when no surrender was forthcoming, Sweeney's mission was launched on August 9. Because his regular plane was still set up to monitor bomb results, Sweeney shifted his crew to Captain Fred Bock's plane, *Bockscar* (also known as *Bock's Car*).

the 509th prepared for its first atomic mission. On August 4, Tibbets briefed his crew, revealing for the first time that a bomb "of unimaginable destructive force" would be dropped; the words "atomic" and "nuclear" were never mentioned. The target was Hiroshima on southern Honshu, a previously unbombed city that included the headquarters of the Second General Army. At 2:42am, Tibbets's B-29 *Enola Gay* (named for his mother) took off. The aircraft, code-named "Dimples 82" for radio communications, approached the target as Tibbets learned from the weather scouts that the skies over Hiroshima were clear. There were no fighter defenses; by this point in the War, Japanese defensive fighters rarely scrambled to intercept a single aircraft.

In the bomb bay sat the device known as "Little Boy," which engineers calculated would cause the most damage if detonated 1,900ft (579m) above the ground. Beginning their bomb run at 31,000ft (9,449m), bombardier Tom Ferebee released the weapon and Tibbets threw the aircraft into a steep, hard-diving, right-hand turn. Some 45 seconds later, the bomb exploded, missing its aim point by fewer than 200 yards (185m). First came the light, and then the shock wave from 10 miles (16km) astern. Tibbets describes what happened: "As it releases, I pulled my goggles down over my face and I'm blind. I can't see a damned thing. How am

Above left: *Following the Hiroshima mission, the* Enola Gay *crew was debriefed by the Commander of the US Strategic Air Forces in the Pacific, General Carl Spaatz (at the head of the table), Lieutenant General Barney Giles (to Spaatz's right), and Lieutenant General Nathan Twining (to Giles's right).*

Inset above: *Bockscar's artwork, added following the Nagasaki mission.*

Left: *Hiroshima from 20,000ft (6,096m) on the morning of August 6, 1945. As Enola Gay turned for home, she was hit by three separate shock waves created by the atomic bomb blast.*

Left: *Never as well known as Paul Tibbets, Major Charles Sweeney was the commander of the atomic bomb mission that destroyed Nagasaki.*

Below: *V-J Day—Victory over Japan Day—came shortly after Nagasaki. At the time, most Americans—and the Emperor of Japan—noted that Japan's surrender could not have happened without the devastation caused by the nuclear weapons. Today, historians debate that conclusion.*

Beahan spotted a break in the clouds and took over. His visual bomb run was a mere 25 seconds at 31,000ft (9,449m). The Mitsubishi Steel and Arms Works was the aim point. Beahan's deft hand put Fat Man just 500ft (152m) to the south of the plant; the plutonium explosion destroyed about 60 per cent of the city.

But Sweeney still had to make it home and, unable to transfer fuel from the bomb bay tank, he set course for Okinawa, more than 400 miles (644km) to the south. His navigator calculated they would fall 50 miles (80km) short of their destination, and, due to a communications mix-up with Guam, no rescue plane was on station to provide aid. Sweeney recalled a conversation he'd had with Tibbets regarding "flying the step"—bringing down a bomber in stages to gain airspeed with each descent, trading altitude for distance. In desperation, Sweeney tried it, and with some success. However, the crew's good luck was short lived; on approach to Yontan, Okinawa, one engine failed, followed by yet another on the airstrip. Shoving the props into reverse and standing on the brakes, Sweeney stopped the plane just yards from the end of the runway. Then the third engine sputtered and died; *Bockscar* had just 7 usable gallons (32 liters) of fuel remaining—enough for less than one minute of flight time!

Air operations continued over Japan: on the night of August 14–15, B-29s struck Kumagaya, Isezaki, and Tsuchizakiminato. As they headed home, the Eighth Air Force's first B-29 mission headed north from new bases in Okinawa. Before making landfall, the Eighth's

Sweeney's primary target was Kokura, with a secondary target of Nagasaki. But, even before the mission began, an inoperable fuel pump made 600 gallons of fuel inaccessible. Given the option to cancel the mission, Sweeney realized that repairing the problem would take too long, and the complicated download-upload sequence precluded moving the Fat Man plutonium bomb to another B-29. And there were further problems with the mission; after hitting his first navigation checkpoint, Sweeney was forced to circle for 40 minutes waiting for the photo aircraft, ultimately wasting valuable fuel because it never arrived.

Unable to wait any longer, Sweeney headed almost due north to Kokura; he arrived there to find the primary target covered by smoke from the previous night's attack on the city of Yawata. Three aborted runs later, and with fighters in sight, Sweeney diverted to the secondary target. *Bockscar*—now 90 minutes late—arrived to find Nagasaki 80 per cent covered by low cloud. Ordered to drop visually, Commander Fred Ashworth, the weaponeer, consulted with Sweeney about dropping by radar; Sweeney was certain it could be done, and Ashworth prepared for a radar approach. But just seconds before the release, bombardier Kermit

aircraft received their recall order—Japan had finally surrendered. Japanese leaders had hoped to make every victory too costly—primarily in the number of casualties—for the Allies to continue, but the atomic bombs had made further delay too costly for the emperor to contemplate.

The B-29s became forever identified with the atomic bombings of Hiroshima and Japan. For those preparing to invade Japan, and for those at home awaiting the return of loved ones, the missions were a gift: the war was over, and fewer Americans would die fighting it. For others, the atomic bombs represented an unspeakable evil, and were a mistake that represented a failure of diplomacy. The debate will continue.

Rest and Recreation

"There was nothing to do off the base, no amusement areas, theaters, bars, gambling casinos, and no decent eating places. Nothing, nothing, nothing. It was the pits."

—Technical Sergeant Jerome Harold Goldwyn, 461st Bomb Squadron, 346th Bomb Group, Eighth Air Force

Sergeant Goldwyn's observations recalled his air base at Kadena, Okinawa, but his sentiments were echoed by thousands of other B-29 crewmen regarding every other overseas Superfortress base, and many of the US bases as well. It's not unusual for soldiers to complain—Napoleon even referred to his vaunted Old Guard Grenadiers as "*les Grognards*" ("the Grumblers")—and B-29 crews certainly had many causes for complaint. The crews were taking an unproven aircraft to war, and they were struggling with the plane's many mechanical deficiencies even as they attempted to prove its combat worthiness; most crewmen recognized, especially during their early missions, that the B-29 was as likely to kill them as were their Japanese adversaries. Their morale was

further tested by issues of leadership, the dearth of promotion and recognition, and the quality of their off-duty hours. The crews fought and worked to complete their missions under trying circumstances, and returned to uncomfortable living conditions; it's hardly surprising that they would complain about their rest-and-recreation options.

Nearly everyone wanted to be home, or anyplace where there wasn't someone trying to kill them, and they weren't required to kill someone else. Denied that option, crews wanted some degree of comfort, good food, and interesting things to do—nearly all of which required logistical support. In India and China, they would compete with their own aircraft for even the most basic resources. The bases in India—Kharagpur, Chakulia, Piardoba, and Dudhkundi—were still under construction when the aircraft arrived, and first priorities centered on maintaining and protecting the Superfortresses; all else would come when time and resources allowed. Initially, troops were quartered in tents, which were eventually replaced by "basha" huts, made with packed soil or concrete for the floors, plastered bamboo walls, and thatched roofs.

The proximity of Calcutta's port facilities allowed the navy and merchant marine to deliver supplies and equipment to within about a hundred miles (about 160km) of the Indian B-29 bases, but disorganization at the port, and the lack of available local transport, often kept the most basic supplies from reaching the units in a timely manner. Aircraft of the Air Transport Command could deliver personnel and supplies from the US, and XX Bomber Command's three organic

Left: *Ingenuity was often the best cure for boredom. Based on Saipan in November 1944, assistant crew chief Sergeant Dick Wilken fashions a watch band out of metal salvaged from wrecked Japanese aircraft.*

in the Marianas Islands. It would be from this island group that the first sustainable B-29 raids would target Japan.

Logistically, the Marianas eliminated many of the supply bottlenecks and local concerns that had plagued the strategic air war flown out of China and India. The islands had no local landowners with whom to negotiate; engineers simply built the bases wherever they felt the facilities should be built. Nor was there any local labor or management to circumvent at port facilities. The navy decided where to position the port and its storehouses, built them, and managed them. Airfields were located within an easy drive of the supply depots, using roads created for that purpose and vehicles delivered for the same purpose. The Marianas became all-American facilities, and if the US forces failed to deliver as promised (as they often did), the response came through the military chain of command rather than a new round of negotiations. By May 1945, the last India-based B-29s had transferred to new bases in the Marianas.

Although logistical support at these new bases proved a boon to Superfortress operations and greatly improved the living conditions for the crews, the off-duty situation was by no means perfect. For most, the novelty of the island paradise wore thin after a short time, and there was

Above: During a break in construction of a B-29 airfield in China, workers get a view of the US from the photos in a copy of Life *magazine shared with an AAF lieutenant.*

Right: The C-47 in the background of this image sprays DDT to kill Saipan's mosquitos; decades would pass before DDT's side effects would be discovered.

transport squadrons were able to fly *matériel* in from as far away as North Africa—but only the most critical items could be delivered by air, with creature comforts much farther down the supply chain.

Unable to strike at the Japanese home islands from India, the B-29s were to stage those missions through four bases (Kiunglai, Pengshan, Hsinching, and Kwanghan) that were being built around Chengtu, China, where the supply situation was even worse. If the supply chain was weak around Calcutta, it was nonexistent at Chengtu; anything that could not be secured locally (which was nearly everything) had to be flown in from India. The landing strips were built by local labor—comprising some 350,000 men, women, and children—with amazing speed. At Kwanghan, for example, work began on January 24, three months to the day before the first B-29 landed there. It was not surprising, then, given the limited time and resources, that there was very little left with which to provide for the crews' comfort or entertainment.

June 7, 1944, would prove a turning point both in the history of the B-29 and in the course of World War II. On that day, the first Superfortresses to hit Japan would bomb the steel mills at Yawata, slightly damaging Japan's war-making potential and—perhaps more critically—signaling a new vulnerability to the country's people and leadership. That same day, American forces began their assault on Saipan

nowhere else to go. Knowing that there was little chance to rotate his crew off the islands for any sort of extended leave, General Curtis LeMay had begun efforts to anchor two former ocean liners in the Marianas, outfitting them as floating rest areas to provide the crewmen with some relief. (The war would end before LeMay could put the plan into effect.)

Whatever recreational support was available in the Pacific, men of the Army Air Force were all too aware that any island's best facilities, supplies, and activities were usually found on the navy side of the island. Clearly, with control over shipping and the ports, navy leaders made certain that their own men were fully supported; equally understandably, the air force personnel usually resented the inequities.

In the CBI theater

As one officer wrote: "Every single goddam thing that we send into China has to be flown in." For much of its time in India, the XX Bomber Command burned far more fuel transporting supplies for its missions than it did attacking the Japanese. Another described XX Bomber Command as "a goddam trucking outfit." Life in India was difficult for most of the US fliers, but living conditions in China were nearly impossible. The XX Bomber Command historian wrote in 1944:

"Faced with the necessity of executing a combat mission on the directed date, despite its reduced transport capacity, the command had only one alternative: to reduce the delivery of equipment, supplies and personnel to all units in the forward area to the bare essentials required to sustain life and permit the airplanes to take off for the target. These instructions were so stringent that all surface transportation to the forward area ceased with the exception of one vehicle per base. No supplementary rations were supplied to the garrisons in the area. All supplies of PX [Post Exchange] rations were eliminated. There

Above: "Harvey's Drive-In," a Red Cross coffee and doughnut shop built by the 444th Bomb Group in Dudhkundi, India.

Left: On Iwo Jima, a 314th Bomb Wing crewman tautens the guy lines to a tent while, in the background, his B-29 awaits repairs for the trip back to Guam.

was no shipment of clothing, less than 25 per cent of the mail. No hospital rations and no additional personal or organizational equipment were supplied. Indeed, insofar as supply was concerned, personnel in the forward area were as isolated and limited as if they had been in a desert island. Full colonels walked two miles to their airplanes."

In fact, the remark about the desert island might have fallen somewhat short of the mark—for most crews, the quality of life would improve once they moved to the Marianas! A diary entry from Willard Wayne Holder, navigator with the 793rd Bomb Squadron, runs: "We are one of the first combat crews to arrive at our new base [Camp Salua, also known as B-1, in northeast India] so we are now doing much physical labor. The Japanese have warned by radio of a bombing and strafing attack to be held during April 16th, 17th or 18th. So we are digging slit trenches. The ground is hard as rock and the sun is hot as hell and the sweat comes off in rolls."

Ralph M. Robert, Flight Engineer, 468th Bomb Group, was assigned to the China theater and remembers a very different kind of "rest home" for crewmembers who couldn't cope:

"There were a lot of people who went overseas, from all branches, and there were those who just couldn't take it. For whatever reason they decided to bug out of whatever assignment they had. So they gave them a choice; if they faltered, they sent them back to the United States for an automatic dishonorable discharge. If they went to the disciplinary training center and came through that, they could be reassigned to some group and fight the war normally. The place was packed. But this had a real influence on a lot of people that were there. It was an eye opener. Still, when we got over there, we had people doing it. I don't know whatever happened to them, but there were those who, unfortunately, couldn't take it."

WHAT IS THE MAGIC IN A LETTER FROM HOME?

Cavalier Corporation
CHATTANOOGA   TENNESSEE

Left: Manufacturers advertised their contributions to the war effort. This advertisement from Cavalier urged US civilians to write to the troops.

Below: Sergeant Richard M. Miller catches up on his reading on the tail of his B-29 in Saipan, November 1944. Hundreds of thousands of books were distributed to all the military services.

If it wasn't combat, it was the primitive living conditions and complete lack of mental stimulation that could drive a person over the edge. Once more, this entry from Willard Wayne Holder's diary graphically describes the situation during the early days in India:

"July 10th, 1944. Today has been a very wet, dismal, sweat-giving day. It seems to rain all of the time. Nothing new is happening and time drags by very slowly. We have little to read or do and thus few things to absorb our thoughts except home and what a 'Shangri-La' it is, and our wives, children, new homes, new hopes in a war-ridden world.

Left: Aircrews eating on Makin Island in the Pacific. In the background, men are washing mess gear in oil drum halves over a fire. Meals were served where the men worked and lived; dining halls, tables, and chairs usually came after maintenance facilities and supply depots had been completed.

stands out above all others was the performance of Andre Kostelanetz, his orchestra, and his wife Lily Pons. Unfortunately, they arrived on the day of the accident, an explosion that killed nine men and wounded 21 from the 44th Squadron. The performance had to be held over until the following night. What a thrill for me to have this lovely lady as a roommate! The following afternoon, Mr. Kostelanetz appeared at the Red Cross Club and said, 'Lily has a dry throat. She needs pineapple juice in order to sing tonight.' There wasn't a chance our shelves held such a delicacy. I contacted Colonel Blanchard who called around and finally located a small can in Calcutta. A plane flew to Calcutta, arriving back at the base just an hour before the performance. Good thing the taxpayers back home didn't know the cost of that little can! It was well worth it; her beautiful voice soared to the heavens, and you guys yelled and screamed for more."

Left: *A group of Chinese laborers pauses to take a break near a B-29 of the 678th Bomb Squadron, 444th Bomb Group.*

Above right: *Inflated mattress covers served as rafts for aircraft crews relaxing on Marianas beaches.*

Below: *Major General Claire Chennault thanks Lily Pons and Andre Kostelanetz after the pair visited China to entertain the troops.*

We sleep in British, 'Indian-built barracks,' which [are] very quickly being eaten by wood ants. We have a wood and sawdust icebox for which we seldom get ice. We drink bad-tasting, heavily chlorinated water. We have an officers' shower for which we are all very thankful. We are sleeping under mosquito nets. Most food and supplies are brought in from American ships docking at Calcutta, by plane. The roads are all very poor here except for a few railroads. We use rupees here as a medium of exchange. One rupee is worth 30 cents in American money. We are making some rough tables and chairs for our thatched straw roof barracks."

With so much energy devoted to the building and supplying of bases, it is no wonder there were few distractions for B-29 crews. But it wasn't all work and no play: those based in India could visit the ancient city of Calcutta; crews, both air and ground, began construction projects; officers' and enlisted men's clubs, theaters, and baseball diamonds soon sprouted up with scrounged materials, often from a burgeoning black market. But there were also short moments of grace and beauty. Kate Van Hogendorp, a Red Cross nurse based in Chakulia, recalls a visit by the Andre Kostelanetz Orchestra and Kostelanetz's wife, Lily Pons, and describes how the 40th Bomb Group redefined the saying "The show must go on." "The show that

The Marianas

Most of the crews that arrived at these new island homes were given an army-published pamphlet titled *Meet the Marianas—A Pocket Guide*. This gave the crews a short history of the Marianas and surrounding area, and warnings about flora and fauna, the native populations, and enemy civilians. There was also a recreation section that described a number of "activities" in which the airmen could indulge: "You'll want to go swimming. Don't try it on the weather side of the islands. There is a heavy surf, the reefs are jagged, the shores rocky. But the larger islands have some fair beaches with light surf. If you go boating, stay inside the reefs.

"You'll want to go hunting. In the open season for wild cattle, goats, and deer, there is plenty of game. But the favorite sport on the islands is pig hunting. For this purpose the islanders unleash a pack of native dogs, which look like small great Danes.

"You'll want to go fishing. You can do it practically anywhere off the shores and reefs of Guam, but the good places are the lagoons near Sumay and Merizo."

Left and below: Booklets produced by several military agencies helped instruct, entertain, and protect the troops who were assigned to the numerous new locations where Americans were based during the war.

are jagged, the shores
have some fair beaches
boating, stay inside the
canoe is not too safe. It is generally an outrigger dug-
out, with a plow-shaped paddle. Sometimes the Cham-
orros rig up a bamboo mast with a cotton sail for speed,
but they are not the navigators their ancestors were.

You'll want to go hunting. In the open season for
wild cattle, goats and deer, there is plenty of game.
But the favorite sport on the islands is pig-hunting.
For this purpose the islanders unleash a pack of native
dogs, which look like small Great Danes. When the
dogs corner a wild pig, a Chamorro finishes him off
with a blow of the machete. They net fruit pigeons,
and use slip-noose snares to catch wild ducks and
jungle fowl.

You'll want to go fishing. You can do it practically
anywhere off the shores and reefs of Guam, but the
good places are the lagoons near Sumay and Merizo.
In the fresh-water streams you'll find perch and eels,
which you can eat. There are plenty of fish in the
lagoons and out in the open waters. Along the shores
and reefs you'll spot lots of shellfish. No pearl oysters,
though. Between January and March, you may see
sperm whales offshore.

Practically any deepwater fish around the Marianas can be eaten. But don't touch the fish living
in the shallow flats along the shore. They feed on
polluted matter from the land. Watch out for a small
grey species of land crab. It's poisonous. On the other

, or who know
Japanese civilian may be something of a surprise. He
turns out to be a human being, and may even be a
rather likeable person. Probably you will have very little personal dealings with him. But, if you do, you
should be careful not to allow your personal feelings
toward him to interfere with your duties as an American citizen and soldier.

The Soldier's Emily Post. At no time will you
"fraternize" with enemy civilians. This means that you
must have no friends among them. Some enemy
civilians may be looking for important military information. They may try to get it by making friends with
a soldier. You won't want to take any chances and
therefore you will avoid taking any enemy civilian into
your confidence. Naturally, you will respect their
privacy, but you will make sure that they respect yours
even more.

If you run across an enemy civilian who speaks
some English, don't get involved in lengthy conversa-
tions with him. Don't start an argument so that you
can tell him your opinion of Japan. Wars are not won
with oratory.

You are expected to be especially careful to respect
the property rights of the enemy population. No
American soldier, under any circumstances, is allowed
to loot or pillage. Enemy troops may do that. We
don't. If you like souvenirs, there are legal and proper

ways of getting them. Don't swipe them from civilians.

The same rule holds for other things belonging
to them. You will not invade their property, or seize
anything on it, or molest their persons, unless a superior authority orders you to do so. Such orders will
be given only if they are necessary for the protection
and maintenance of our forces.

Never touch an enemy civilian, unless you must
in self-defense. Many Orientals resent physical contact with strangers. Treat the women with politeness
and the children with kindness. Don't jostle other pe-

RECREATION

You'll want to go swimming. Don't try it on the
weather side of the islands (generally the northern
and eastern shore.) There is a heavy surf, the reefs

28

29

12

13

How useful this pamphlet was, or indeed how much it was used, is open to debate. For many crews, life on base was a monotonous, fatiguing existence of hot days and long missions. Nolan Strange, aircraft commander, comments: "When we weren't flying we were sleeping. There was nothing else to do. The barracks were primitive and there were still Japanese on the island. The navy had it pretty well; they had a big base down on the west side of the island. All we had to drink was beer. We had an officers' club, if you could call it that. I think Tinian was a bit better off than we were. They built that base like they were going to stay awhile."

Charles Gilson remembers playing cards for hours on end: "Life on Saipan was pretty quiet between missions, which were only a couple of times a week as I recall. I did a lot of bridge playing, sometimes ten hours a day. And we built our own officers' club on a lovely location, looking out over the rocks and the sea below. (When I say 'we', I should really say 'they'—I think the volunteer builders had just completed the officers' club before we arrived in early April.)"

The stress of combat also had a telling effect on the men. Their island homes were primitive and not without danger. On many of the islands Japanese soldiers were active, especially at night. William H. Carter, a gunner with the 60th Bomb Squadron, describes an elaborate routine required when nature called:

"In the northern part of the island of Guam, a number of Japanese hid in the many caves on the island. If we had to go several feet away from our Quonset huts to the latrine—that's the toilet—at night, we would strap on our .45 automatics, carry a flashlight, and wake a buddy to accompany us for protection. There were several instances when Japanese

killed an American and stole their supplies and anything else that was available. While I was on the island, some of these Japanese soldiers managed to get into the mess tent of the black engineers and killed some of them. They escaped with all the food they could carry. The next day a squad of marines captured a group of Japanese soldiers from the caves."

There was also the ever-present danger from air attack. John Mitchell of the 3rd Photo Squadron describes being forced to hit the dirt:

I turned the switch off—if people didn't know there was an air raid on now they would never know—and went outside to see what was going on. People were running from the tent area toward the trees and brushy area that we used as an air raid shelter . . . As I looked toward the flight line I could see one Zero making a run down the line of parked B-29s. On the end of the field I could see smoke boiling up from burning planes.

"The Zero completed his run down the flight line, banked sharply and reversed course and headed again for the camp area. He was bearing down directly on me but this time the gun emplacements to the east of our area opened up and I could see the tracers tearing into him. He slowed, wobbled a bit, then smoke and flame poured from his fuselage. I saw he was going down and I thought if he hits and bounces he will come down right on top of me. It took me two jumps to be through the orderly room and hit the dirt on the other side where I could look back through the hut and see what happened. The Zero staggered and then, engulfed in flames, hit the ground and exploded."

Far left and left: *Carroll "Mark" Markowski photographed exiting an abandoned Japanese cave; a head-on view of a Mitsubishi A6M Zero.*

Below: *Corporal Robert L. Sherman collects a souvenir. He is seen here cutting a tail number from an A6M Zero on Saipan.*

"I stepped to the door of the orderly room to look toward the motor pool—over by the mess hall the men were lining up for the noon meal. I paid scant attention to the two fighter planes I saw making a sweep over the ridge and heading toward our area. Just a couple of navy boys, I thought, pulling a buzz job before landing. But then one plane banked slightly and I saw the big rising sun emblem on the side of the fuselage; at the same instance I saw the winks of light as his wing guns opened up. As I made a leap for the switch to turn on the air-raid alarm I remember seeing the little puffs of dust in front of the orderly room as the slugs tore into the ground. The first two Zeros swept past to be followed by another pair.

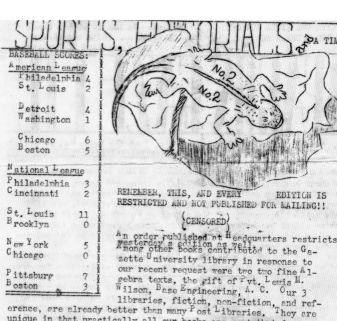

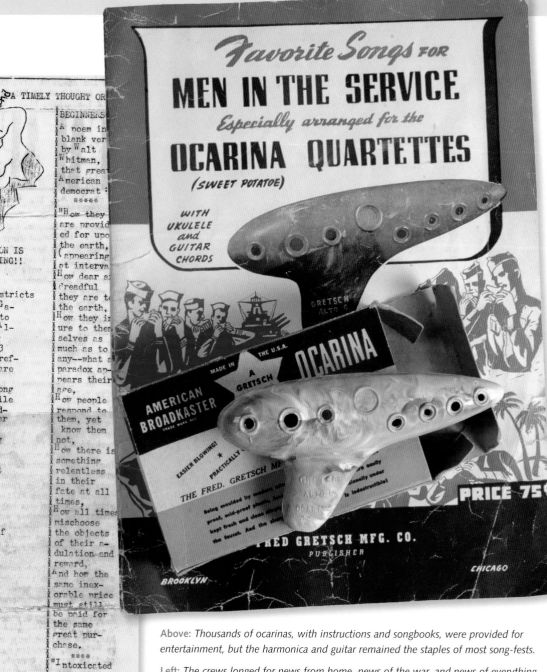

Above: *Thousands of ocarinas, with instructions and songbooks, were provided for entertainment, but the harmonica and guitar remained the staples of most song-fests.*

Left: *The crews longed for news from home, news of the war, and news of everything going on around them. Base- and unit-level newspapers were essential to morale; they were produced locally to fill the gaps left by imported newspapers and magazines.*

The B-29 crews had nowhere to go. They were stuck in the middle of the Pacific with very few creature comforts and the certainty that if they flew long enough most would not make it home. The fatigue of combat and their monotonous existence began to take its toll. XXI Bomber Command flight surgeons viewed these trends with alarm. The following is an extract from the *Medical Support of the Army Air Forces in World War II* (Office of the Surgeon General, USAF, 1955):

"During the three and one half months of operations against the Japanese prior to the March incendiary raids, some very subtle but significant psychological problems developed among flying personnel of XXI Bomber Command. It was obvious that the combat personnel had accumulated a high coefficient of operational combat experience during the months of December, January and February, and yet the operational losses due to mechanical failure of the B-29 and technical failure of personnel persisted in exceeding the losses due to enemy action.

Consequently the combat crews, finding only a minimum of evidence to support confidence in their airplane, began to fear their own aircraft and field orders more than the devices of the enemy. Moreover, small bomb loads and poor bombing results afforded them no compensation or satisfaction commensurate with the operational risks entailed.

"Yet as a tribute to small-unit leadership and to the maturity of the individual combat airmen, very few cases of childish hysteria or indications of personal inadequacies were manifest, and individual disintegration from anxiety was rare. Rather, the crews developed a dull, dutiful attitude toward the flying of missions. They discerned their duty and set about performing it, technically, to the best of their ability, but with an emotional tone so hopeless and devoid of luster that operational efficiency could not but suffer. A monotonous and determined demand arose for a rotation policy. A fixed number of combat missions was termed a necessary 'something to shoot for.' Symbolically, this 'something to shoot for' was not connected with waging the war or defeating the enemy, but with home, security, and reward for the dutiful completion of a task."

William H. Carter from the 60th Squadron remembers, "Most of us developed a fatalistic attitude about being shot down over Japan. We knew the odds were against us. This would happen one day if you flew enough missions, but somehow this attitude seemed to keep us going."

Not surprisingly, those in charge still had not developed a definite rotation policy, but this was simply because they never had enough men to be able to do so. A memorandum dated February 1945 and titled "Policy for Selection of Combat Crews for Return to the US" reveals a command still grappling with the issue:

"The problem of selection of combat crews for return to the United States is one of the utmost concern to combat crews themselves and to this Headquarters. It is now known that it will be impossible to lay down a fixed rotation policy based on hours or on a fixed number of combat missions. The rotation of crews must of necessity be geared to the rate of arrival of replacement crews and to the maintenance of the prescribed strength of crews with the group."

After the war, tail gunner Andy Doty from the 19th Bomb Group wrote about his experiences and what everyday life was like while based on Guam: "My earliest impressions of our new home were of jungle, rain and mud. We lived in tents surrounded by high rows of uprooted trees and got about on wooden walkways. After a few weeks we moved into newly constructed Quonset huts that were high and dry. We settled into a routine on Guam that spring and summer, playing boyhood games while waiting to wage war. Our days were actually quite pleasant . . . we teamed up in after hours for softball, made our way to the beach near the middle of the island, busied ourselves in our Quonset huts, or attended

movies. Much of our time was spent in shorts and sneakers as we turned bronze under the warm sun. We strolled over to the PX tent where we could buy Zagnut candy bars and Fort Pitt beer. It was a terrible combination, but it was all that was available.

Above: *Clark's Zagnut® bars—now made by Hershey's—were popular with many troops. Often coming directly from high school, some of the younger men showed more interest in a good candy bar than in cigarettes and liquor.*

Left: *Religion played an important part in the lives of most aircrew. The army provided chaplains, supplies, and facilities to support many denominations.*

"A movie played every night at the crude outdoor theater. The seats were empty ammunition boxes. Everyone carried a flash light, a poncho and a helmet liner, for it rained every evening. One day a touring group of major league baseball players arrived for an exhibition game. Hundreds of airmen gathered along the baselines to watch 'Birdie' Tibbetts, 'Flash' Gordon, Enos Slaughter, 'Pepper' Martin and other major league stars."

Slowly, life at each base became organized and somewhat comfortable, but the US forces' advance through Japanese-held islands continued, and new bases were opening even as the war drew to a close.

Okinawa was one of the last islands taken by the US. Soon after the occupation, B-29 units from the 316th Bomb Wing began to arrive, but, as with Guam, Saipan, and Tinian before, the early living conditions on Okinawa were primitive. Gunner Jerome Harold Goldwyn was

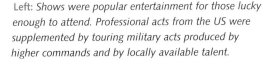

a staff sergeant with the 461st Bomb Squadron. An excerpt from his memoir reveals a world of vile smells and the ever-present danger of attack:

"I left the States on August 4, 1945 with a squadron of B-29s [bound] for Guam. After a short stay we went on to Tinian, then finally Kadena Field, Okinawa. Our quarters were laid out with about 20 pyramid tents for all the air crew, plus a mess tent, rec hall, briefing tent, headquarters, PX [Post Exchange or military store], and tents for all other personnel. It was called 'tent city.' Our living area slept six to a tent. Each tent had three double-decker bunk beds. We had our 'B4s,' which were like garment bags, and foot lockers near every cot. Our foot lockers were shipped before us and arrived at our tents before we did. The name footlocker came from the fact that these chests were kept at the foot of each bunk. Each footlocker was about 3ft [91.4cm] long, 18 inches [45.7cm] wide, and 18 inches deep with a hasp for a lock. They were always kept locked.

"The worst part was the smell of fertilizer mixed with human feces that the Okinawans used in their fields. It was so intense that we began to walk around with gas masks on. Every once in a while, even today, I will be somewhere and I swear I can still smell the stink of those islands. Our quarters and ready rooms (where we got our instructions), plus mess hall and rec areas were in a newly planted field that always had this wonderful smell of human fertilizer.

"On some bases overseas as well as Stateside we had what we called creepy crawlers on the floor, which was either dirt or concrete. To protect

Left: This game between the "Tinian Flyers" and the "Saipan Bombers" was played on Saipan the day before the first atomic bomb mission against Japan.

Right: The proximity of women, which increased as B-29 crews moved to Okinawa, also increased the incidences of venereal diseases. Troops were provided with condoms, and, for those who eschewed condoms, personal VD kits.

Right and below: *Locally printed cards: membership (below) of a NCO (non-commissioned officers) club on Okinawa and (right) a Christmas card dating from just after the end of the war.*

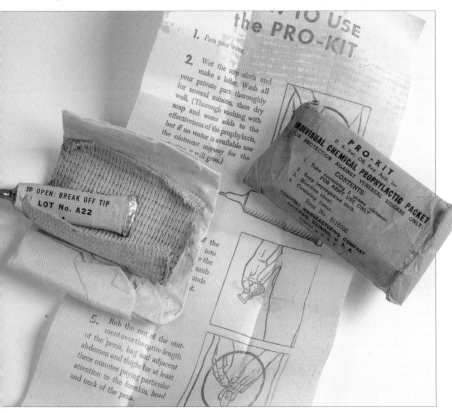

our beds we got whatever tin cans or containers without any holes that we could beg, borrow, or buy from the mess hall, or that we could find, and filled them with any kind of liquid. We put the legs of the beds in the cans. Anything that crawled up the cans would fall in the water and drown. This worked well until a couple of smart guys poured gasoline in the containers and set them ablaze in the middle of the night. The guys who did it stood by with buckets of water. The other tricks were to put bugs or snakes in

a guy's bunk when he was out late. But not in Okinawa; there were no snakes, so sometimes a rope would be substituted for the same effect. As a precaution against the creepy crawlers, we shook everything out before using it or putting it on.

"Periodically we would get Red Cross packages which would contain . . . four cigarettes with a label (Camel, Chesterfield, etc.), a piece of cheese (like a rock), a piece of hard chocolate, and several packages of squares of toilet paper, which we dropped in our foot lockers. When we had enough chocolate we would melt the chocolate into one big chunk. When you wanted a piece you took your knife and sliced off a piece.

"At one end of our area, but in the middle of all the tents, was our toilet, a 20-holer. These were long planks of wood facing each other, chair height. They were set over trenches that had been dug to catch our waste. Each hole had a peg to hold your toilet paper roll, which you brought with you. It looked really funny to see 20 bare guys sitting over a hole. When it rained, and it did rain, we'd wear ponchos, and of course the toilet paper got all wet. So you would pay two or more cigarettes to have someone get you some dry paper. Between every two holes there was a tin of disinfectant powder, which you would dump into your hole when you were finished. The urinal was just one big hole with a wooden walkway all around it.

"We wore .45 caliber pistols and carried carbines wherever we went. We stood guard at our airfield, guarding our planes. We got word that the Japanese had a few tricks. They had captured and rebuilt a DC-3. They landed at our airfield and came out wearing white head bands, yelling "banzai"! They had belts on with lots of grenades. Then they ran to our planes, hugged them, and pulled the pins on their hand grenades. In order to protect our aircraft we had our engineering outfit make a sandbag fort on the side of the plane and we had to take turns standing guard."

Time Off in Korea

When the communists of North Korea attacked South Korea on June 25, 1950, the US's Far East Air Forces commanded a single B-29 unit: the 19th Bomb Group. Based on Guam, the 19th was quickly moved to Kadena Air Base, Okinawa, flying its first strike against North Korean targets on June 28. By the year's end, four more B-29 groups would deploy from the Strategic Air Command in the US: the 22nd and 307th bomb groups (both sent to Okinawa) and the 92nd and 98th bomb groups (both sent to Japan).

Flying combat missions out of Japan and Okinawa was, at that time, a unique experience for US military air power. The bases were established facilities, though new structures were required to accommodate all of the new arrivals. The local population was friendly, for the most part, and not involved in the undeclared war being flown from their bases. There were no great worldwide strategic campaigns being waged, so sea lanes were open to deliver supplies, equipment, and reinforcements without threat of enemy attack or seizure. Contact with the folks back in the US was greatly improved through ham radio sets, trans-Pacific telephone and telegraph cables, and regular mail service. And, in some cases, dependents—wives and children—accompanied the units to the Far East for the duration of the war or for prolonged visits.

Below: By no measure did the B-29 crews have an easy time during the Korean War. But unlike some of their comrades based on the Korean peninsula, they were not shot at during their off-duty hours; they were able to clean up and change into dry clothes after missions; and their sleep was more likely to be interrupted by an alarm clock than by gun fire. As many ground troops and aviation units liked to point out, when they needed a break from the fighting, they were sent to Japan!

Left: Food was improved over what was offered in World War II. Fresh produce was readily and locally available and unrationed. New in-flight box lunches (first introduced during the Berlin Airlift in 1948) added to crew comfort during combat missions. On-base clubs had few problems keeping liquor in stock, and off-base restaurants and clubs offered local favorites and interesting attempts at delivering meals in line with American tastes.

Above: Daddy's home! Several B-29 crews had the advantages of seeing their families after each mission. Wives and children could travel to Japan and Okinawa by ship or commercial air lines without danger from enemy action. However, despite the message behind this posed photo, most families could not wait by the operations shack for their returning heroes.

Glossary

A/C Aircraft Commander

AF Air Force

AMC Air Materiel Command

AN Army-Navy

AN/APG Airborne Fire Control Radars (as in the AN/APG-15 S-Band tail gun radar system)

AN/APQ Airborne Multipurpose/Special Radars (as in the AN/APQ-7 Eagle bombardment radar system)

AN/APS-15 X-band bombing and navigational radar for B-29; nicknamed Mickey

APU Auxiliary Power Unit (see Putt-Putt)

BC Bomber Command

BG (M) Bomb Group (Medium)

BG (VH) Bomb Group (Very Heavy)

BS (M) Bomb Squadron (Medium)

BS (VH) Bomb Squadron (Very Heavy)

BW (VH) Bomb Wing (Very Heavy)

Capt Captain

CBI China-Burma-India theater of operations

CFC Central Fire Control

CSFC Central Station Fire Control

CO Commanding Officer

CP Copilot

Col Colonel

Cpl Corporal

FE Flight Engineer

1/Lt First Lieutenant

1/Sgt First Sergeant

HE High Explosive

HEI High Explosive Incendiary (bomb)

IAS Indicated Air Speed

IFF Identify Friend or Foe

IP Initial Point (at the start of a bomb run)

KIA Killed in Action

KIAS Knots Indicated Air Speed

LG Left Gunner

LORAN LOng RANge Navigation

Lt Col Lieutenant Colonel

Maj Major

MIA Missing in Action

M/Sgt Master Sergeant

MX Material, Experimental

NCO Non-Commissioned Officer

P Pilot

PFC Private First Class

POW Prisoner Of War

PRS Photographic Reconnaissance Squadron

PTO Pacific Theater of Operations

Putt-Putt Colloquial term for the APU: a small gasoline generator to provide electrical power before number three engine is started

PX Post Exchange

R Radial engine (as in R-3350)

RO Radio operator/radar operator

R&R Rest and Recreation/Relaxation/Recuperation

RG Right Gunner

SAC Strategic Air Command

SAF Strategic Air Force

2/Lt Second Lieutenant

Sgt Sergeant

S/Sgt Staff Sergeant

TG Tail Gunner

T/Sgt Tech(nical) Sergeant

UHF Ultra-High Frequency

USAF United States Air Force

USAAC US Army Air Corps

USAAF US Army Air Forces (see right)

USO United Service Organizations

XX BC 20th Bomber Command

XXI BC 21st Bomber Command

Organizational Titles

In 1926, the US Congress passed the Air Corps Act, establishing the Army Air Corps (the Air Corps, AAC or AC) to manage the US Army's aviation assets. The General Headquarters Air Force (GHQAF) was created by the army in 1935 to command all army bomber, fighter, and attack units in the US. (Observation squadrons and combat squadron based in Panama, Hawaii, and the Philippines remained assigned to local US Army authorities.)

In June 1941, the army responded to a lack of coordination between the Air Corps and GHQAF, placing both under the control of a new organization, the Army Air Forces (officially abbreviated AAF, though commonly listed as USAAF for clarity). As an organization, the Air Corps ceased to exist in 1942, when all authority and responsibilities were delegated to other commands. With the formation of the Army Air Forces, GHQAF was renamed Army Air Forces Combat Command, then, in 1942, disestablished and replaced by geographically based numbered air forces. Numbered air forces and commands were always expressed in Roman numerals or spelled out: Twentieth Air Force (for example, XX Air Force, XXI Bomber Command), but never 20th Air Force or 21st Bomber Command. Combat wings, groups, and squadrons were always expressed in Arabic numerals: 73rd Bomb Wing, 40th Bomb Group, 676th Bomb Squadron, etc.

The army's air arm achieved independence in 1947, when Congress created the US Air Force (USAF). At the same time, the superfluous Army Air Corps was disestablished.

Further Reading

Anderton, David A.: *B-29 Superfortress at War* (Scribner, 1978)

Birdsall, Steve: *Saga of the Superfortress* (Double Day, 1980)

Birdsall, Steve: *Superfortress, The Boeing B-29* (Carrollton, TX: Squadron/Signal Publications, 1980)

Bodie, Warren M. and Ethell, Jeffrey L.: *WWII Pacific War Eagles in Original Color* (Widewing Publications, 1997)

Bowers, Peter M.: *Boeing B-29 Superfortress* (North Branch, MN: Specialty Press, 1999)

Bowman, Martin W.: *USAAF Handbook 1939–1945* (Stackpole Books, 1997)

Bradley, F. J.: *No Strategic Targets Left* (Paducah, KY: Turner Publishing Company, 1999)

Campbell, Richard H.: *The Silverplate Bombers* (Jefferson, NC: McFarland & Company, 2005)

Davis, Larry: *B-29 Superfortress in Action* (Carrollton, TX: Squadron/Signal Publications, 1997)

Dick, Ron and Patterson, Dan: *American Eagles—A History of the United States Air Force* (Howell Press, 1997)

Dorr, Robert F.: *B-29 Superfortress Units of the Korean War* (Osprey Publishing, 2003)

Dorr, Robert F.: *B-29 Superfortress Units of World War 2* (Osprey Publishing, 2002)

Doty, Andy: *Backwards into Battle* (Tall Tree Press, 1995)

Doty, Andy: *Backwards Into Battle* (Palo Alto, CA: Tall Tree Press, 1997)

Freeman, Roger A.: *Camouflage & Markings: United States Army Air Force* (Ducimus Books, 1974)

Herbert, Kevin: *Maximum Effort—The B-29s Against Japan* (Sunflower University Press, 1983)

How to Fly the B-29 Superfortress: The Official Manual for the Plane that Bombed Hiroshima and Nagasaki (Stackpole Books, 1995)

Howlett, Chris: *Washington Times Newsletter* (Taunton, Somerset, United Kingdom, fall 2001 and on)

Kohn, Leo J.: *Pilot's Manual for B-29 Superfortress* (Appleton, WI: Aviation Publications, 1999)

Link, Mae Mills and Hurbert Coleman: *Medical Support of the Army Air Forces in World War II* (Office of the Surgeon General, USAF, 1955)

Maguire, Jon A.: *Gear Up! Flight Clothing & Equipment of USAAF Airmen in World War II* (Schiffer Military/Aviation History, 1995)

Marshall, Chester W. with Thompson, Warren: *Final Assault on the Rising Sun* (North Branch, MN: Specialty Press, 1995)

Marshall, Chester: *B-29 Photo Combat Diary: The Superfortress in WWII and Korea* (Specialty Press Publishers and Wholesalers, 1996)

Nijboer, Donald: *Cockpit—An Illustrated History of World War II Aircraft Interiors* (Boston Mills Press, 1998)

Nijboer, Donald: *Graphic War—The Secret Aviation Drawings and Illustrations of World War II* (Firefly Books, 2005)

Nijboer, Donald: *Gunner—An Illustrated History of World War II Aircraft Turrets and Gun Positions* (Boston Mills Press, 2001)

Pace, Steve: *B-29 Superfortress* (United Kingdom: Crowood, 2003)

Ross, Stewart Halsey: *Strategic Bombing By the United States in World War II* (McFarland & Company, Inc Publishers, 2003)

Sakai, Saburo: *Samurai* (Ballantine Books, 1958)

Sakaida, Henry: *Imperial Japanese Navy Aces 1937–45* (Osprey Publishing, 1998)

Sakaida, Henry: *Japanese Army Air Force Aces* (Osprey Publishing, 1997)

Takaki, Loji and Sakaida, Henry: *B-29 Hunters of the JAAF* (Osprey Publishing, 2001)

Tillman, Barrett: *Whirlwind: the Air War Against Japan 1942–1945* (Simon & Shuster , 2010)

Websites

www.40thbombgroup.org

www.346bg.com

www.B-29.org

www.444thbg.org

www.315bw.org

Picture Credits and Acknowledgments

Page number and position are indicated as follows: L = left, TL = top left, TR = top right; C = center; CL = center left; B = bottom, etc:

Bendix Corporation via Steve Pace: 57BL. **Boeing via Steve Pace**: 45TL. **Peter M. Bowers collection**: 8. **B-29Saipan.com**: 19BR; 104CT; **Richard H. Campbell via Steve Pace**: 138BR; 139BR; 139CR. **The family of Joe Caner Swann**: www.cygnuschronicles.com: 114BL; 145CR. **Cavalier Corporation via Steve Pace**: 147CT. **Champion via Steve Pace**: 129CT. **Chrysler Corporation via Steve Pace**: 70BL. **Bill Copeland Collection**: 43BR; 63TL; 64BR; 103TR; 105BL; 105CB; 56T. **C. E. Daniel Collection**: 92CT. **Department of History, US Military Academy**: 35TL. **Jim Ewen collection**: 45BL. **B. F. Goodrich via Steve Pace**: 77CT. **Paul D. Guttman**: 119BL. **Hersch via Jason Liebig**: 153CR. **Via Chris Howlett of the *Washington Times***: 149C. **Carroll Markowski collection via Steve Pace**: 31CR; 61BL; 64BL; 104CR; 130BR; 151CL. **Ray Martin collection**: 154CT. **National Museum of the United States Air Force**: 17TR; 17BL; 18TR; 19TR; 20TL; 21BL; 28BR; 29TR; 32; 33R; 33BL; 35R; 42CR; 42L; 60BL; 65R; 71TL; 72CT; 75R; 84BL; 86BL; 94BL; 108TR; 115TR; 118TL; 120BL; 122BL; 131TR; 133C; 133BL; 133TR; 134BR; 135TL. **Donald Nijboer**: 37BR; 48R; 49R; 62T; 84CT; 89TL; 100BL; 106B; 107TR; 107C; 109BL; 128TL; 129TR; 135BR; 135BL; 151C. **Steve Pace**: 40BR; 47BR; 56BR; 65C; 105TR; 109BR; 134CL. **Dan Patterson**: 3; 16C; 16TC; 17C; 17C; 18L; 20CB; 21CT; 23; 24; 26BL; 26CB; 27TL; 27BR; 27TR; 27BL; 29C; 29TL; 30CB; 34BL; 38; 41CB; 41C; 41BR; 41BL; 41TL; 43T; 45TR; 46TR; 46BL; 48T; 48BL; 49TL; 50BL; 50C; 51TR; 52L; 55TR; 55CT; 55TL; 55B; 57T; 58TR; 58T; 59TR; 60TR; 66L; 69TL; 69BR; 69BL; 69TR; 73TL; 74BR; 75CB; 77BR; 78L; 79TL; 80; 82B; 83TR; 83TL; 83B; 84TR; 87CT; 87R; 88CT; 91TL; 96; 98BR; 99BR; 99BL; 99CB; 99TR; 99TL; 102CB; 110L; 113BL;

113TL; 113R; 115CL; 117CT; 119TL; 121B; 122TR; 123BL; 124; 124R; 127TR; 127TL; 127BL; 128BL; 130CB; 131C; 132C; 132TR; 134C; 137TL; 143; 144T; 152TR; 152TL; 155TR; 155BL; **Stan Piet**: 30TR; 31TL; 35BR; 41TR; 43CB; 44T; 50TR; 51BL; 56TL; 56L; 58CR; 61TR; 64TR; 73BR; 76BR; 77BL; 79CT; 85BL; 91C; 95TL; 102TR; 114CT; 120CT; 121TL; 123TL; 123C; 131TL; 132CT; 137CR; 140CT. *Popular Mechanics*: 117BL; 118BR. **Taigh Ramey**: twinbeech.com: 14TR; 101BL; 108CB. **Robert M. Robbins estate**: 11TR. Scott A Willey: 63BR; 127BR; **The family of Charles D. Mulligan**: 74C; 74CT. **Bill Streifer collection via Steve Pace**: 22. **The family of Stanley Tecoma**: 94CT; 95BR; 95TR. **USAF Collection, National Archives and Records Agency**: 11BL; 12L; 13TL; 13BR; 14C; 30BL; 34T; 36B; 37TL; 47T; 49T; 57BR; 59BL; 59BR; 62BR; 63R; 65TL; 68CB; 71BR; 75TL; 75CT; 76BL; 86TR; 88CR; 88BL; 90BR; 91TR; 92BL; 93CL; 93C; 93TR; 101TR; 103CL; 109CT; 112BL; 112BR; 116CB; 116TR; 116BL; 116CL; 117BR; 119CR; 121CR; 121C; 126B; 129TL; 136BL; 136BR; 138CT; 138BL; 139TL; 140TL; 140BR; 141TL; 141C; 142; 144BL; 145TL; 146BL; 146TR; 147BL; 147TR; 148BR; 148TL; 149T; 150CR; 150TL; 151BR; 151TL; 153BL; 154BL; 156B; 157BL; 157T. **The family of Jean VanDruff**: 89CB. **Via Carl Weidenburner**: http://cbi-theater.home.comcast.net: 85C. **Westinghouse War Production Coordinating Committee via Steve Pace**: 10C. **Dick Windler collection via Steve Pace**: 32T; 78R; 79BR.

Jacket and front cover illustration:

Jacket and front cover illustration: *Spearhead to Victory* by Roy Grinnell (www.roygrinnell.com).

Editors' and authors' acknowledgments

The editors and authors wish to thank the following for their help in preparing this book: Gina McNeeley; Stan Piet; Nicolaas Kitsch, The Korean War National Museum; Jean and Carey VanDruff; Taigh Ramey, Proprietor, Vintage Aircraft, www.twinbeech.com; Joe Swann; Michael Mulligan; Alan Reeter; Nolan Strange; Charles Gilson; Bert Kortegaard—excerpts from Ralph Livengood's diary; Alan K. Reeter; William Atkinson; Craig Goldwyn—excerpts from Jerry Goldwyn's diary; Robert Wachs; Mike Speciale and the 40th Bomb Group Association and the John W. Ramsay Research Library, New England Air Museum; Friends Journal National Air Force Museum; Robert F. Door; Barrett Tillman.

Grateful acknowledgment is made to the following for permission to reprint previously published material: *Saga of the Superfortress: The Dramatic Story of the B-29 and the Twentieth Air Force* by Steve Birdsall, copyright c.1980 by Steve Birdsall. Used by permission of Doubleday, a division of Random House, Inc. *B-29 Superfortress Units of World War 2* and *B-29 Superfortress Units of the Korean War*, 2003, 2003 Osprey Publishing. *Backwards into Battle* by Andy Doty, Tall Tree Press, 1995.

Thanks also for kind efforts and access to their oral history databases: Veterans History Project Collection, American Folklife Center, Library of Congress; The Air Force Historical Research Center; The Rutgers Oral History Archives.

Museums

Special thanks go to the Air Force Museum Foundation, and George Mongon, Development Director there (www.nationalmuseum.af.mil).